CASES IN CORPORATE GOVERNANCE AND BUSINESS ETHICS

CASES IN CORPORATE GOVERNANCE AND BUSINESS ETHICS

Collette Kirwan, Hugh McBride
and Chris O'Riordan

CHARTERED
ACCOUNTANTS
IRELAND

Published in 2018 by
Chartered Accountants Ireland
Chartered Accountants House
47–49 Pearse Street
Dublin 2

www.charteredaccountants.ie

This publication is designed to provide accurate and authoritative information in regard to the subject matter covered. It is provided on the understanding that The Institute of Chartered Accountants in Ireland is not engaged in rendering professional services. The Institute of Chartered Accountants in Ireland disclaims all liability for any reliance placed on the information contained within this publication and recommends that if professional advice or other expert assistance is required, the services of a competent professional should be sought.

The cases in this book are entirely fictional and any resemblance between featured people and organisations and any real people or organisations, living or dead, is entirely coincidental.

ISBN 978-1-912350-14-8

Typeset by Datapage
Printed by Replika Press Pvt. Ltd.

To colleagues who contributed directly and indirectly to this book and to Ciarán – thank you.

Collette Kirwan

Grá agus ómós do Mary, Tomás, Ellen, Mary Frances agus Tom a'Bhungalow; agus ag cuimhne ar mo chara sár-eiticiúil Deirdre McMahon.

Hugh McBride

To my mother and father, for always being there. To Fiona, Cillian, Tara and Richard – thank you for your love, support and endless patience.

Chris O'Riordan

Contents

Authors and Contributors

Collette Kirwan

Collette Kirwan FCA, BBS, PhD is a first class honours graduate of Waterford Institute of Technology (WIT). She trained as a Chartered Accountant with PricewaterhouseCoopers where she subsequently worked as a manager in Audit Services. Collette first joined the School of Business at WIT in 2005. In 2011, she was awarded the Waterford Institute of Technology Teaching Excellence Award. Between 2012 and 2016, Collette was a lecturer in accounting at University College Dublin (UCD). Over her career, Collette has lectured at undergraduate, postgraduate and executive education levels. Her main subject areas include auditing, financial reporting, financial management, corporate governance and business research methods. In 2013, Collette was awarded her PhD from UCD, which examines the role of non-executive directors on boards of private family firms. Collette's research interests include corporate governance, boards of directors, governance of family firms, governance of not-for-profit organisations, financial reporting and auditing. During her academic career, Collette has presented at a number of international conferences and national conferences, and has published articles in *Accounting, Auditing and Accountability Journal* and *Accounting in Europe*, as well as *Accountancy Ireland*.

Hugh McBride

Hugh McBride is a senior lecturer in business at the Mayo campus of Galway–Mayo Institute of Technology (GMIT). A member of CIMA since 1987, he graduated from UCD with a B.Comm (in 1976) and an MBS (in 1977). Hugh has also lectured at DCU, NUIG, the Copperbelt University (Zambia), the University of Malawi, the University of Dar es Salaam (Tanzania), and at the Fachhochschule Vorarlberg (Austria). He also worked for a year at the Centre for Cooperative Studies, UCC (in 1981). He has a long-standing interest in the areas of corporate ethics and governance. The topic of his MBS dissertation (1977) was "Corporate Social Responsibility and Social Accounting". In 2002, he designed a Level 8 module in Corporate Ethics & Governance, which he first delivered in the academic year 2003/04. He also integrates ethical issues into the undergraduate curriculum as embedded elements of modules in financial management, management accounting and management control systems. He has been a member of GMIT's Academic Council for 20 years, and also served as a member of the Institute's governing body for five years.

Chris O'Riordan

Chris O'Riordan FCA, BA, MBA, PhD, is a lecturer in accounting at Waterford Institute of Technology (WIT) since 2004. Prior to this, he worked in a variety of financial and managerial roles in family businesses, SMEs and multinational companies, having first trained as a Chartered Accountant with PricewaterhouseCoopers in Waterford. He lectures at undergraduate, postgraduate and executive levels in a range of subjects, including financial reporting, management accounting, finance, knowledge management and managing change, and supervises students at doctoral level. Chris is also Head of the Centre for Management Research in Healthcare and Healthcare Economics, Course Leader for the Higher Diploma in Business in Management, and Accounting Stream Leader on the Bachelor of Business (Hons) programme at WIT. With Dr Pat Lynch, Chris co-edited *Managerial Challenges in Irish Organisations: A Case Study Collection* (2010), to which he also co-contributed two cases. He has twice won European Foundation for Management Development case study competitions with co-authored cases and is a previous winner of the 'Best Postgraduate Paper' award at the Irish Academy of Management Annual Conference. Chris publishes articles in ABS-ranked journals and professional publications, including *Accountancy Ireland*.

Niamh Brennan

Niamh Brennan, FCA, CDir, BSc, PhD, is Michael MacCormac Professor of Management at University College Dublin (UCD). In a survey of alumni, Niamh was voted one of UCD's top three lecturers for the 2000s onwards. She has served as Head of Accounting and Associate Dean for Research at the UCD College of Business. A first class honours, first place in class, UCD Science (Microbiology & Biochemistry) graduate, Niamh qualified as a Chartered Accountant with KPMG, holds a PhD from the University of Warwick and is a Chartered Director of the Institute of Directors (London). She is an Inaugural Honorary Fellow of the Institute of Directors in Ireland and an Honorary Fellow of the Society of Actuaries in Ireland. Having established the UCD Centre for Corporate Governance in 2002, Niamh plays a leading role in the public discourse in Ireland and internationally on corporate governance. The Centre has provided executive and professional training to thousands of Irish company directors.

Former chair of the National College of Art and Design and the Dublin Docklands Development Authority, Niamh holds/has held non-executive directorships with the Children's Hospital Group, the Health Service Executive, Ulster Bank, Co-operation Ireland, Coillte and Lifetime Assurance (Bank of Ireland's life assurance subsidiary). She serves/has served on the audit committee of An Garda Síochána, Dun Laoghaire Rathdown County Council, the Department of Agriculture and Food and is former chair and member of the UCD Audit Committee. She chaired the Commission on Financial Management and Control Systems in the Health Services and was vice-chair of the Review Group on Auditing.

Anthony Burke

Anthony Burke, ACA, BBS, is a Chartered Accountant with over 10 years' experience working in practice, industry and academia. Anthony is currently in the final stages of his doctoral thesis at Waterford Institute of Technology (WIT). His research focuses on the nature of contemporary accounting work in organisations and the current issues facing accountants in the workplace. Anthony also lectures a number of accounting and management modules at both WIT and Trinity College Dublin, where he was the recipient of a Teaching Excellence Award in 2018.

Richard Burke

Richard Burke, BBS, H.Dip Ed., MBSI, PhD, is a lecturer in finance at Waterford Institute of Technology. He teaches a wide range of modules and has supervised students conducting research at both undergraduate and postgraduate levels. His research interests include corporate governance, equity release schemes and public private partnerships. Richard completed his doctoral thesis on public private partnerships at Queen's University, Belfast in 2014. Richard has contributed to a number of books and has published in a number of peer-reviewed journals.

John Casey

John Casey, FCA, BComm, MSc, is a Chartered Accountant and has an MSc in finance. Having previously worked as an auditor with PwC, John lectures at Waterford Institute of Technology (WIT), where he is programme director for the MSc in Global Financial Information Systems (GFIS). He has served as an examination moderator for the professional accounting institutes. He is a former committee member of the Irish Accounting and Finance Association (IAFA) and is currently a member of the AIB Centre for Finance and Business Research at WIT. John is co-author of the *South East Economic Monitor*, an annual publication that tracks key economic indicators, capturing data on the economy of the five counties of Ireland's South East. He is also co-author with Clare Kearney of *Advanced Cases in Financial Reporting* (Chartered Accountants Ireland, 2012).

Margaret Cullen

Margaret Cullen, BA, MSc, PhD, is a specialist in the areas of corporate and investment fund governance. She holds a BA in economics from University College Dublin (UCD), an MSc in Investment and Treasury from Dublin City University and a PhD in corporate governance from UCD. Her doctoral research explored the role and effectiveness of boards of directors in investment fund governance. Prior to completing her doctoral research, Margaret worked for 12 years in the financial services industry. She has held senior positions at ABN AMRO International Financial Services Company, the Central Bank of Ireland, JP Morgan Bank Ireland plc and RBC Dexia Investor Services Ireland Ltd. Margaret is CEO and Academic Director of the Certified Investment Fund Director Institute (CIFDI), a specialist institute of the Institute of Banking (IoB) which focuses on raising professional standards in investment fund governance through its flagship Certified Investment Fund Director Programme and the on-going professional development of CIFDI members. Margaret also lectures on bank governance on the IoB's Certified Bank Director Programme. She is an associate lecturer for the UCD Centre of Corporate Governance, lecturing on the Professional Diploma in Corporate Governance since 2007 in the areas of executive remuneration and behavioural aspects of boards. Margaret is a former non-executive director of the Qualifications and Quality Authority of Ireland. She is a non-executive director on the board of The Progressive Building Society in the UK and of BNP Paribas Fund Administration Services (Ireland) Ltd.

Clare Kearney

Clare Kearney, FCA, BSc (Mgmt), MA, is a lecturer in financial reporting and corporate finance at Waterford Institute of Technology (WIT), where she has also been involved in the management and co-ordination of academic programmes. In 2017, she completed a Master's in Education. Before joining WIT, Clare trained as a Chartered Accountant with Deloitte. She has lectured at all levels of accounting education including undergraduate, postgraduate and professional. She is currently an acting external examiner at Dundalk Institute of Technology and served as an examiner for Chartered Accountants Ireland for a number of years. Clare is currently a member and a former chair of the Irish Accounting and Finance Association (IAFA). She is also a member of the AIB Centre for Finance and Business Research at WIT. She is co-author with John Casey of *Advanced Cases in Financial Reporting* (Chartered Accountants Ireland, 2012).

Rosemarie Kelly

Rosemarie Kelly FCA, BComm, Dip Prof Acc, MBS, PhD qualified as a Chartered Accountant with PricewaterhouseCoopers and worked in industry in the United Kingdom and Australia for a number of years prior to joining Waterford Institute of Technology as a lecturer in finance. She has lectured a wide variety of modules at undergraduate and postgraduate levels, including finance, auditing, management accounting, corporate governance and forensic accounting. She has also supervised postgraduate students at Masters and PhD level. Her research interests primarily relate to management accounting and public sector organisations.

Introduction

This book is structured as follows: Part I provides an overview of the topics of corporate governance and ethics and Part II presents case studies addressing corporate governance and/or ethical matters. Part I does not attempt to provide a deep-dive, comprehensive review of corporate governance and ethics. Rather, the aim is to introduce some of the philosophical and/or practical corporate governance and ethics matters that a reader may find useful when addressing the case studies in Part II. While knowledge of corporate governance best practices, moral philosophy and ethical theories is necessary to explore and examine the complexities of corporate governance and ethics, we fundamentally believe that such matters are inherently practical.

In total, 10 authors have come together to develop the case studies presented in Part II. Thirty case studies have been designed to provide the reader with opportunities to gain insights into the corporate governance and ethical challenges that may arise in real life. Each case is fictitious. However, by examining and exploring the issues presented in each case, the reader, we hope, will gain an insight into the practical challenges and dilemmas that can emerge. Thus, when reading the case studies, some common themes will be evident, while in other case studies issues unique to the setting will be present. Moreover, the line between a corporate governance issue and an ethical issue will be at times difficult, if not impossible, to determine or define. Not all the matters presented in the case studies are negative. Thus, the reader is encouraged to think, not only about possible negative issues presented in the cases but also about the positive insights that may be drawn from them. Each case is designed to encourage discussion and debate; as such, there are no model solutions to the questions posed in or by the cases. That said, certain 'rules-of-thumb', 'best-practices' or 'norms' will assist the reader to navigate the, often complex, issues addressed in and by the cases. It is intended that the cases will encourage readers to reflect upon the complexities that can and do arise in practice. In this way, we hope to assist the reader to develop an informed, sophisticated understanding and appreciation of corporate governance and ethical issues and dilemmas.

Acknowledgements

We would like to thank Michael Diviney and Susan Rossney at Chartered Accountants Ireland for all of their help, support and wonderful guidance throughout the production of this book. We would also like to express our sincerest gratitude to all of the contributors, who so willingly gave up their time to produce an excellent set of cases that we believe are an invaluable resource for those who are using this book as part of their studies. Their professionalism, attention to detail and all-round collegiality made each and every contributor a pleasure to work with.

PART I

CORPORATE GOVERNANCE AND BUSINESS ETHICS: AN INTRODUCTION

Chapter 1

Corporate Governance

Collette Kirwan and Chris O'Riordan

1.1 What is Corporate Governance?

Corporate governance is concerned with directing or steering a corporate entity (the word 'governance' comes from the Latin word '*gubernare*', meaning 'to steer'[1]). The *Cadbury Report* (1992), a precursor of the *UK Corporate Governance Code* (see **Section 1.2** below), defines corporate governance as "the system by which companies are directed and controlled".[2] Thus, emphasis is given to the structures and processes (i.e. systems) that facilitate the board of directors, who are "responsible for the governance of their companies", to direct **and** control. The *Cadbury Report* further explains that the "shareholders' role in governance is to appoint the directors and the auditors and to satisfy themselves that an appropriate governance structure is in place".[3]

However, corporate governance is not confined to the structures and processes operating within a company. Indeed, "what is going on in the engine of the company underneath [the] structures and systems is arguably more important, i.e. culture".[4] In 2016, the Financial Reporting Council (FRC) published a report on how boards of directors and executive management might steer

---

[1] Solomon J. and Solomon, A., *Corporate Governance and Accountability* (John Wiley & Sons, 2004).

[2] *Report of the Committee on the Financial Aspects of Corporate Governance* ("The Cadbury Report") (Gee Publishing, 1992), para. 2.5.

[3] *Ibid.*

[4] Brennan, N.M., "What is corporate governance?", *Business and Leadership*, 28 July 2014. Available at https://www.businessandleadership.com/leadership/item/46921-what-is-corporate-governance/ (accessed March 2018).

corporate behaviour to create a healthy corporate culture.[5] Sir Winfried Bischoff, Chair of the FRC, states in the foreword to the report that: "Strong governance underpins a healthy culture, and boards should demonstrate good practice in the boardroom and promote good governance throughout the business".[6]

As can be seen, corporate governance is a complex topic and its reach extends beyond the inner structures and processes of an entity. Although shareholders, the board of directors and executive management are considered to be the central players in corporate governance,[7] its scope extends to and incorporates others such as external auditors, contractual stakeholders (e.g. employees, suppliers, customers, lenders, etc.), regulators and the wider society. Perhaps now more than ever, we can see the broad societal impact of good corporate governance and the wide-reaching implications of corporate governance failures.

1.2 Corporate Governance Codes and Recommendations

Entities can take different forms and the corporate governance regimes that apply differs between entity types. In this section, the governance regimes of listed UK/Irish entities, private entities and not-for-profit organisations are considered.

1.2.1 Listed Entities

The first UK corporate governance report (or code) was published in 1992 by a committee chaired by Sir Adrian Cadbury. The report, entitled *The Financial Aspects of Corporate Governance* but generally known as the "Cadbury Report", was published in response to a number of corporate governance failures in the UK. Since 1992 numerous other reports have been published. **Figure 1.1** summarises the main UK corporate governance codes/reports and key developments between 1992 and 2016.[8]

As did its predecessors (see **Figure 1.1**), the *UK Corporate Governance Code* (2016),[9] adopts a 'comply or explain' approach. As such, the Code does not

---

[5] Financial Reporting Council, *Corporate Culture and the Role of Boards* (2016). Available at https://www.frc.org.uk/getattachment/3851b9c5-92d3-4695-aeb2-87c9052dc8c1/Corporate-Culture-and-the-Role-of-Boards-Report-of-Observations.pdf (accessed March 2018).

[6] *Ibid*. p. 2.

[7] Tricker, B., *Corporate Governance: Principles, Policies, and Practices* (3rd Edition, Oxford, 2015).

[8] In July 2018, the Financial Reporting Council released the 2018 *UK Corporate Governance Code*. Because the 2018 Code applies to accounting periods beginning on or after 1 January 2019, in the sections that follow, unless otherwise indicated, reference is made to the 2016 *UK Corporate Governance Code*.

[9] Financial Reporting Council, *The UK Corporate Governance Code* (FRC, 2016). Available at https://www.frc.org.uk/getattachment/ca7e94c4-b9a9-49e2-a824-ad76a322873c/UK-Corporate-Governance-Code-April-2016.pdf (accessed May 2018), hereinafter referred to as the *UK Corporate Governance Code* or, simply, the 'Code'.

represent a list of corporate governance rules. Rather, the Code includes a number of principles (main and supporting) and provisions. Under the UK Listing Authority (UKLA) *Listing Rules*,[10] all companies with a premium listing of equity shares must disclose in their annual report how they have applied the Code. If a company decides not to comply with the Code, clear and meaningful explanations must be included in the annual report. The explanations should outline why the company decided not to comply with the Code. This 'comply or explain' approach accommodates the dynamic nature of corporate governance and the Code acknowledges that non-compliance "may be justified in particular circumstances if good governance can be achieved by other means".[11] In Ireland, the corporate governance regime is similar to that in the UK. However, in addition to complying with the *UK Corporate Governance Code*, companies listed on the Main Securities Market are required to comply with the "Irish Corporate Governance Annex".[12]

On 16 July 2018, the FRC released the 2018 *UK Corporate Governance Code*.[13] The 2018 Code continues to provide flexibility through the application of principles and 'comply or explain' provisions and supporting guidance (supporting principles have been removed). The 2018 Code emphasises the importance of positive relationships between companies, shareholders and stakeholders and calls for companies to establish a corporate culture that aligns with the purpose of the company and its business strategy, promotes integrity and values diversity. It incorporates a new provision recommending greater engagement between the board and the workforce of the company. In addition, it recommends that remuneration committees should consider workforce remuneration when setting the remuneration of directors. Because the 2018 Code applies to accounting periods beginning on or after 1 January 2019, in the sections that follow, unless otherwise indicated, reference is made to the 2016 *UK Corporate Governance Code*.

---

[10] The UK Listing Authority *Listing Rules* are available at https://www.handbook.fca.org.uk/handbook/LR.pdf

[11] *Ibid*. p. 4.

[12] Irish Stock Exchange, *Main Securities Market Listing Rules and Admission to Trading Rules*, Appendix 4, "Irish Corporate Governance Annex" (ISE, 2011).

[13] Further details of the 2018 *UK Corporate Governance Code* are available from https://www.frc.org.uk/news/july-2018/a-uk-corporate-governance-code-that-is-fit-for-the (accessed July 2018).

FIGURE 1.1: EVOLUTION OF UK CORPORATE GOVERNANCE REPORTS AND CODES 1992 - 2016[14]

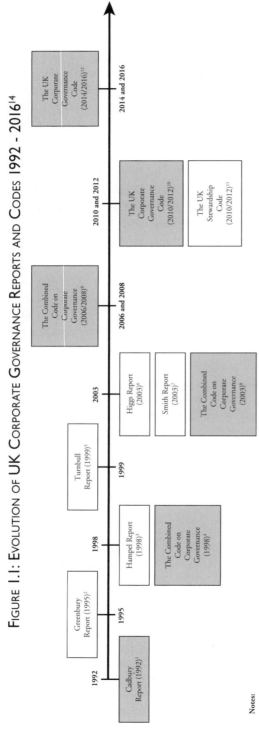

Notes:

1. The *Cadbury Report* (1992) introduced the principle of 'comply or explain' and addressed matters such as the role of non-executive directors and audit committees, the division of responsibilities between the chair and the chief executive officer, and financial aspects of corporate governance.
2. The *Greenbury Report* (1995) addressed directors remuneration.
3. The *Hampel Report* (1998) reviewed the *Cadbury* and *Greenbury Reports*.
4. The *Combined Code on Corporate Governance* (1998) consolidated the *Cadbury, Greenbury* and *Hampel Reports*.
5. The *Turnbull Report* (1999) addressed internal controls including financial, operational, compliance and risk management. It was revised in 2005.
6. The *Higgs Report* (2003) addressed the role and effectiveness of non-executive directors.
7. The *Smith Report* (2003) addressed the role of audit committees.
8. The *Combined Code on Corporate Governance* (2003) revised the 1998 Code to incorporate the *Higgs* and *Smith Reports*.
9. Following two consultation exercises, the *Combined Code on Corporate Governance* (2003) was revised in 2006. It was further revised in 2008 to reflect new EU requirements relating to audit committees and corporate governance statements.
10. The *UK Corporate Governance Code* (2010) updated the *Combined Code on Corporate Governance* of 2006. The 2010 Code addressed five areas: (i) leadership; (ii) effectiveness; (iii) accountability; (iv) remuneration; and (v) relations with shareholders. The 2010 Code was further updated in 2012. The changes included confirmation by boards that the annual report and accounts taken as a whole are fair, balanced and understandable, and that companies explain and report on progress with their policies on boardroom diversity.
11. The *UK Stewardship Code*, first issued in 2010 and revised in 2012, provides guidance on good practice for investors and should be considered a companion piece to the *UK Corporate Governance Code*.
12. The *UK Corporate Governance Code* (2014) updated the 2012 Code. It was revised to enhance the quality of information received by investors about the long-term health and strategy of listed companies. In 2016, the *UK Corporate Governance Code* was revised to implement the EU Audit Regulation and Directive.

14 A detailed account of the origins and evolution of the *UK Corporate Governance Code* is available from the FRC at https://www.frc.org.uk/directors/corporate-governance-and-stewardship/uk-corporate-governance-code/history-of-the-uk-corporate-governance-code (accessed May 2018).

As outlined, the *UK Corporate Governance Code* incorporates a number of principles (main and supporting) and provisions. **Table 1.1** below reproduces from the Code the main principles listed according to the five sections of the Code.

TABLE 1.1: MAIN PRINCIPLES OF THE UK CORPORATE GOVERNANCE CODE (2016)[15]

"Section A: Leadership
- Every company should be headed by an effective board which is collectively responsible for the long-term success of the company.
- There should be a clear division of responsibilities at the head of the company between the running of the board and the executive responsibility for the running of the company's business. No one individual should have unfettered powers of decision.
- The chair is responsible for leadership of the board and ensuring its effectiveness on all aspects of its role.
- As part of their role as members of a unitary board, non-executive directors should constructively challenge and help develop proposals on strategy.

Section B: Effectiveness
- The board and its committees should have the appropriate balance of skills, experience, independence and knowledge of the company to enable them to discharge their respective duties and responsibilities effectively.
- There should be a formal, rigorous and transparent procedure for the appointment of new directors to the board.
- All directors should be able to allocate sufficient time to the company to discharge their responsibilities effectively.
- All directors should receive induction on joining the board and should regularly update and refresh their skills and knowledge.
- The board should be supplied in a timely manner with information in a form and of a quality appropriate to enable it to discharge its duties.
- The board should undertake a formal and rigorous annual evaluation of its own performance and that of its committees and individual directors.
- All directors should be submitted for re-election at regular intervals, subject to continued satisfactory performance.

Section C: Accountability
- The board should present a fair, balanced and understandable assessment of the company's position and prospects.
- The board is responsible for determining the nature and extent of the principal risks it is willing to take in achieving its strategic objectives. The board should maintain sound risk management and internal control systems.

---

[15] *The UK Corporate Governance Code* (*op. cit.* above, n. 9), pp. 5 and 6.

- The board should establish formal and transparent arrangements for considering how they should apply the corporate reporting, risk management and internal control principles and for maintaining an appropriate relationship with the company's auditors.

Section D: Remuneration

- Executive directors' remuneration should be designed to promote the long-term success of the company. Performance-related elements should be transparent, stretching and rigorously applied.
- There should be a formal and transparent procedure for developing policy on executive remuneration and for fixing the remuneration packages of individual directors. No director should be involved in deciding his or her own remuneration.

Section E: Relations with Shareholders

- There should be a dialogue with shareholders based on the mutual understanding of objectives. The board as a whole has responsibility for ensuring that a satisfactory dialogue with shareholders takes place.
- The board should use general meetings to communicate with investors and to encourage their participation."

In the Code, the main principles are informed by supporting principles and more specific provisions. For example, the Code incorporates provisions addressing the composition of boards of directors and its committees. **Table 1.2** provides a summary of these provisions.

TABLE 1.2: UK CORPORATE GOVERNANCE CODE (2016) – COMPOSITION OF THE BOARD OF DIRECTORS AND ITS COMMITTEES[16]

Board of Directors

- The chair and chief executive should not be the same individual (Provision A.2.1).
- The chair should be independent on appointment (Provision A.3.1).[17]
- The chief executive should not go on to become chair unless all major shareholders are consulted (Provision A.3.1).
- The board should appoint one of the independent non-executive directors to be the senior independent director (Provision A.4.1).
- For FTSE 350 companies, at least half of the board, excluding the chair, should comprise independent non-executive directors. Smaller companies should have at least two independent non-executive directors. A smaller company is one that is below the FTSE 350 throughout the year immediately prior to the reporting year (Provision B.1.2).[18]

---

[16] *The UK Corporate Governance Code* (FRC, *op. cit.* above, n. 9).

[17] 'Independence' is defined in Provision B.1.1 of the Code.

[18] The "Irish Corporate Governance Annex" (*op. cit.* above, n. 12) includes interpretative provisions for companies that are of an equivalent size to companies that are included in the FTSE 100 and FTSE 350 indices. Details are available at http://www.ise.ie/Products-Services/Sponsors-and-Advisors/MSM-Listing-Rules.pdf (accessed June 2018).

Nomination Committee
- The nomination committee should comprise majority of independent non-executive directors (Provision B.2.1).

Audit Committee
- The audit committee should comprise at least three independent non-executive directors (two for smaller companies) (Provision C.3.1).
- The audit committee should comprise at least one member with recent and relevant financial experience (Provision C.3.1).

Remuneration Committee
- The remuneration committee should comprise at least three independent non-executive directors (two for smaller companies) (Provision D.2.1).

Section 1.3 below describes the roles and responsibilities of the board of directors, board committees, the chair, non-executive directors, the chief executive officer and the Company Secretary. (Readers are advised to consult the full text of the *UK Corporate Governance Code*.)

1.2.2 Private Entities

Although the corporate governance of listed entities receives significant attention from policy-makers, practitioners and academics, globally, most corporate entities are unlisted. Unlisted entities may include start-ups, founder-owned and managed companies, family companies, private equity-owned companies, joint ventures, subsidiaries and state-owned entities.[19]

A large proportion of unlisted entities are founder- or family-owned.[20] Internationally, and in Ireland, the family business sector is significant. Family businesses are a vital part of the Irish economy and a significant source of job creation.[21] Given the economic importance of private family companies, their governance environment has important practical implications. The basic principles of good corporate governance are relevant to private family companies; however, the unique characteristics of private family companies present unique corporate governance considerations and challenges.

---

[19] Institute of Directors (UK), *Corporate Governance Guidance and Principles for Unlisted Companies in the UK* (Institute of Directors (UK), 2010), p. 9. Available at https://www.iod.com/news/news/articles/Corporate-Governance-for-Unlisted-Companies (accessed May 2018).

[20] Tricker, B., *op. cit.* above, n. 7.

[21] PwC Ireland, '*The Missing Middle*: Bridging the Strategy Gap in Family Firms' (PwC Ireland, 2016). Available at https://www.pwc.ie/publications/2016/family-business-survey.pdf (accessed April 2018).

The existence of three overlapping core systems, or dimensions, influences the governance of private family companies (see **Figure 1.2**):

1. family;
2. business, and
3. ownership.

Understanding the three separate but inter-related dimensions is fundamental to understanding the governance challenges of private family companies. Each dimension requires consideration. In his book, *Family Enterprises: The Essentials*, Peter Leach suggests that the family dimension is based on emotion.[22] Family members are "bound together by deep emotional ties that can be both positive and negative".[23] Often, family members will emphasise values such as long-term loyalty[24] and creating a legacy for the next generation.[25] The business dimension is concerned with the production/supply of goods and services, contractual relationships (e.g. suppliers, customers, employees), attainment of tasks,[26] and operational needs.[27] The ownership dimension is concerned with maintaining adequate control over the business so as to guide it towards long-term success.[28]

FIGURE 1.2: THE THREE-CIRCLE MODEL OF A FAMILY BUSINESS[29]

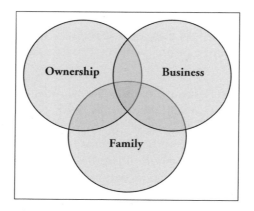

---

[22] Leach, P., *Family Enterprises: The Essentials* (Profile Books, 2015).
[23] *Ibid.* pp. 37–38.
[24] *Ibid.*
[25] McCarthy, K., *Family Business: A Survival Guide* (Chartered Accountants Ireland, 2014).
[26] Leach, P., *op. cit.* above, n. 22.
[27] McCarthy, K., *op. cit.* above, n. 25.
[28] *Ibid.*
[29] Family companies are often depicted as three intersecting circles. Here, we use the three-circle model presented by Kieran McCarthy (*op. cit.* above, n. 25). The original model was developed by Renato Tagiuri and John Davis (see Leach, P., *op, cit.* above, n. 22).

The ownership of private family companies is often depicted as progressing through three lifecycle stages[30]:

1. owner-managed firms;
2. sibling partnerships; and
3. cousin consortiums.

The ownership evolution of a private family company has important implications for its governance. For instance, at the owner-managed stage, it is likely that management and governance of the company will be intertwined with little, if any, separation between owners, directors and senior managers.[31] However, it is important at this stage (and indeed at all other stages) to recognise that the company is not an extension of the owners' personal property.[32] Assuming the company transitions to the next lifecycle stage – 'sibling partnership' (i.e. two or more siblings inherit their parents' shares in the company) – it becomes necessary to develop processes and procedures for sharing decision-making power and control among siblings. By the time the company transitions to the third stage – 'cousin consortium' – there may be multiple family members, representing different branches of the family, with ownership stakes in the company. Some owners may have a significant ownership stake while others may not. Some owners may work in the company while others may not.[33] The involvement of multiple generations can present challenges. For example, multiple opinions and expectations can cause tensions and conflicts. However, good governance can ease complexities and promote sustainability.[34]

The governance of private family companies involves the governance of the company itself (i.e. corporate governance) and the governance of the family (i.e. family governance). Family governance is concerned with:

1. defining the roles, responsibilities and rights of family members;
2. establishing how the family interacts with the business; and
3. establishing how the owners interact with the board of directors and management of the company.[35]

Family governance mechanisms may include family constitutions and family councils. A family constitution is "a written statement (gained by consensus) of the family's shared values and policies in relation to ownership and operation of the business".[36] A family council is a group of family

[30] Leach, P., *op. cit.* above, n. 22.
[31] Tricker, B., *op. cit.* above, n. 7.
[32] Institute of Directors (UK), *op. cit.* above, n. 19 (accessed May 2018).
[33] Leach, P., *op. cit.* above, n. 22.
[34] McCarthy, K., *op. cit.* above, n. 25.
[35] *Ibid.*
[36] Leach, P., *op. cit.* above, n. 22, p. 133.

members that meet in a forum separate to the business. Its role is to represent the interests of the family and to act as a bridge between the family (shareholders) and the board of directors.[37]

In 2010, the Institute of Directors in the UK published *Corporate Governance Guidance and Principles for Unlisted Companies in the UK*,[38] which provides a set of voluntary best practice principles for unlisted companies. The Institute of Directors argue that, in the absence of their own specific corporate governance code, unlisted entities may "refrain from developing an appropriate governance framework, with negative implications for their long-term effectiveness and success".[39] **Table 1.3** lists the principles identified in the *Corporate Governance Guidance and Principles for Unlisted Companies in the UK*.

TABLE 1.3: CORPORATE GOVERNANCE GUIDANCE AND PRINCIPLES FOR UNLISTED COMPANIES[40]

Phase 1 Principles: Applicable to all unlisted companies

1. Shareholders should establish an appropriate constitutional and governance framework for the company.
2. Every company should strive to establish an effective board, which is collectively responsible for the long-term success of the company, including the definition of the corporate strategy. However, an interim step on the road to an effective (and independent) board may be the creation of an advisory board.
3. The size and composition of the board should reflect the scale and complexity of the company's activities.
4. The board should meet sufficiently regularly to discharge its duties, and be supplied in a timely manner with appropriate information.
5. Levels of remuneration should be sufficient to attract, retain, and motivate executives and non-executives of the quality required to run the company successfully.
6. The board is responsible for risk oversight and should maintain a sound system of internal control to safeguard shareholders' investment and the company's assets.
7. There should be a dialogue between the board and the shareholders based on a mutual understanding of objectives. The board as a whole has responsibility for ensuring that a satisfactory dialogue with shareholders takes place. The board should not forget that all shareholders have to be treated equally.

---

[37] McCarthy, K., *op. cit.* above, n. 25.

[38] The *Corporate Governance Guidance and Principles for Unlisted Companies in the UK* (Institute of Directors (UK), *op. cit.* above, n. 19) is the UK edition of pan-European guidance developed by the European Confederation of Directors' Associations (ecoDa).

[39] Institute of Directors (UK), *op cit.* above, n. 19, p. 9.

[40] *Ibid.* p. 7.

8. All directors should receive induction on joining the board and should regularly update and refresh their skills and knowledge.
9. Family-controlled companies should establish family governance mechanisms that promote coordination and mutual understanding amongst family members, as well as organise the relationship between family governance and corporate governance.

Phase 2 Principles: Applicable to large and/or more complex unlisted companies

10. There should be a clear division of responsibilities at the head of the company between the running of the board and the running of the company's business. No one individual should have unfettered powers of decision.
11. All boards should contain directors with a sufficient mix of competencies and experiences. No single person (or small group of individuals) should dominate the board's decision-making.
12. The board should establish appropriate board committees in order to allow a more effective discharge of its duties.
13. The board should undertake a periodic appraisal of its own performance and that of each individual director.
14. The board should present a balanced and understandable assessment of the company's position and prospects for external stakeholders, and establish a suitable programme of stakeholder engagement.

Acknowledging the dynamic nature of governance, the Institute of Directors in the UK list the 14 principles on the basis of a phased approach, taking into account the size, complexity and level of maturity of individual entities. Principles 1 to 9 are applicable to all unlisted companies. Principles 10 to 14 are applicable to large and/or more complex companies.

1.2.3 Not-for-profit Organisations

Not-for-profit organisations are both socially and economically significant. Charities, a subset of not-for-profit organisations, will often serve those who are most disadvantaged and deliver critical public services.[41] In the Republic of Ireland,[42] the Charities Act 2009 aims to achieve greater accountability and to enhance public trust and confidence in charities. Moreover, the Act provides for the establishment of the Charities Regulatory Authority and a Register of Charities. It should be noted that in the not-for-profit sector, the governing body of the organisation may be given a variety of names

---

[41] Connolly, C., Hyndman, N. and Liguori, M., *Charity Accounting and Reporting at a Time of Change* (Chartered Accountants Ireland, 2017).

[42] In the UK, the main pieces of legislation are: the Charities Act (England and Wales) 2011; the Charities and Trustee Investment (Scotland) Act 2005; and the Charities Act (Northern Ireland) 2008 (see Connolly *et al.*, *op. cit.* above, n. 41).

including council, management committee, board of governors, board of trustees, or board of directors.[43]

Organisations in the not-for-profit sector (e.g. charities, sports associations, cultural organisations and other entities in the public and voluntary sectors) require sound governance policies and procedures.[44] In the Republic of Ireland, *The Governance Code*[45] is a resource developed for community, voluntary and charitable (CVC) organisations. It is a voluntary code of practice for good governance and provides governance practices tailored for very small, medium and large CVC organisations. *The Governance Code* is based on five principles:

1. leading the organisation;
2. exercising control over the organisation;
3. being transparent and accountable;
4. working effectively; and
5. behaving with integrity.

Readers should refer to *The Governance Code* itself for more information.

1.3 Company Boards of Directors and Board Committees[46]

In the Republic of Ireland,[47] the eight principal fiduciary duties of company directors are set out in section 228 of the Companies Act 2014 (previously these were recognised only in common law).[48] These principal fiduciary duties of company directors are summarised below in **Table 1.4**.

---

[43] Tricker, B., *op. cit.*, above, n. 7, pp. 136 and 276.

[44] Tricker, B., *op. cit.*, above, n. 7.

[45] *The Governance Code* (October 2016) ("A Code of Practice for Good Governance of Community, Voluntary and Charitable Organisations in Ireland") is available from www. governancecode.ie (accessed May 2018).

[46] In writing **Section 1.3**, the authors have made use of David W. Duffy's book, *A Practical Guide to Corporate Governance* (Chartered Accountants Ireland, 2014). Where direct quotations have been used, we have referenced these in the text. However, to avoid being overly repetitious, we have not directly cited this publication otherwise. We encourage readers, who are interested in exploring corporate governance further, and particularly in a practical context, to read this publication.

[47] In the UK, the seven general duties of directors are set out in the Companies Act 2006. For further information, refer to Sturgeon, L., *An Introduction to Business Law in Northern Ireland*, 2nd Edition (Chartered Accountants Ireland, 2016) and https://www.legislation. gov.uk/ukpga/2006/46/contents.

[48] Chartered Accountants Ireland, "Codification of Directors' Duties under the Companies Act 2014". Available at https://www.charteredaccountants.ie/Member/Technical/Companies-Act-2014/Corporate-governance-and-Directors-Duties/Changes-in-corporate-governance-requirements-under-2014-Act/Codification-of-Directors-Duties-under-the-2014-Act (accessed June 2018).

TABLE 1.4: PRINCIPAL FIDUCIARY DUTIES OF COMPANY DIRECTORS

1. Act in good faith in what the director considers to be the interests of the company.
2. Act honestly and responsibly in relation to the conduct of the affairs of the company.
3. Act in accordance with the company's constitution and exercise his/her powers only for the purposes allowed by law.
4. Not to use the company's property, information or opportunities for his/her own or anyone else's benefit.
5. Not agree to restrict the director's power to exercise independent judgement.
6. Avoid any conflict of interest between the director's duties to the company and his/her own interests.
7. Exercise the care, skill and diligence which would be exercised in the same circumstances by a reasonable person.
8. To have regard to the interests of the members of the company, in addition to the duty to have regard to the interests of the company's employees in general (referring to section 224 of the Companies Act 2014).

As well as being a legal requirement, in most cases the board of directors is also a critical component in the management of incorporated entities. The board connects the company to key stakeholders, most notably the shareholders, who ultimately elect its members. The board exists at the centre of the organisation and has significant power, holding the ultimate authority over all decisions. While many of these decisions, particularly the more routine ones, are delegated to lower levels of management, the board remains accountable for the outcomes of these decisions and the performance of the company. The directors together must put in place proper functioning controls to satisfy themselves that they are able to carry out their role and to manage risks that the company faces.

Consequently, it is essential that the board are properly informed about what is happening internally and externally, in a timely manner and in a format that they can utilise effectively and understand fully. In doing this, board members meet regularly and collectively to consider all of this information and the implications that this has, particularly at a strategic level. This is because a key part of the remit of any board is strategy setting and monitoring and, stemming from this, ensuring that appropriate actions are taken when either the strategy itself is no longer fit for purpose or its achievement is wavering.

If the board is not working effectively, the company will suffer, and it is incumbent on all members of the board to act in the best interests of the company. The board should not operate as a 'clique' or become overly comfortable, nor should it be laced with recurring conflict or hostility. A middle ground should be aspired to where members of the board work well together and deal with matters and any disagreements in a non-personal, mature and constructive manner. This also sets an example for the rest of the organisation, as the board represents the values and ethical compass of the company, setting the 'tone from the top'.

1.3.1 Board Members

The configuration and composition of boards of directors can vary. For example, the boards of directors of larger entities tend to include both executive (see **Section 1.3.1.3**) and non-executive directors (**Section 1.3.1.2**), while in smaller, founder-owned and managed companies the board of directors may be comprised of executive directors only. The presence of non-executive directors can provide additional perspectives and independence in decision-making, though this does give rise to an additional cost for the business. In this section, the roles and responsibilities of members commonly found on the boards of directors of companies are considered.

1.3.1.1 The Chair

As the head of a board, typically filled with both executive and non-executive directors, the chair sits, metaphorically, somewhat removed and he or she is often independent of the executives (though not always, if they are an executive chair). In this respect, organising, overseeing and arranging are key elements of a chair's work, ensuring that plans, processes and information, among other aspects, are in place. The chair's attitude to leadership must be one of clear impartiality. While their tenure may end up being more akin to that of an executive director – and thus they may have a long relationship with the executive directors if they are in situ for many years – they must maintain the independence of a non-executive in how they operate.

The chair strives to maintain order and discipline (when needed) so that the board can function in a manner that is efficient, effective, fair and accountable. If the board appears to be no longer delivering in these areas, or is underperforming as a board, the chair will be central to remedying this through discussions with board members and others (such as consultants and advisors, where relevant), and prompting appropriate action. The chair should be comfortable in engaging with different groups and stakeholders, internally and externally, and typically comes to the role from elsewhere with extensive and established knowledge and experience as a company director. This gives them credibility both within and outside the organisation. **Table 1.6** in **Appendix 1.1** to this chapter summarises the roles and responsibilities of the chair.

1.3.1.2 Non-executive Directors

While the independence of the chair is a valuable asset to any board of directors, if the chair is the only independent voice among a dominant group of executive directors, their capacity to influence and balance decision-making in the interests of the company will be diluted. Therefore, it is important for companies to ensure that independent perspectives are heard and are prominent at board level. (See **Section 1.3.3.1** for a discussion of the meaning of 'independence' in this context.) This can be achieved through the prominent presence on the board of a number of 'non-executive directors', who will strive to serve and protect the best interests of the company.

As their title suggests, 'non-executive directors' are not part of the executive management of the company and are therefore not employees in the traditional sense. While they are remunerated for their work, it is typically in the form of fees (an annual sum as a retainer and/or a sum per meeting attended) instead of a salary or incentive payment.[49] As a result, non-executive directors generally do not have a direct, vested financial interest in the performance of the company, which has the effect of reducing the risk that they will act in their own interests rather than those of the company.

However, the value that non-executive directors bring to a board of directors is likely to involve much more than just protecting the interests of the company, as they will bring their different experiences, insights and perspectives, as well as new knowledge, expanded networks and business contacts. In other words, a key contribution non-executive directors can make is to provide alternatives to the perspectives and priorities of the executive members of the board, challenging the status quo that would otherwise persist, raising issues that the executives might not have been aware of or asking questions that they may not want to address.

When effectively leveraged through its board, this combination of executive directors' detailed knowledge of the business with the informed, expert and challenging views of the non-executive directors can create a competitive advantage for any organisation. Of course, the selection of the right

---

[49] Provision D.2.3 of *The UK Corporate Governance Code* (FRC, *op. cit.* above, n. 9) states that "The board itself or, where required by the Articles of Association, the shareholders should determine the remuneration of the non-executive directors within the limits set in the Articles of Association. Where permitted by the Articles, the board may however delegate this responsibility to a committee, which might include the chief executive."

people as non-executive directors is critical and this is part of the remit of the board's nomination committee (see **Section 1.3.2.3**). Some companies may decide to appoint one of their independent non-executive directors as a senior independent director, who has added responsibilities in helping to address issues, conflicts and disputes that may arise between board members. The *UK Corporate Governance Code* specifies that the senior independent director acts as "a sounding board for the chairman", is "an intermediary for the other directors when necessary" and "should be available to shareholders if they have concerns which contact through the normal channels of chair, chief executive or other executive directors has failed to resolve or for which such contact is inappropriate".[50] **Table 1.7** in **Appendix 1.1** summarises the roles and responsibilities of non-executive directors.

1.3.1.3 Executive Directors

While it was mooted above that non-executive directors act as a counter-balance to the potential for executive directors to put their interests before the interests of the company, this is not to suggest that self-interested behaviour on the part of executive directors is inevitable. As with all directors, executive directors are required to act in a manner that is independent, objective and for the benefit of the company as a whole. Moreover, it is now established best practice that the remuneration of executive directors should be set only by non-executive directors, on the basis that no-one should decide their own pay (see **Section 1.3.2.2**). Again, this is not to say that executives *will* behave in a manner counter to the company's interests, but by virtue of their roles and power, this risk exists and is then mitigated by a greater representation of non-executives as protectors of the company's interests.

Larger companies (particularly listed entities) may have multiple executive directors, often with their own functional specialism (such as marketing, HR, production/operations, finance, etc.). These specialisms are important and represent the detailed knowledge of, and connection to, aspects of the business that such executive directors, as executive managers, bring to the board. In this respect, as the leaders of and representatives for their areas of responsibility within the company, executive directors might seek to use their position on the board to access resources and further their priorities. However, the interests of the company come first and, as directors, the executives need to be able to make that distinction (i.e. between the department/function they represent and the company as a whole) in how they act. Executive directors should seek to contribute to the board beyond their specialism because, as a member of the board of directors, they have collective responsibility for decisions taken; silence or inactivity is not an excuse

---

[50] *The UK Corporate Governance Code* (*op. cit.* above, n. 9) p. 9.

or a defence if poor actions result. That said, with the additional knowledge that their area of specialism gives them, it is imperative that they take extra care around decisions that directly or indirectly involve this knowledge, whether the decisions impinge on them or not. For example, during any boardroom discussions on advertising campaigns, one would expect all members to contribute some perspective, but this would be expected even more so from the marketing director. **Table 1.8** in **Appendix 1.1** summarises the roles and responsibilities of executive directors.

1.3.1.4 The Chief Executive

The pivotal executive director on the board is typically the chief executive officer (CEO) who runs the company on a day-to-day basis, and implements and reports on board-approved strategic plans that he or she will have had a key role in developing. However, it is worth noting that the chief executive does not necessarily have to be a member of the board and that some companies use instead the title 'managing director' to denote this distinction, i.e. that the person concerned is a director.[51] All of the specialist executive directors will generally report directly to the chief executive, who will thus lead and direct their work in a tactical and operational sense. In most organisations, with the chief executive at the helm, the executive management team, which often includes executives who are not on the board, will work and meet separately from the board with greater regularity. While the executive management team will make executive decisions, the board retains authority over these and will determine the extent to which the executive management team can act in a delegated capacity, i.e. what decisions require board approval and what decisions do not.

The chief executive is the connector between the board and the executive management team; indeed, in some companies, they may well be the only individual sitting on both the board of directors and the executive management team. Consequently, it is imperative that the chief executive is kept informed of all relevant matters that are being discussed within both groups so that he or she can communicate and report effectively between and on them. In particular, the chief executive will report regularly against agreed budgets and plans, with the nature of the plan determining the frequency of reporting (e.g. annual budgets on a monthly basis, strategic plans up to quarterly). It is worth noting that the chief executive, while an employee of the company, is appointed by the board and thus can also be removed by the board. **Table 1.9** in **Appendix 1.1** summarises the roles and responsibilities of the chief executive.

[51] Duffy, D.W., *A Practical Guide to Corporate Governance* (Chartered Accountants Ireland, 2014). See above, n. 46.

1.3.1.5 The Chair and the Chief Executive – Key Similarities and Differences

The relationship between the chief executive and chair is an important one and ideally should be respectful, constructive and effective. In essence, this means that they should work well together without unduly encroaching on each other's respective responsibilities. Where one seeks to dominate or undermine the other, this often translates into a dysfunctional board where little is achieved. Being typically the two most senior members of the board, it is important that the roles of chair and chief executive knit well together as a collective, but also that they are sufficiently demarcated to avoid duplication and undue interference. **Table 1.5** outlines some of the key similarities and differences between the two roles.

TABLE 1.5: CHAIR COMPARED TO CHIEF EXECUTIVE	
Chair	**Chief Executive**
Appointed by the board	Appointed by the board
Paid a salary or fee, typically fixed without performance incentives	Paid a salary and performance incentives
Not part of the executive management team[52]	Heads the executive management team
Works in a largely part-time capacity in the company	Works on a full-time basis in the company
Maintains order at board meetings	Maintains order at executive level
May hold shares in the company	May hold shares in the company
Staff do not report to the chair	Staff report to the chief executive

1.3.1.6 The Company Secretary

The Company Secretary "is responsible for supporting the board and the governance process, providing advice and guidance to the board on company law and regulations, its own policies and best practice in corporate governance".[53] In the Republic of Ireland, the duties of the Company Secretary are typically a combination of those that are set out in the Companies Act 2014[54] (such as preparing the minutes of board meetings, maintaining company registers and sending relevant documentation

---

[52] In some instances (e.g. private family companies), the chair might be an executive chair. In such instances, the executive chair will play a more active role in the day-to-day operations of the business.

[53] Duffy, D.W., *op. cit.* above, n. 46, p. 75.

[54] In the UK, the duties of the Company Secretary are set out in the Companies Act 2006, available from https://www.legislation.gov.uk/ukpga/2006/46/contents.

to the Companies Registration Office (Companies House in Northern Ireland) and those duties and responsibilities that the board delegate to the office holder). These will often include ensuring that board members receive relevant, accurate information in advance of board meetings, keeping the board updated on new legislation/regulations about which it needs to be aware, arranging board meetings and taking care of their administration, and reviewing the company's governance procedures to ensure they are functioning properly.

While the Company Secretary will generally attend board meetings and be an active contributor, particularly on matters directly related to their office, they do not necessarily have to be a director. Indeed, in some cases, the work performed by the Company Secretary is outsourced to professional advisors or professional services firms, which may prove to be more efficient for smaller companies as opposed to employing a specific person in the role. If they are not a director, they will therefore not be eligible to vote on board decisions. In recent years, the role of Company Secretary has increased in importance and it is incumbent on the company to ensure that the person/firm appointed has the necessary skills to perform the required duties and that these skills remain current. The guidance that the Company Secretary gives to board members in the context of their various obligations is critical, as they have expertise (particularly those with third-level or professional qualifications) that board members may not possess. Therefore, the Company Secretary needs to be suitably current in this knowledge to be able to provide appropriate and up-to-date advice and insight. In their capacity as the company's legal and compliance officer, the Company Secretary should also ensure that proper procedures – both those that are legally required and those that are self-imposed – are followed by the board so that its decisions are valid.

1.3.2 Board Committees

In order to discharge its considerable responsibilities, the board of directors of a company will form sub-committees of the board or 'board committees' that are tasked with areas of particular importance. As a sub-committee of the board, the powers of a board committee are derived from the board and it must therefore always remain under the board's control. Each committee's status and functions should be specified clearly in written terms of reference. The membership of board committees is usually made up either mostly or entirely of non-executive director members of the main board. This is to ensure the committees' independence and objectivity in making decisions in the best interests of the company.

While some board committees may be ad hoc and temporary in nature, others, partly because they are viewed as best practice under the *UK Corporate*

Governance Code, appear more commonly in the governance structures of most listed entities:

- the audit committee[55];
- the remuneration committee;
- the nomination committee; and
- the risk committee.

1.3.2.1 The Audit Committee

All listed companies are subjected to an external (statutory) audit by firms of independent auditors and, typically, to internal audit carried out by the internal department or function of their own organisation. External auditors report on the financial statements of the company and whether its financial statements give a true and fair view of its financial performance and position. Internal auditors seek to ensure that the internal controls within the organisation are fit for purpose and operating effectively such that its assets are protected, risks are minimised and information generated by its various systems is reliable, among other outcomes. The audit committee takes on the responsibility to provide assurance to the board that this is happening, and that action is being taken on the back of anything established from such audits.

An effective working relationship therefore needs to be established by the audit committee with both the company's external and internal auditors. To achieve this, it is imperative that the membership of the audit committee be carefully selected to include a balance of directors with financial backgrounds and knowledge, with directors from other backgrounds to ensure that a range of perspectives is considered when making decisions, but also that a specialist skill set is available when required. **Table 1.10** in **Appendix 1.1** summarises the roles and responsibilities of audit committees.

1.3.2.2 The Remuneration Committee

One of the challenges that all boards face is the remuneration (and how remuneration is constituted in terms of fixed and variable elements) of its executive members and chair. This is particularly so for listed entities, when details of such packages are matters of public record through the company's annual report. There is a clear need to balance the reality of having to pay amounts that encourage executive directors to perform at high levels in a fair manner with the understanding that such payments may reduce the profits available to shareholders. It is unrealistic to expect an executive director to

---

[55] In the Republic of Ireland, for companies of a certain size (turnover > €25m, balance sheet > €50m), section 167 of the Companies Act 2014 requires there to be an audit committee or that the company explains in its annual report why it has decided not to appoint such a committee.

impartially determine his or her own pay and so a board committee is formed consisting solely of non-executive directors (if structured in accordance with the *UK Corporate Governance Code*). By virtue of not being executives, and thus not typically availing of incentive-based pay, non-executive directors do not have a vested interest in who is paid what and as a result will be, theoretically at least, unbiased in the choices they make. Such choices should be rational and made using facts, such as benchmark salaries and packages being offered by similar companies. Directors' remuneration is further discussed below in **Section 1.3.4**. **Table 1.11** in **Appendix 1.1** summarises the roles and responsibilities of remuneration committees.

1.3.2.3 The Nomination Committee

While the election/re-election of executive and non-executive directors is typically handled at the annual general meeting (AGM) and voted on by shareholders, the appointment of board members in the interim is the remit of the board itself and the process of nominating directors is driven by the nomination committee. As a committee of the board, the nomination committee is tasked with ensuring that potential directors are suitable to join the board of the company. In this respect, new directors should bring something of value to the board, in the form of experience, knowledge, specialist skills, contacts, diversity, and other features that will benefit and advance the organisation into the future.

By being vetted through a nominations committee, existing directors and shareholders will have reasonable confidence as to the suitability and compatibility of proposed directors and that they are not 'token' appointments driven by the agendas of vested interests. While the board does not have to accept the nomination committee's recommendations, it is generally expected that it would in the normal course of events.

In its work, the nomination committee should seek to take a proactive approach to ensuring that the appointment of new directors is timely and appropriate, that the company's board composition requirements are anticipated and aligned with its strategy so that the introduction of new members is planned and not reactionary and that, as much as is reasonably possible, succession management plans are in place for key roles (see also **Section 1.3.3** below on board composition). **Table 1.12** in **Appendix 1.1** summarises the roles and responsibilities of nomination committees.

1.3.2.4 The Risk Committee

All organisations are exposed to risks and it is critical that appropriate actions are taken to identify, assess and manage these. While overall responsibility for risk rests with the main board of the company, it is considered best practice to establish a board committee that can focus greater attention on this area. Appropriate risk assessments and plans can then be conducted and developed, with the help of external professional advice when required, to mitigate adverse impacts of risks as they arise and – where necessary – deal with any crises that occur. **Table 1.13** in **Appendix 1.1** summarises the roles and responsibilities of risk committees.

1.3.3 Board Composition

Given the importance of the board of directors and the work that it does, it is vital to get its composition right. In a practical sense, this means that the board and its members should have a good blend of backgrounds, qualifications, cultures, genders, personalities, and youth and maturity if it is to function effectively. An alignment between what directors bring to the table in terms of skills, competencies and experience, and what the organisation needs is essential and does not happen by accident. Too much 'sameness' in the membership can narrow the perspective of the board and mean that decisions are not fully contemplated or challenged. While this may, at times, create a degree of conflict, this is not necessarily something that needs to be avoided as long as it is addressed in a constructive manner for the betterment of the organisation and its stakeholders. For example, it is obvious that having directors with financial experience and knowledge on the board is an advantage, but *only* having directors with such experience and knowledge is hugely limiting and creates a risk of 'groupthink'.

Various corporate governance codes (see **Section 1.2**) provide guidelines that should be considered when structuring the membership of a board. In summary, best practice recommends that a board include a sufficient number of non-executive directors with proven track records from various backgrounds, who are independent of the executive directors/executive management team. This will help to keep the board focussed on important strategic issues rather than getting bogged down in operational matters that can be addressed by executive management. Clearly, the selection of such individuals is important and the nomination committee (or equivalent) has a key role in identifying any skills gaps and in following a rigorous, transparent process to recruit the most suitable individuals available. For example, it would be advisable for a domestic company entering export markets to introduce at least one non-executive director with international marketing or business development experience, or a non-executive director who is a national of a key country targeted for sales.

When recruiting non-executive directors, it can be tempting for organisations to go after 'big names', high-profile individuals who may be leading up (or have previously led) large businesses, or who have multiple directorships in well-known companies, or have a particularly high status in society. Certainly, having such people as non-executive directors can generate publicity or create valuable networking opportunities for the company and they may have a wealth of experience, but this needs to be balanced with their ability to devote the necessary time to their non-executive director role. Questions will need to be asked as to how many meetings they will be able to attend, if they will be able to take an active role in decision-making, have the time to read and digest material distributed before board meetings, and how available they will be to their board colleagues for advice and consultation. This issue is recognised in the *UK Corporate Governance Code* and the *Governance Code for Credit Institutions and Insurance Undertakings*,[56] where there are limits placed on how many directorships an individual should take on to avoid over-diluting their ability to contribute.

It is important also to recognise the value in recruiting 'up-and-coming' individuals as non-executive directors, whose profiles may not be as widely known but who are energetic and enthusiastic, and who possess both contemporary thinking and, crucially, the time to prepare for and actively attend board meetings. Of course, such younger, or less experienced, non-executive directors may lack the high-level connections of their more senior colleagues and they may not yet carry the same gravitas in debates around the boardroom table. However, a company can benefit from having a mix of experienced and less experienced members on its board. For such boards, the inexperience risk can be managed by the more senior members providing a ready-made mentoring facility to bring less senior members on in their development.

1.3.3.1 Director Independence

While company directors, executive and non-executive directors have the same overall fiduciary duties, they do differ in terms of the extent to which they can be perceived as independent. Executive directors, by virtue of being employees of the company and involved in its day-to-day management, cannot be considered wholly independent, as their behaviours as directors may be influenced by their roles and needs as managers. This can create a difficult situation where decisions need to be made by the board that may be disliked by managers, such as cutting budgets or salaries, or introducing compulsory redundancies. The challenge of wearing 'two hats' and having potentially divided loyalties (shareholders vs self/staff) cannot be ignored and this is an area where the presence of non-executive directors is crucial.

---

[56] *Governance Code for Credit Institutions and Insurance Undertakings* (Central Bank of Ireland, 2013).

As discussed in **Section 1.3.1.2**, though part of the company, non-executive directors work outside any function, division, department or team in the organisation by virtue of not being 'executive' managers. Thus, theoretically, they are able to bring perspectives that are not biased in any direction and they only consider what is in the best long-term interests of the company as a whole. The *UK Corporate Governance Code* defines an independent non-executive director as an individual who is "independent in character and judgement".[57] The Code also identifies circumstances and relationships that can threaten the independence of a non-executive director, i.e. when he or she:

1. has been an employee of the company or group within the last five years;
2. has, or has had within the last three years, a material business relationship with the company either directly, or as a partner, shareholder, director or senior employee of a body that has such a relationship with the company;
3. has received or receives additional remuneration from the company apart from a director's fee, participates in the company's share option or a performance-related-pay scheme, or is a member of the company's pension scheme;
4. has close family ties with any of the company's advisers, directors or senior employees;
5. holds cross-directorships or has significant links with other directors through involvement in other companies or bodies;
6. represents a significant shareholder; or
7. has served on the board for more than nine years from the date of their first election.[58]

While executive directors are typically remunerated through packages that incorporate performance-related pay (PRP) in order to motivate increased performance (see **Section 1.3.4**), this would not be best practice for non-executive directors. Instead, non-executive directors (in the UK and Ireland) are usually paid for the work that they do. As mentioned above, this could be a flat sum amount and/or be based on meeting attendance. Crucially, though, the remuneration is not dependent on the performance of the business, which helps to ensure that non-executive directors are not compromised in making decisions that may have short-term benefits but that are wrong for the company in the long term. In addition, the sum itself should not represent a major portion of the non-executive director's total annual income, as this helps to ensure that decisions they make are financially independent and not self-interested. While a non-executive director

---

[57] *The UK Corporate Governance Code* (*op. cit.* above, n. 9) p. 10.
[58] *Ibid.* pp. 10–11.

could have a small shareholding in the company, which is not therefore influential, holding large shareholdings individually or in concert with others could, however, be highly compromising in terms of non-executive directors' independence and might not be viewed favourably by either internal or external stakeholders. This could also potentially arise where non-executive directors are rewarded with share options.

1.3.3.2 Board Size

According to David W. Duffy in his book, *A Practical Guide to Corporate Governance,*

> "while there is no 'right size' for a board, its size will be influenced by the size of the organisation, the range of skills and experience required to support it strategically, the stage of its development and the work to be carried out, either at board meetings or in committees. Larger boards tend to be less efficient. Consequently, smaller boards with the right composition tend to be more effective".[59]

From this, we can establish that there is no specific 'magic number' to aspire to and that it is largely down to what works best for the organisation. The nomination committee (or equivalent, e.g. the board itself in a smaller company) have an important role to play in considering what an appropriate size is. Of course, a global business that is listed on major stock exchanges will have a much larger board than a micro entity or a single-owner private company. This reflects the complexity of the organisation and the need for multiple skills to be present in the larger company for it to achieve its mission and objectives. Equally, a mature company is likely to have more board members than a start-up business, again due to complexity, but also because as a business grows and develops, new directors will join to compliment the membership of the board and the number of directors largely stabilises at a level that is manageable and effective.

David W. Duffy does suggest that a board size of between eight and 12 directors is preferable, which provides a reasonable range within which to set the appropriate numbers of members, though understandably these numbers could be too high for small companies (five to seven is considered a good target for the boards of start-up businesses). What this highlights is that large numbers of directors can be unwieldy and slow down or prevent decisions being made because a consensus cannot be reached. The voices of individual members can become lost in the 'noise' and they might shy

---

[59] Duffy, D.W., *op. cit.* above, n. 46, p. 21.

away from taking responsibility or initiative, believing that they are not being listened to.

However, if the board is too small, it may lack the range of skills and experiences that are needed currently by the company and in the future. The risk of taking a limited or restrictive approach to board size is that key abilities and knowledge that the company requires for its development may be denied to it. (The same thinking is also likely to have an adverse effect at an operational level; for example, not having a marketing manager may save money today, but who will drive the company's product development and sales of the future?) In addition, fewer directors means more work for those currently on the board, which can be problematic, particularly for non-executive directors who are already 'part time' in the sense that they can often have extensive executive responsibilities elsewhere. Companies need to carefully consider these issues from all angles and decide on a reasonable board size that allows the work of the board to be carried out efficiently and effectively in a way that is also fair to board members, their capabilities and capacities.

1.3.3.3 Board Tenure

Tenure of membership is another aspect of board composition where it is important to aspire to and achieve some balance. Board tenure pertains to the length of time that a director spends on a board. There are obvious advantages in having long-serving directors on boards. Such board members have extensive knowledge of the organisation, its people, mission and objectives; in this sense, preserving that knowledge is both good for the business and helps directors in their effective execution of their role.

In addition, it can be argued that a regular turnover of directors and influx of new board members will mean that much time is spent on getting such directors 'up to speed' with the company, its governance structures and processes, and the existing board. New relationships have to be formed and during this period there is a risk that the efficiency of the board will suffer. The knowledge and experience that is lost when a director leaves a board may be irreplaceable as much of it can be tacit or intangible in nature, and very difficult to retrieve or recreate. Furthermore, if a prospective director feels that his or her tenure with a company is going to be short, it is questionable whether they will take on the role as the level of investment in terms of time and effort may not be worth it. If they do take on the role knowing that they will have to depart in a year or two, it is difficult to know how much of themselves they will then put into the often arduous work of a director. While acknowledging that no director should take on the requisite duties if they are not going to undertake them to the best of their abilities, human nature does come into play.

This is not to say that board membership should be for life. There are obvious benefits to introducing new people. New directors bring with them new knowledge, new ideas and perspectives, and an energy and freshness that may be lacking if the board has been together for too long. In many sectors today, this is essential, as cutting-edge innovations and thinking need to be introduced and contemplated at a strategic level. New directors may be connected and networked in different ways to how the existing board members are and this can represent a valuable opportunity for the company.

In addition, introducing new board members on a regular basis can help to 'shake up' the board in a positive way. Over time, complacency can set in and board members can become overly comfortable in their roles. While solid relationships built over years can be helpful and enhance trust, they can also create a situation in which board members find it difficult to challenge each other for fear of conflict. In the case of non-executive directors who have served with executive directors for many years, there is a risk that their independence and objectivity may be compromised, or that this is, at least, potentially the perception of other stakeholders. All of this can stifle challenge and vigorous debate, even though – as noted earlier – some conflict (in a measured and fair way) can be healthy. The introduction of new directors, perhaps because they are not used to 'the way things are done around here', or simply because they see things differently, can help to avoid such stasis, thereby helping to maintain board effectiveness and the long-term success of the company. And, again taking human nature into account, because tensions can flare and negativity thrive in situations involving change, a strong and effective chair is essential, to keep order and ensure that matters are handled fairly and constructively between all members of the board.

What, then, is an appropriate tenure for board membership? As with board size, it is difficult to be definitive on this matter as all organisations are different. However, best practice should be considered and this is provided in the *UK Corporate Governance Code*. In general terms, for both executive and non-executive directors, their terms should not exceed three years without the approval of shareholders by way of re-election (see B.7 of the *UK Corporate Governance Code* for further details). This means that an executive director can serve for many years – and some do spend much of their working lives in such a role – but only when they wish to, and the majority of shareholders show their satisfaction with this by voting to such effect in director elections at the relevant AGM. In the case of non-executive directors, their appointments should be for a fixed term and not be indefinite. Best practice[60] suggests that non-executive directors serve for

---

[60] Duffy, D.W., *op. cit.* above, n. 46.

two terms of three years each and this may be extended by a further three years. However, shareholders would again have the final say on this at the AGM through the election process. As discussed above, it is important the board ensures that the succession process for departing directors is handled in an orderly and relatively seamless manner, which will entail identifying and introducing replacement directors at the right time to facilitate an effective handover. Having a board composition profile consisting of a range of more experienced and less experienced directors, and effectively creating a pipeline of talent, can greatly assist in this.

1.3.3.4 Board Diversity

In **Section 1.3.3**, when discussing board composition, we mentioned the issue of excessive 'sameness' among board members. As David W. Duffy notes:

> "When a board becomes overly homogenous, there is a real danger that its effectiveness will be greatly reduced as the breadth and depth of thinking and insight that is required to make it successful could be compromised".[61]

It is advisable for boards to embrace the concept of diversity, which entails having 'outsiders' as members who come from a range of different backgrounds and sectors, different disciplines and skills, different cultures and nationalities. The thinking here is that such heterogeneity will enhance the capacity of the board to make better, more informed and more nuanced decisions than if everyone thinks and acts in the same way. As suggested in **Section 1.3.3**, having a multinational and multicultural board can help when the business is looking to internationalise or expand into other territories as board members from these regions and countries can bring a wealth of otherwise hard-to-acquire knowledge, experience and contacts. It is important to note, however, that such directors are of equal standing and importance to their 'insider' colleagues, and that their directors' duties and responsibilities are no different. Indeed, as boards diversify, the distinction between 'insiders' and 'outsiders' should become much less significant and even insignificant in time; they are all board members with a common goal and purpose.

Currently, an area of great interest and debate in the context of board diversity is that of gender diversity. As in many countries, there is a significant imbalance in the representation of men and women on boards of directors

---

[61] Duffy, D.W., *op. cit.* above, n. 46, p. 135.

in Ireland. While women account for just over 50% of the population,[62] they represent far less than half of company board members. According to the *Women on Boards in Ireland Report 2015*,[63] which surveyed female board members, the majority of respondents to their survey (59%) estimated the proportion of women on boards to be between 11% and 40% of the boards of which they are members. In the EU, women make up approximately 23% of board members of the largest listed companies.[64] There are many different reasons suggested for why this is the case, including the existence of an 'old boy's network' in some organisations, a lack of equal access to information about available positions, commitments outside of the workplace being greater for women, a reluctance on the part of women to apply for board positions, and insufficient mentoring for younger women.[65]

Strong arguments are being made that this imbalance needs to be addressed. In 2012, the European Commission noted that greater diversity would mirror the market (women control most consumer spending), improve decision-making and enhance corporate governance and ethics.[66] Darrin Hartzler has indicated that gender diversity may lower the risk profile of a company and increase the interest of investors.[67] Michael Casey has reported on research showing that more gender-diverse boards are less likely to take risks, decide on larger dividend payments, show lower volatility in stock and accounting returns, and engage in less aggressive acquisition strategies.[68] Considerable research has been conducted into the economic argument for having greater representation of women on boards by examining whether higher numbers/percentages of women on boards have a positive effect on business performance. Linda-Eling Lee indicates that a strong female representation (at least three members) on the board can be linked to improved return on equity and earnings per share,[69] while Corinne Post and Kris Byron have found a positive

---

[62] Central Statistics Office, *Census 2016 Summary Results – Part 1* (CSO, 2017).

[63] Institute of Directors in Ireland, *Women on Boards in Ireland 2015* (IOD Ireland, 2015).

[64] European Commission, "Gender balance on corporate boards: Europe is cracking the glass ceiling", Fact Sheet, July 2016. Available at https://ec.europa.eu/newsroom/document.cfm?doc_id=46280 (accessed February 2018).

[65] Institute of Directors in Ireland, *op. cit.* above, n. 63.

[66] European Commission, *Women in economic decision-making in the EU: Progress report* (Publications Office of the European Union, 2012).

[67] Hartzler, D., "So you want to add women directors to your board?" (2016) *Ethical Boardroom*, Winter 12–13.

[68] Casey, M., "Study finds a diverse corporate board reigns in risk, good for shareholders", *Fortune*, 30 July 2014. Available at http://fortune.com/2014/07/30/study-finds-a-diverse-corporate-boards-rein-in-risk-good-for-shareholders/ (accessed January 2018).

[69] Lee, L-E., "The Tipping Point: Women on Boards and Financial Performance", MSCI 2016 [Online]. Available at https://www.msci.com/www/blog-posts/the-tipping-point-women-on/0538249725 (accessed January 2018).

relationship between female representation and accounting returns.[70] Positive results have also been identified in studies by Mijntje Lückerath-Rovers[71] and Lone Christiansen *et al.*,[72] among others.

However, some argue that attempting to deal with this lack of diversity can be damaging or counterproductive. One issue is that seeking to positively 'enforce' diversity can give rise to a degree of tokenism, where women are being appointed to board positions primarily to comply with policies, rules or regulations, as opposed to appointing the person on merit. It has been argued that token representation can adversely affect the appointee's potential to perform as they face challenging expectations and pressures.[73] In an economic sense, there is also evidence that greater gender diversity either lowers performance measures or has no notable impact. Renée Adams and Daniel Ferreira note that adding female directors to a board where strong governance already exists will not necessarily improve performance,[74] while Sabri Boubaker *et al.* have determined a negative relationship between representation and financial performance of the business.[75] Moreover, based on Frank Dobbin and Jiwook Jung, increasing gender diversity on the board has a negative effect on share price,[76] while David Carter *et al.* indicate that there is no significant relationship between gender diversity and financial performance.[77]

Interestingly, policy-makers in some countries seem to have taken the view that gender diversity is something not only to be sought but actually mandated. A number of European countries – including Norway, France, Spain, Iceland, Italy, Finland, the Netherlands, and Belgium – have introduced legislated quotas for women on boards in varying contexts. In some of these countries, at least 40% of board members must be women and companies can face sanctions for

---

[70] Post, C. and Byron, K., "Women on boards and firm financial performance: A meta-analysis" (2015) *Academy of Management Journal*, Vol. 58 No. 5, 1546–1571.

[71] Lückerath-Rovers, M., "Women on boards and firm performance", (2013) *Journal of Management & Governance*, Vol. 17 No. 2, 491–509.

[72] Christiansen, L., Lin, H., Pereira, J., Topalova, P. and Turk, R., *Gender Diversity in Senior Positions and Firm Performance: Evidence from Europe*, International Monetary Fund Working Paper 16/50 (IMF, 2016). Available at https://www.imf.org/~/media/Websites/IMF/imported-full-text-pdf/external/pubs/ft/wp/2016/_wp1650.ashx (accessed January 2018).

[73] Dobbin, F. and Jung, J., "Board diversity and corporate performance: Filling in the gaps: corporate board gender diversity and stock performance: The competence gap or institutional investor bias?" (2011) *NCL Review*, Vol. 89, 809–2228.

[74] Adams, R.B. and Ferreira, D., "Women in the boardroom and their impact on governance and performance" (2009) *Journal of Financial Economics*, Vol. 94 No. 2, 291–309.

[75] Boubaker, S., Dang, R. and Nguyen, D.K., "Does board gender diversity improve the performance of French listed firms?" (2014) *Gestion 2000*, Vol. 31 No. 1, 259–269.

[76] Dobbin, F. and Jung, J., *op. cit.* above, n. 73.

[77] Carter, D.A., D'Souza, F., Simkins, B.J. and Simpson, W.G., "The gender and ethnic diversity of US boards and board committees and firm financial performance" (2010) *Corporate Governance: An International Review*, Vol. 18 No. 5, 396–414.

not achieving this. The logic of such quotas is clearly to make organisations take diversity more seriously and it puts the onus on them to address the issue at source. However, the approach is not universally popular. In Ireland – where legislated quotas do not exist – only 23% of respondents to the *Women on Boards in Ireland 2015* survey felt that gender quotas are the most effective way of increasing representation; 40% were in favour of targets instead, while 28% contended that quotas are the wrong approach and that merit is what matters.[78]

One of the big challenges arising from gender quotas is that for companies to fill quotas initially, they can find themselves competing with each other for the same small pool of existing candidates and thus those who are appointed may end up on multiple boards.[79] This creates workload problems for successful directors, and is hardly 'diversity' in its true meaning. Additionally, where companies recruit women solely at non-executive director level to satisfy a quota, this may mean that female representation within and at the heart of the organisation is not being increased and executive management decisions remain male-dominated. To date, the evidence as to whether quotas work is mixed and largely inconclusive, with Renée Adams and Daniel Ferreira, for example, noting that the suggestion of enforced quotas needs to be driven by reasons other than firm financial performance.[80] Some of this research has been in Norway, who introduced quotas in 2006. Kenneth Ahern and Amy Dittmar have found that the enactment of quotas has had a negative effect on share price (on announcement) and on financial performance in subsequent years.[81] Harald Dale-Olsen *et al.* have indicated that, although improving gender equality has the potential for long-term positive effects, there was no notable impact of the quota on company financial performance in the short term.[82]

1.3.4 Directors' Remuneration

An aspect of corporate governance that regularly generates debate is the remuneration or pay of company directors. Consequently, this is a prominent theme in many of the governance codes that have been developed and

---

[78] Institute of Directors in Ireland, *op. cit.* above, n. 63.
[79] Zillman, C. "French Companies are Scrambling to Get Women Onto Their Boards", *Fortune* 22 March 2016. Available at http://fortune.com/2016/03/22/french-women-corporate-boards-quota (accessed January 2018).
[80] Adams, R.B. and Ferreira, D., *op. cit.* above, n. 74.
[81] Ahern, K.R. and Dittmar, A.K., "The changing of the boards: The impact on firm valuation of mandated female board representation" (2012) *The Quarterly Journal of Economics*, Vol. 127 No. 1, 137–197.
[82] Dale-Olsen, H., Schøne, P. and Verner, M., "Diversity among Norwegian boards of directors: Does a quota for women improve firm performance?" (2013) *Feminist Economics*, Vol. 19 No. 4, 110–135.

continue to be developed. The fact that directors receive such payments is entirely appropriate – they are performing important duties on behalf of the company that demand a sizable time input and effort, and they should be rewarded for this. Indeed, for executive directors, this is their 'job' and usually their main source of income. However, issues and controversies can arise around the amount of these payments and how they are decided upon.

1.3.4.1 Remuneration of Non-executive Directors

In the case of non-executive directors, such difficulties arise less frequently due to the fact that – as mentioned in **Section 1.3.1.2** – they are usually paid either a fixed annual fee and/or a fee for attending meetings. For those non-executive directors who take on additional responsibilities (such as chairing a board committee – see **Section 1.3.2**), they may receive an additional payment for this. As previously noted, the fees paid to non-executive directors are usually decided by the board, and should not be at a level that represents a significant proportion of any individual non-executive director's income. In addition, it would be unusual and potentially problematic if non-executive directors received payments linked to the performance of the organisation as this could compromise their independence.

The chair is typically paid a salary and may well receive other benefits from the company. Whether this extends into an element of performance-related-pay (PRP) depends on what is agreed, though this could have implications for their perceived independence as the head of the board, and as a voice for and representative of the company's interests. The remuneration committee determines the remuneration package (and the components of this) of the chair.

1.3.4.2 Remuneration of Executive Directors

Remuneration is not as straightforward when it comes to executive directors, for whom PRP is considered an essential element. For some chief executives and executive directors, the remuneration that they receive can amount to substantial amounts each year, paid in different ways including basic salary, bonuses, share options, pension contributions, long-term incentive plans, benefits-in-kind (e.g. a company car), etc. (By way of illustration, Tim Cook – the CEO of Apple – earned total remuneration of just under $145 million in 2016.[83])

Typically, the rationale behind how executive director remuneration packages are structured is that a substantial proportion is in the form of PRP, which means that the director will only earn the relevant amounts if targets

[83] Meisler, L., Ritcey, A. and Zhao, J., "Apple's Cook Reaped $145 Million Last Year, Most of S&P 500 CEOs", Bloomberg (Online), 29 June 2017. Available at https://www.bloomberg.com/graphics/2017-ceos-take-home-pay/ (accessed February 2018).

have been met or surpassed. Thus, share options or bonuses will only be granted or paid if, for example, a certain profit is achieved; and failure is not rewarded. Such targets should be set so that they are challenging but also to be of benefit to the organisation. In this way, the director does well only if the company does well, which should motivate the director to work harder for mutual gains. To protect against short-termism, companies will often ensure that share options are granted at an agreed point in the future, so that the recipient strives to grow the share price in the interim. Bonuses and other incentive elements may also be deferred or phased for similar reasons.

The appropriateness of paying large sums of money to executives is regularly debated in the media, and questions are asked about whether executives deliver real value for such payments. There is a view that increased remuneration to executives should lead to increased performance by the organisation. This can help to address agency issues that arise due to the separation of ownership (shareholders) and control (executives),[84] i.e. directors (as agents) satisfy the interests of shareholders because this is also in their interests. Michael Armstrong and Helen Murlis have indicated that incentivised pay can act as a motivation for improved individual performance leading to improved company performance, rewarding those who are committed and attracting and retaining the right calibre of executive.[85] However, PRP can also have negative implications, including recipients being too money-focused to the cost of everything else, feeling controlled by the incentive and experiencing reduced intrinsic rewards.[86] Considerable empirical research has been conducted to establish if a relationship exists between directors' remuneration and financial performance of their companies, and how strong this relationship is. The results have been largely mixed and not entirely conclusive, which suggests that both positive and negative outcomes can arise in practice. Kevin Murphy, Michael Jensen and Kevin Murphy, Rachel Merhebi *et al.*, and Siew Peng Lee and Mansor Isa have found relationships between higher director/ chief executive pay and improved company financial performance.[87]

[84] Fama, E.F. and Jensen, M., "Separation of ownership and control" (1983) *Journal of Law and Economics*, Vol. 26 No. 2, 301–325.

[85] Armstrong, M. and Murlis, H., *Reward Management: A Handbook of Remuneration Strategy and Practice* (4th Edition, Kogan Page, 1998).

[86] Baker, G. P., Jensen, M. C. and Murphy, K. J., "Compensation and incentives: Practice vs. theory" (1988) *The Journal of Finance*, Vol. 43 No. 3, 593–616.

[87] Murphy, K.J., "Corporate performance and managerial remuneration: An empirical analysis" (1985) *Journal of Accounting and Economics*, Vol. 7 Nos. 1–3, 11–42; Jensen, M.C. and Murphy, K.J., "Performance pay and top-management incentives" (1990) *Journal of Political Economy*, Vol. 98 No. 2, 225–264; Mehrebi, R., Pattenden, K, Swan, P.L. and Zhou, X., "Australian chief executive officer remuneration: pay and performance" (2006) *Accounting and Finance*, Vol. 46 No. 3, 481–497; Peng Lee, S. and Isa, M., "Directors' remuneration, governance and performance: the case of Malaysian banks" (2015) *Managerial Finance*, Vol. 41 No. 1, 26–44.

In an Irish context, Tongyu Cao *et al.* seem to indicate that any relationship between CEO remuneration and company performance is of limited significance.[88] At the other extreme, scholars have also found that a negative relationship can exist.[89]

The decision in larger/listed companies as to how much is paid to executive directors and how this is structured rests with the remuneration committee (see **Section 1.3.2.2**), which should include only non-executive directors as members. This helps to maintain their independence in the decisions that they make, as they do not set their own pay. Typically, members of the remuneration committee will look to set pay and any associated targets at levels that will incentivise higher performance and retain quality executives. A helpful action is to examine pay levels in the company in the context of what competitors are paying, as this will give an indication as to what is generally acceptable in the market. This may require the input of outside consultants who have expertise in this area as it can be difficult to obtain information to properly compare companies in this respect. Ensuring that packages are comparable with market rates while targets are challenging should help to ensure that the right people are in the senior leadership roles, that they want to be there and remain there, and that they are being pushed on to higher performance.

However, there is also a shareholder interest dimension to director's remuneration that cannot be ignored. While the company needs to be fair to, and value the work of, its executives, this involves paying out what is in effect shareholders' funds and their interests, collectively, have to be protected. Ultimately, this is a challenge for all remuneration committees and whether they get this right or not is often only established over time when shareholders voice either their approval or disapproval through their votes for director election/re-election at the AGM.

As previously noted, remuneration packages for board members are disclosed in the annual financial statements of listed companies, which helps to keep this process and its outcomes suitably transparent. In addition, levels of directors' remuneration and any increases should align with what is happening at other levels in the organisation. If directors are receiving pay increases that in percentage terms significantly exceed those paid to other staff, this is likely to give rise to dissatisfaction and

---

[88] Cao, T., Donnelly, R. and McCarthy, J., "Pay, performance and governance in Irish PLCs" (2012) *Irish Accounting Review*, Vol. 19 Nos. 1 & 2, 1–22.

[89] For example: Core, J. E., Holthausen, R.W. and Larcker, D.F., "Corporate governance, chief executive officer compensation and firm performance" (1999) *Journal of Financial Economics*, Vol. 51 No. 3, 371–406; Brick, I.E., Palmon, O. and Wald, J.K., "CEO compensation, director compensation, and firm performance: Evidence of cronyism?" (2006) *Journal of Corporate Finance*, Vol. 12 No. 3, 403–423.

may affect the motivation and the retention of such staff. Thus, directors' remuneration is an area that should be handled with sensitivity and objectivity.

Appendix 1.1: Summary of Roles and Responsibilities

TABLE 1.6: ROLES AND RESPONSIBILITIES OF THE CHAIR[90]

Role of the Chair
- Leadership of the board and ensuring its effectiveness in all aspects of the board's role.
- Ensure that the company achieves a satisfactory return on investment for its shareholders.
- Set and maintain the highest standards of integrity and probity, set clear expectations concerning the company's culture, values and behaviours and the style and tone of board discussions.
- Oversee the orderly operation of the board of directors.
- Ensure appropriate interaction between the board, its shareholders, and executive management.

Responsibilities of the Chair
- Chair board meetings.
- Serve as the company's primary representative to key external and internal stakeholder groups. (This responsibility could be shared with the chief executive.)
- Take a leading role in determining and reviewing the composition, structure and performance of the board.
- Ensure that the board determines the nature and extent of the significant risks that the company is willing to embrace.
- Ensure that the company has a risk management plan that is reported against on a regular basis.
- Foster a good relationship of mutual trust with the chief executive and develop strong working relationships with all executive directors and the rest of the executive management team.
- Ensure that decisions are reached in the best interests of the company.
- Ensure that the board undertakes a thorough analysis of all issues and concerns.
- Ensure that board committees are properly established and operated with appropriate terms of reference.
- Exploit board members' knowledge and experience and ensure that all board members contribute during meetings.
- Ensure that the company has a strategic plan, supported by an annual business plan and budget.
- Ensure that all members of the board have access to accurate, timely and clear information.

[90] Adapted from Duffy, D.W., *op. cit.* above, n. 46, pp. 59–60.

- Put in place the appropriate plans to facilitate succession of the chief executive.
- Develop agendas for board meetings for the year in consultation with the chief executive and the Company Secretary.
- Ensure that a process is put in place to assess the performance of the board.
- Ensure that the board is up to date with relevant corporate governance issues.
- Create the appropriate environment to foster constructive debate and effective decision-making by the board.

TABLE 1.7: ROLES AND RESPONSIBILITIES OF NON-EXECUTIVE DIRECTORS[91]

Role of Non-executive Directors
- Provide objective and independent advice to the board to enable it to make better decisions in the interest of all shareholders and stakeholders.

Responsibilities of Non-executive Directors
- Bring a genuine independent and external perspective to stimulate board debate and enhance decision-making.
- Provide value-added input to strategy and strategic development.
- Act in the best interests of the company as a whole rather than any one particular group of shareholders.
- Assist in carrying out the duties of the board such as:
  - reviewing, approving, and ongoing monitoring of the strategic plan;
  - reviewing organisational capability in relation to stated objectives;
  - reviewing financial performance against targets;
  - raising capital;
  - reviewing any major changes in the company, such as the financial and organisation structure;
  - providing advice on major investments/divestments to be made;
  - monitoring legal, ethical, risk and environmental compliance where appropriate.
- Act as a catalyst for change and challenge the status quo, when appropriate.
- Maintain the highest ethical standards, probity, and integrity in the company.
- Ensure that financial controls and systems of risk management are robust and operating effectively.
- Monitor and constructively challenge the performance of the executive management team.
- Assess and assist the executive management team to address and manage risk.
- Play a leading role in the nomination, remuneration, audit and risk committees, where applicable.
- Play an active role in assisting the chief executive in the replacement of key senior management and in planning for management development and succession.
- Attend board committee meetings, as appropriate.

[91] Adapted from *ibid.* pp. 63–64.

- Attend board meetings, ad hoc meetings with the chair, and meetings of non-executive directors, as appropriate.
- Ensure that the financial information is accurate, timely and clear, and that financial controls and systems of risk management are robust and defensible.
- Maintain the confidentiality of information received.
- Carry out functions with due skill, care, and diligence.
- Devote sufficient time to their responsibilities.
- Undergo specific and relevant training for the role.

TABLE 1.8: ROLES AND RESPONSIBILITIES OF EXECUTIVE DIRECTORS[92]

Role of Executive Directors
- Provide independent, objective advice and the benefit of their day-to-day experience to enable better decisions to be made in the strategic interests of the company.

Responsibilities of Executive Directors
- Support the chief executive in the management of the company.
- Provide first-hand, in-depth knowledge of the organisation.
- Act in the best interests of the company as a whole even when this might conflict with their role as a member of the executive management team.
- Be fully informed with regards to all issues relevant to the work of the board.
- Participate in board meetings and decision-making.
- Ensure that the company's compliance and risk management policies are being maintained.
- Remain detached from considerations of self-interest.
- Constructively challenge opinions of colleagues on the board.
- Maintain the confidentiality of information received.
- Carry out functions with due skill, care and diligence.
- Participate in the day-to-day management of the organisation.
- Insist on receiving full, accurate and timely information from the executive management team, even if this may reflect poorly on their role on the executive management team.

TABLE 1.9: ROLES AND RESPONSIBILITIES OF THE CHIEF EXECUTIVE[93]

Role of the Chief Executive
- Develop and deliver on the company's strategic plan in the most effective and efficient manner.
- Be accountable for the overall performance of the company and for the day-to-day running and management of the company's business, under delegated authority from the board.

[92] Adapted from *ibid.* p. 72.
[93] Adapted from *ibid.* pp. 37–38.

Responsibilities of the Chief Executive

- Develop and present the strategic and annual business plans to the board for approval.
- Implement the board's policies and strategies.
- Report to the board on progress against the strategic and annual business plans on a regular basis. (Typically, reporting against the annual plan will be monthly, while reporting against the strategic plan will be less frequent, although it should be at least two or three times a year.)
- Ensure that the information to the board is well presented, easily digestible, relevant, timely and accurate, and is sufficient for the board to perform their role and fulfil their responsibilities.
- Manage the day-to-day operations of the company.
- Ensure that financial results, business strategies and targets are communicated to those who need to know.
- Monitor the financial and operating results against plans and budgets.
- Manage, motivate, develop, and lead members of the executive management team.
- Manage resources efficiently and effectively to achieve the company's objectives.
- Chair executive management team meetings.
- Take a leadership role in establishing or developing the company's cultures and values.
- Ensure that there is a fit between the ethics and values of the organisation, its strategy and the company's processes and structure.
- Ensure that the appropriate internal audit processes and procedures are in place (in liaison with the head of internal audit and/or the external auditors, if a board committee is not in place).
- Develop and maintain an effective framework of internal controls over risk in relation to business activities and report to the board as appropriate.
- Develop processes to ensure that investment proposals are reviewed thoroughly, that risks are identified, and steps are taken to manage them.
- Ensure that there is a succession plan in place for the executive management team.

TABLE 1.10: ROLES AND RESPONSIBILITIES OF AUDIT COMMITTEES[94]

Role of Audit Committees

- Monitor and review internal controls, external audit, financial controls, accounting, and external reporting.

Responsibilities of Audit Committees

- Report to the board on all matters covered by its terms of reference and how it has discharged its responsibilities.

[94] Adapted from *ibid.* pp. 81–82.

- Monitor the integrity of the financial statements of the company and any formal announcements relating to the company's financial performance and review significant financial reporting issues contained therein.
- Review the company's internal financial controls and risk management systems, unless addressed by another board committee.
- Monitor and review the effectiveness of the company's internal audit function.
- Approve the appointment or removal of the head of the internal audit function, where it exists, or an outsourced internal audit function.
- Review major audit issues and accounting policies.
- Review the content of the annual report and accounts and advise the board on whether they are fair, balanced and understandable, and provide adequate information for the shareholders.
- Review company compliance with ethical standards, regulations, policies, and practice reviews.
- Act as the link between the board and the external auditors.
- Review and monitor the external auditor's independence, objectivity, and effectiveness of the audit process, taking into account professional and regulatory requirements.
- Monitor the supply of non-audit services by the external auditors, taking into account relevant ethical guidance regarding the provision of non-audit services by an external audit firm.
- Make recommendations to the board to be put to the shareholders for their approval in relation to the appointment of the external auditor and to approve his or her remuneration and terms of engagement.
- Meet with the external auditors twice a year, once at the planning stage and once post-audit at reporting stage.

TABLE 1.11: ROLES AND RESPONSIBILITIES OF REMUNERATION COMMITTEES[95]

Role of Remuneration Committees
- Advise the board on the remuneration policies for the chief executive, the chair, executive directors, the Company Secretary and the other members of the executive management team it is designated to consider.

Responsibilities of Remuneration Committees
- Determine and agree with the board the framework or board policy for the remuneration of the chief executive, chair, the Company Secretary and such other members of executive management as are designated to the committee.

---

[95] Adapted from *ibid.* pp. 85–86.

- In determining such policy, the remuneration committee takes into account all factors that it deems necessary. The objective of such policy should be to ensure that members of the executive management team of the company are provided with appropriate incentives to encourage enhanced performance and are, in a fair and responsible manner, rewarded for their individual contributions to the success of the business.
- Within the terms of the agreed policy, determine the remuneration packages of the chair, chief executive and the executive management team, including salary, bonuses, pension rights, incentive payments and share options. The committee may/shall consult the chief executive about proposals relating to the remuneration of senior management.
- Review the ongoing appropriateness and relevance of the remuneration policy.
- Approve the design of, and determine targets for, any performance-related-pay schemes operated by the company and approve the total annual payments made under such schemes.
- Review the design of all share incentive plans for approval by the board and shareholders.
- Determine the policy for, and scope of, pension arrangements for the chief executive and other senior management (as determined by the board).
- Ensure that contractual terms on termination, and any payments made, are fair to the individual and the company, that failure is not rewarded and that the duty to mitigate loss is fully recognised by the company.
- Oversee any major changes in employee benefits structures throughout the company.
- Be exclusively responsible for selecting, appointing and setting the terms of reference for any remuneration consultants who advise the committee.

TABLE 1.12: ROLES AND RESPONSIBILITIES OF NOMINATION COMMITTEES[96]

Role of Nomination Committees

To assess the director requirements of the board going forward. This will include:
- Monitor, review and evaluate the structure, size and composition of the board.
- Identify new skills and experience requirements.
- Plan for orderly rotation of directors.
- Lead the process for all board appointments (executive, non-executive and the chair), and make recommendations to the board in this regard.

Responsibilities of Nomination Committees
- Review the structure, size and composition of the board and make recommendations to the board.
- Ensure the board and its committees have the appropriate balance of skills, experience, independence, and knowledge to achieve its strategic goals and discharge its duties effectively.

[96] Adapted from *ibid.* pp. 88–89.

- Identify and nominate candidates to fill board vacancies when required. The board will subsequently review and approve the nominations, as appropriate.
- Give full consideration to succession planning for directors and other senior executives.
- Ensure that appointments to the board display the appropriate degree of diversity of gender, backgrounds, skills, social connections, and nationalities necessary.
- Prepare a description of roles and responsibilities for particular appointments.
- Assess the time commitments of each board position and ensure that the individual candidates have sufficient available time to undertake them.
- Ensure that on appointment to the board, non-executive directors receive a formal letter of appointment setting out clearly what is expected of them in their role.
- Assess the leadership needs of the company in terms of its ability to compete in its industry/sector.

TABLE 1.13: ROLES AND RESPONSIBILITIES OF RISK COMMITTEES[97]

Role of Risk Committees
- Provides oversight and advice to the board on the current risk exposures and future risk strategy of the company.

Responsibilities of Risk Committees
- Assess and estimate the likely impact of the full range of risks to which the organisation is exposed, including financial, operational, commercial, reputational, data loss, cybersecurity, brand, legal, safety and environmental risks.
- Advise the board on risk appetite and tolerance for future strategy, taking account of the board's overall risk appetite, the current financial position of the institution and its capacity to manage and control risks.
- Communicate regularly with the board in relation to ongoing risk assessment and advise them on the effectiveness of strategies and policies in place.
- Ensure the ongoing maintenance of risk management and reporting systems.
- Consult external experts where necessary, depending on the industry and risk exposure.
- Ensure compliance with any regulatory requirements in relation to risk.
- Ensure that there is a crisis management plan in place.

---

[97] Adapted from *ibid.* pp. 91–92.

Chapter 2
Ethics
Hugh McBride

> *"'... you're an ethical man, Don Felícito. Ethical down to the soles of your feet. One of the few I've known, in fact.' What could that mean, 'an ethical man'? ... He was always hearing words whose meaning he didn't know."*[1]

2.1 What is Ethics?

Imagine you are on a short visit to a less-developed African country, working on the evaluation of a proposed aid project for an Irish, state-funded development agency. Driving a rented jeep, you and the local guide accompanying you are stopped by armed police at a checkpoint in a remote rural area. The battery on your smart phone is dead, besides which there is no coverage in the area. After an hour waiting, the police officer in charge informs you that there may be a problem with your driving licence and that they will have to impound the car to prevent you travelling further until the matter is adjudicated upon by the regional chief of police. He is not due to return from attending a funeral for another three days, so you will have to wait until then for the matter to be resolved. The local guide who is accompanying you has a further conversation with the police officer. "She says there may be an informal way of resolving the problem", the guide tells you. "You could make a goodwill payment now, rather than waiting to be fined later." The guide recommends that you make the payment, pointing out some of the police appear to be drunk and the situation could get very nasty, especially for him. You are scheduled to have a few final meetings

[1] Vargas Llosa, M., *The Discreet Hero* (Faber & Faber, 2015), p. 338.

later that evening in the capital city, which is 350 kilometres away, and to fly back to Ireland from there the next day. You enter into negotiations with the police officer and agree on an amount that you then pay in US dollars. On the plane home the following day, you experience a twinge of guilt about having made the payment. You feel a bit of a hypocrite as you have previously been critical of people and corporations who pay bribes. But you quickly dismiss these negative thoughts and do not mention the incident in your report on the trip, which is deemed to be very successful overall.

Imagine again, this time that you are at a car-boot sale on Sunday morning. You have an interest in antiques and often find items of interest at these casual, open-air markets, at which you also really enjoy the social interaction. You spot an item on sale you think could be very valuable. Closer inspection confirms your initial impression. You fall into conversation with the seller, who is an elderly widow at the car-boot sale for the first time, selling-off "some of the junk my husband accumulated on his travels". She plans to use any money she makes to help fund her grand-daughter's music studies. Trying hard to contain your excitement, you ask her to quote a price for the item. "You seem like a nice person", she says; "do you think €50 would be fair?" You pay her the money and wish her well. A few months later you re-sell the item for €4,500, an amount far exceeding your expectations. You fleetingly wonder whether you should have told the widow about your suspicions as to the real value of the item, but you dispel any pangs of conscience with the thought that in the market, both the buyer and the seller need to be wary.

Now imagine you are a student and that you have promised your sister you will mind her children for the weekend. You are not particularly close to your sister, but after a few drinks following an anniversary mass for your parents you have agreed to help her out. She and her husband plan to go to a wedding on the Saturday afternoon, stay the night in the hotel and come home at their leisure on the Sunday. On the Tuesday beforehand, you are unexpectedly invited to the Accountancy Society Ball by someone you have fancied for a long time. The tickets have all been paid for and will not cost you a cent. You phone your sister on the Wednesday explaining that, unfortunately, you will not be able to mind your niece and nephew after all because you have to work on a major project all weekend to meet a submission deadline. Your sister is really disappointed to be let down but is understanding of your priorities. You attend the ball and have the night of your life. You hear from your brother a few weeks later that your sister did not go to the wedding after all as she was unable to find someone to mind her kids.

Each of the above anecdotes raises questions about the morality of personal behaviour. They are illustrative of the kind of stories that people tell each other in everyday conversation and of types of situation that many of us will have experienced personally. The stuff of everyday living, they are the kind of stories typically featured in the plot lines of TV soap operas and of confessional interviews on talk shows. Such incidents, involving petty corruption, passive deception and promise-breaking, may seem relatively trivial and insignificant in the grand scheme of things. However, imagining ourselves in such situations can challenge us (even if only fleetingly) to **question**:

- our character and the virtues manifest in our motivations and actions;
- what it is that we value;
- the manner in which we ought to balance our self-interest with the interests of others;
- the nature of our obligations to others, and what people should expect from each other and from themselves;
- the way we are and the way we ought to be in the world;
- the way we behave and live, and the way we ought to behave and live;
- the reasons for our behaviour and whether we should consider it to be acceptable, right or wrong, good or bad, admirable or contemptible.

These kinds of issues, raised by such incidents, are the same as those raised by the more complex, demanding and significant moral challenges and dilemmas people inevitably and inescapably encounter in their private and public lives, both individually and collectively, as members of families, as friends, neighbours, members of clubs and organisations, colleagues, employees, employers, members of communities and social groups, as citizens and as fellow human beings sharing the Earth. And addressing such issues, leads to another, more fundamental question: what guides our moral direction and choices? Addressing this question is a fundamental purpose of **ethics**.

> Are we *obliged* to help other people? For example: what is the nature and extent of our obligation to give our time and resources to helping people trapped in extreme poverty and distress? The philosopher Peter Singer[2] has suggested that rather than spending our money on unnecessary things, we should voluntarily give more than 5% of our income towards this purpose.

2.2 Ethics is Moral Philosophy

Ethics is the branch of philosophy concerned with the study of morality (*moral philosophy*). It involves a disciplined inquiry into the nature, source, purpose, content and validity of moral principles and norms, of moral perspectives and moral claims, and of morality itself. It is an inquiry into *whether* and *why* people's beliefs, attitudes, dispositions, intentions and behaviour should be judged good or bad, right or wrong.

[2] Singer, P., *The Life You Can Save: Acting Now to End World Poverty* (Picador, 2009).

Ethics involves asking questions about how people *ought* to act (what should be?), and about the moral adequacy of how they actually *do* act (what is?) when tested against such a normative standard. What constitutes *good* or *right* behaviour? What makes for a *good life,* a life *lived well?* What ought one to strive to become? What is, and what should be, expected from people in their relationships with others and in their engagement with the world? How should we reconcile our interests and desires with those of others? What are people's responsibilities, obligations and duties as *moral agents?* On what basis should people, individually and collectively, make moral choices and exercise moral judgement? Are the moral choices and judgements people make justifiable?

Ethics is not about specifying and prescribing a particular set of universally applicable commands or rules for right and good behaviour, a list of 'dos and don'ts'. Rather, its central concern is with inquiring into *how* people ought to think about moral issues in order to determine their obligations and duties to themselves, to other people, to society in general and the environment. Ethics is about exploring, identifying, articulating, clarifying, balancing, evaluating and challenging conceptions of *the good* and *the right;* of the *ends* we ought to pursue, and the principles, norms and reasoning that ought to govern the *means* and behaviour we choose.[3] At its core is a concern with reasoned justification,[4] not only with *what one ought to do* but, more importantly, with *why one ought to do it.*

(***Note***: The terms 'ethics' and 'morals' are often used interchangeably, which is consistent with our definition here of ethics as moral philosophy.)

2.2.1 Values

Our *values* reflect 'the things that we hold dear'; what we should, and do, care about; what we believe should be sought after and cherished by everyone; what is worthwhile in life and makes life worthwhile. Values are abstract ideals about desirable and desired states of being that are important determinants of the human condition and of how we should and do live. They shape our worldview and influence our thoughts, intuitions, attitudes, feelings and actions. They are closely linked to our sense of individual and collective identity; shared values are what binds us together with other people and promotes social cohesion and harmony.

Ethical inquiry necessarily raises questions about values. Ethics is values-based and values-driven. Values underpin our conceptions about what is good and right; they provide a reference point for the determination of moral principles, a foundation and a guide for moral reasoning. The evaluation

---

[3] Audi, R. (General Editor), *Cambridge Dictionary of Philosophy* (2nd Edition, Cambridge University Press, 1999) p. 284.

[4] See, for example, Garvey, J., *The Ethics of Climate Change: Right and Wrong in a Warming World* (Continuum International Publishing Group, 2008) pp. 33–46.

of moral claims and the justification for moral choices, for the motives and behaviour of moral agents are grounded in value judgements.

A typical set of values might include some or all of the following: life, happiness, liberty, equality, solidarity, justice, fairness, tolerance, plurality, truth, beauty, love, empathy, individuality, family, community, country/patriotism, privacy, fame, wealth, health, security, serving God.

However, there is no definitive list of values or their relative importance. Values differ across cultures and societies, and they differ over time within any particular culture or society. What people value constantly evolves with individual and collective experience. And even if people agree on the relative importance of a particular value, they might not necessarily agree on its meaning.

Though there is no definitive list, values can be categorised as either desirable in themselves (virtues as *ends*) or as *means* to attain a desirable end. The former have *intrinsic* value, the latter *extrinsic* value. For example, happiness might be considered to be self-evidently good and desirable in and for itself, whereas the goodness and desirability of wealth or fame depend on the happiness that they bring.

Robert Audi[5] opines that all major ethical views take some notion of value as central, or at least very important, for morality. He suggests that value plays at least two guiding roles:

1. Our values act as a set of restraints – that which we value, for instance liberty and justice, must be protected by moral conduct and so limits what we *may* do.
2. Our values reflect ideals expressing our aspirations, thereby directing our energies and challenging us to strive harder and to see what we *can* do and achieve.

2.2.2 Ethical Inquiry

The ultimate purpose of ethical inquiry is enlightenment[6]: to enrich and enhance our understanding so that we can deal better with the moral issues we encounter – issues, many of them difficult and complex, that may impact significantly on our well-being and on the well-being of others. Ethical inquiry will not necessarily provide us clear prescriptions for action;

---

[5] Audi, R., *Moral Value and Human Diversity* (Oxford University Press, 2007) pp. 35–36.

[6] There is a distinction between the purposes of morality and the purposes of studying morality, although they are clearly linked. Understanding the former is the reason for the latter. Pojman suggests five purposes for morality: to keep society from falling apart; to ameliorate human suffering; to promote human flourishing; to resolve conflicts of interest in just and orderly ways; to assign praise and blame, reward the good and punish the guilty: "The goal of morality is to create happy and virtuous people, the kind that create flourishing communities. That's why it is the most important subject on earth." See Pojman, L.P., *The Moral Life: An Introductory Reader in Ethics and Literature* (Oxford University Press, 2000) pp. 39–41.

at first, particularly by challenging previously taken-for-granted moral certainties, it may well add to our confusion about morality. It will, however, provide us with the tools for understanding the nature of our confusion, fostering our confidence in and competence for moral reasoning.

Life, inescapably, has ethical dimensions, and as Simon Blackburn explains: "Every society ... will need some sense of what is expected and what is out of line. For human beings, there is no living without standards of living."[7] Ethics provides us with conceptual frameworks for identifying, analysing and evaluating moral issues; for understanding our obligations and duties and acting accordingly; for guiding our judgement and behaviour; and thereby enabling us to live better and to flourish individually and collectively. Such thinking forms the basis for answering questions about what should be expected and what should be considered 'out of line'. Its purpose is ultimately practical and applied, and it is relevant to everyday life.

People do not approach moral issues and decision-making with a blank slate. We develop ideas about what is good or bad, right or wrong from an early age and these strongly influence our thoughts, feelings, attitudes, convictions and behaviour. Our ideas about morality are mainly shaped by our upbringing and our personal experiences. In addition, however, our moral consciousness and sensibilities may also be influenced by a capacity to imagine our own life in different circumstances, to imagine lives other than our own, to put ourselves in someone else's shoes. Our capacity to imagine and empathise in this way enables us to transcend the limitations of our personal experience, explore the depths and richness of human nature, and become more consciously attuned to the diversity, possibilities and complexities of human experience.

It is in this context, and for this reason, that storytelling and other forms of stimuli to the imagination are important in ethical thinking. It is why we can usefully turn to novels, theatre, film, TV (e.g. soap operas), comics, painting, and music to inform, enliven, inspire and support us in our inquiry. Stories, or narratives, illuminate abstract ideas and help us to know ourselves and others better. They broaden our horizons, enabling us to enter into worlds different from our own, exposing us to a range of different world-views, providing us with a window into the complexity and depths of the human soul. Louis Pojman comments as follows about how literature can contribute to moral inquiry:

> "Literature often highlights moral ideas, focusing on particular people in their dilemmas, awakening our imagination to new possibilities, and enabling us to understand the moral life in fresh and creative ways. Good literature compels us to rethink and revise our everyday

---

[7] Blackburn, S., *Being Good: A Short Introduction to Ethics* (Oxford University Press, 2001) p. 23.

assumptions. It sets before us powerful particularities, which serve both as reinforcers and counterexamples to our sweeping principles… It makes the abstract concrete, brings it home to the heart, and forces us to think with innovative imagination. …

Literature particularises general problems, brings them home to us, enlivening the imagination so that we see and feel nuances that are vital to resolving difficult moral issues, possibilities that we might not have considered in our abstract thinking about moral dilemmas."[8]

Antigone is a play by the Ancient Greek playwright, Sophocles (496–406 BC). It presents a conflict between irreconcilable, absolute moral principles. There is a civil war in Thebes. Two brothers fight for the throne and in the fighting, kill each other. Creon, their uncle, is now King. As a deterrent to anyone contemplating challenging the authority of the state, he decrees that the body of the rebel brother should remain unburied with a sentence of death for anyone defying his order. Antigone, however, considers that she has an irrevocable duty to bury her dead brother, irrespective of the orders of her uncle Creon or of the consequences for her own life, or for society more generally. For Antigone, '*fiat justitia ruat caelum*'.

A version of *Antigone* by French playwright Jean Anouilh was famously produced in Paris in 1942 during the German occupation of France. Antigone's 'No' to Creon, based on an absolute duty regardless of consequence, was an appeal to the French to resist the occupation. (Creon's argument for the necessity of absolute obedience to the authority of the state, because of the threatened consequences, no doubt appealed to the Nazis.)

2.3 Branches of Moral Philosophy

Ethics, or moral philosophy, can be subdivided into five inter-related and overlapping areas of inquiry:

1. meta-ethics,
2. moral psychology;
3. descriptive ethics;
4. applied ethics; and
5. normative ethics,

---

[8] Pojman, L.P., *op. cit.* above, n. 6, p. xii (Preface) and p. 4.

2.3.1 Meta-ethics

Meta-ethics is the branch of moral philosophy concerned with analytical inquiry into the question of what morality is *in itself*, its origins and purpose, rather than *what is moral* (the focus of applied and normative ethics – see below). Meta-ethics is concerned with questions *about* ethics rather than with questions *in* ethics, with the status of ethics rather than with its content.[9] For example:

- Is morality only social custom, beyond which there is no moral truth?
- Is morality essentially a set of psychological adaptations that evolved to enable otherwise selfish individuals with competing interests to cooperate *within groups* in order that they might live happily and prosper?[10]
- Is moral validity essentially a question of social consensus and approval, rather than a question about intrinsic right or wrong?
- Is individual moral choice essentially subjective and arbitrary, grounded in natural impulse, feeling, sentiment, prejudice and self-interest?
- Can we reasonably affirm standards of the right and the good as any more than projections of our own preferences?[11]
- Are there standards of right and wrong that should apply universally?
- Is any moral position intrinsically better than any other?
- How should the moral be distinguished from the non-moral?
- Does morality ultimately lie outside the realm of objective justification through reason?

A question that is core to meta-ethics addresses the issue of *relativism*: can moral claims be objectively validated as universally applicable truths or are they essentially *relative* to the cultural context and social conditioning of the moral agent? Is the authority of moral norms relative to their time and place?[12]

2.3.1.1 The Implications of Relativism

"relativism ... suggests a skepticism about morality itself. Why? Because 'moral relativism' sounds like an oxymoron to someone whose conception of morality is of something universal and absolute. So if the meaning of moral relativism is that there is no absolute morality, then, in effect, there is no morality."[13]

---

[9] Mackie, J.L., *Ethics: Inventing Right from Wrong* (Penguin Book, 1977) p. 9.
[10] Greene, J., *Moral Tribes: Emotion, Reason, and the Gap Between Us and Them* (Atlantic Books, 2014) pp. 22–27.
[11] Audi, R., *op. cit.* above, n. 5, p. 4.
[12] Lukes, S., *Moral Relativism* (Picador, 2008) p. 18.
[13] Marks J., "W(h)ither Morality?" (2011) *Philosophy Now*, Issue 82, Jan/Feb, p. 4.

Consider the possible implications of a relativist perspective on morality. Arguably, it challenges the very idea of human civilisation and progress. Does it mean that all socially and culturally sanctioned practices in a particular society at a particular time are morally legitimate, including, for example: 'laddish' behaviour; strictly enforced dress codes; restricting sexual activity outside of marriage; exacting personal revenge in the name of family honour; discrimination on the grounds of gender, sexual orientation, ethnicity or religion; apartheid; slavery; capital punishment; genocide?

And relativism is one of the seven contemporary 'threats' to the very possibility of ethics identified by Simon Blackburn, the others being the 'death of God', egoism, evolutionary theory, determinism and futility, unreasonable demands and false consciousness.[14]

Chryssides and Kaler, however, suggest that even without recourse to ultimate justification, ethical inquiry remains not only possible but, in terms of social functioning, absolutely inescapable. They claim that we "simply cannot function in society without operating within and reasoning about moral rules, and this ... is a good reason for regarding them as ultimately justifiable."[15]

2.3.2 Moral Psychology

"It is generally recognised that an adequate understanding of desire, emotion, deliberation, choice, volition, character, and personality is indispensable to the theoretical treatment of human well-being, intrinsic value, and duty. Investigations into the nature of these psychological phenomena are therefore an essential, although auxiliary, part of ethics. They constitute the adjunct field of moral psychology."[16]

Ethics is about human behaviour in private and public spheres. It is important therefore to consider how people formulate moral norms, think and feel about moral issues, approach the resolution of moral dilemmas, evaluate competing moral claims, arrive at moral judgements, justify and rationalise the moral choices they do, or do not, make in various situations. Furthermore, it is relevant to examine how people's intuitions and conscience (their 'moral machinery') inform and direct their motives and actions, and how these impact reciprocally on their inner selves.

---

[14] Blackburn, S., *op. cit.* above, n. 7.
[15] Chryssides, G. and Kaler, J., *An Introduction to Business Ethics* (Cengage Learning, 1993) p. 21.
[16] Audi, R. (General Editor), *op. cit.* above, n. 3, p. 289.

Understanding human nature and the psychology of moral behaviour[17] is an important aspect of ethics, providing an essential link between the abstract ideas of ethical theory and their manifestation in the conduct of the moral agent acting in social contexts. This is particularly important as people are not necessarily *rational* agents. And Joshua Greene suggests an even greater importance for moral psychology:

> "Moral psychology is not something that occasionally intrudes into the abstract realm of moral philosophy. Moral philosophy is a manifestation of moral psychology."[18]

One particularly important aspect of moral psychology involves research into and theories on the development and evolution of a person's moral outlook, sensibilities, reflexes, conscience, and capacity for moral reasoning. (The work of the development psychologist Laurence Kohlberg, and in particular his six-stage theory of cognitive development, is highly influential in this area.)

Another important and related aspect is consideration of the nature and scope of *moral agency*, and whether moral responsibility or culpability is ever excusable. A leading area of inquiry in this regard is why ordinary and essentially 'good' people often make 'bad' ethical choices.[19] Landmark studies in this regard (studies which also raised questions about the ethics of research) include: the 1961 Milgram experiment at Yale University into obedience and conformity to perceived legitimate authority;[20] the 'Stanford prison experiment' in 1971; and the experiment conducted in a California high school in 1967 which is portrayed in the 2008 film *Die Welle (The Wave)*.[21]

Understanding the impact on people of the demands and expectations of their personal relationships, work roles and social situations is important to understanding the ethical dimension of their behaviour. Human complexity, imperfections, frailties and perceived powerlessness are evident in how people respond to moral choices. It is sobering to consider that more people have been killed by those who profess to be acting from altruistic

---

[17] See, for example, Wright, D., *The Psychology of Moral Behaviour* (Penguin Books, 1971). See also: Kahneman, D., *Thinking Fast and Slow* (Penguin Books, 2012); Thaler, R., *Misbehaving: The Making of Behavioural Economics* (Penguin Books, 2016); the *Calvin & Hobbes* cartoons of Bill Watterson (Universal Press Syndicate, 1989).

[18] Greene, J., *op. cit.*, above, n. 10, p. 329.

[19] See Gellerman, S., "Why 'good' managers make bad ethical choices" (1986) *Harvard Business Review*, July–August, 85–90.

[20] Milgram, S., *Obedience to Authority: An Experimental View* (HarperCollins, 1974).

[21] See also the film, *The Experimenter* (2015) about the Milgram experiment.

motives than have been killed by those acting out of motives of self-interest (e.g. people killing for love of country rather than hatred of an enemy).

It is also pertinent to ask why rational, self-interested people would *choose* to behave ethically. Game theory,[22] including for example the 'Prisoner's Dilemma', has provided valuable insights into the relationship between individual rationality and collective rationally, highlighting the importance of morality as a rational basis for building trust and enabling cooperation, bringing long-term mutual benefit to the individual actors. Once again, however, it is a sobering to remember that it is the promise of mutually assured destruction that has prevented nuclear war for the last 70 years rather than any appeal to the love of humankind or higher human moral purpose; a thin psychological thread on which to hang the nuclear 'sword of Damocles'.

2.3.3 Descriptive Ethics

Descriptive ethics involves an empirical focus on '*what is*' (compared to normative ethics, the focus of which is '*what ought to be*'). It is concerned with the study of prevailing values, moral principles, norms and approved standards of behaviour in particular societies, cultures, sub-cultures, ethnic communities, and other social sub-groups at a particular time. The focus is on identification, explanation and comparison, drawing on sociological, anthropological and ethnographic perspectives as an external and impartial observer.

Descriptive ethics involves inquiry into what Simon Blackburn calls the 'moral or ethical environment'[23] to render its underlying shared beliefs and values visible and understandable; its climate of ideas that are manifest in how people see and think about the world and in how they live. It involves inquiry into:

- the myths, stories and rituals that shape and reinforce individual and collective identity, and bind members of a society into a shared, cohesive sense of meaning and being;
- the ideas that inspire and govern hearts, minds and imaginations, and that determine and validate modes of behaviour and ways of living;
- the ideas, assumptions and values (espoused, emergent and unstated) underpinning the nature of social, political and economic arrangements and institutions;
- the kinds of behaviour and dispositions of character that a particular environment nurtures and encourages;
- people's sense of their own worth and the worth of others;
- what is generally considered important, desirable, acceptable, admirable or objectionable.

---

[22] See, for example, Gauthier, D., *Morals by Agreement* (Oxford University Press, 1986).
[23] Blackburn, S., *op. cit.* above, n. 7, p. 1.

The ambition of descriptive ethics is "to understand the springs of motivation, reason, and feeling that move us. It is to understand the network of rules or 'norms' that sustain our lives. The ambition is often one of finding system in the apparent jumble of principles and goals that we respect, or say we do. It is an enterprise of self-knowledge."[24]

2.3.4 Applied Ethics

Applied ethics (or 'practical ethics') is concerned with using ethical theory as a basis for investigating, analysing and evaluating the moral dimensions of real and contemporary social, political and economic issues, which are often controversial and divisive. It is, according to Peter Singer:

> "the application of ethics or morality – I shall use the words interchangeably – to practical issues like the treatment of ethnic minorities, equality for women, the use of animals for food and research, the preservation of the natural environment, abortion, euthanasia, and the obligation of the wealthy to help the poor."[25]

The aim is to clarify and explain the nature of, and reasons for, the controversy with a view to proposing morally justifiable resolutions as a basis for practical action. In addition to the issues mentioned above by Peter Singer, set out below are some other issues that pose significant moral challenges and dilemmas for contemporary society:

- balancing freedom with the demands of collective security;
- balancing privacy with the convenience of social media;
- balancing the conflicting rights of different social groups;
- poverty, inequality and economic injustice;
- corporate responsibility and accountability;
- the treatment of asylum seekers and refugees;
- addressing climate change;
- the use of extra-judicial counterterrorism security measures (e.g. enhanced interrogation techniques, extraordinary rendition and lengthy detention without trial);
- the legitimacy of state-sanctioned violence and war.

Applied ethics is also concerned with the application of ethical theories and moral reasoning to the circumstances and problems arising in particular **occupational** areas as a guide for professional practice, for example: politics, business, finance, medicine, social care, sport, law, journalism,

---

[24] *Ibid.* p. 5.
[25] Singer, P., *Practical Ethics* (2nd Edition, Cambridge University Press, 1993) p. 1.

architecture, engineering, IT, science, research, policing and education. There is a debate[26] as to whether each occupational area should be treated as a separate realm of activity, which, because of its particular nature and circumstances, necessitates its own, unique ethical framework for evaluating *whether* and *why* behaviour in that realm should be judged right or wrong. For example, there is an argument that the essential 'rules of the game' in politics or in business justify behaviour that would not be morally acceptable in other spheres of life; therefore, a distinct 'political ethics' or 'business ethics' is necessary and legitimate as a basis for validating principles and norms of behaviour that are unique to those worlds. However, there is no consensus about the validity of the 'separate realm view' or that a special ethics should apply in particular fields of human activity. The 'rules of the game' (if indeed an occupation or profession should be considered to be 'a game') and the special occupational ethics will themselves be subject to ethical evaluation and moral justification using normative ethical theories and meta-ethical frameworks.

2.3.5 Normative Ethics (Ethical Theory)

It is the business of ethics to tell us what are our duties, or by what test we may know them.[27]

John Stuart Mill

Normative ethics is the branch of moral philosophy concerned with elucidating theories that aim to provide systematic explanations and ethical first principles as tests for determining what one *ought* to do and *why*. (A 'normative' statement is about how things should, or ought to be, rather how things are (see **Section 2.3.3**, 'descriptive ethics'.) The focus of normative ethics is inquiry into the fundamental bases for moral judgement and choice. It "is concerned with supplying and justifying a coherent moral system of thinking and judging. Normative ethics seeks to uncover, develop, and justify basic moral principles that are intended to guide behaviour, actions and decisions".[28]

---

[26] See Audi, R. (General Editor), *op. cit.* above, n. 3, p. 35.

[27] Mill, J.S., *Utilitarianism* (1861; Warnock, M. (Ed.) Fontana, 1962), p. 269.

[28] Carroll, A. and Buchholtz, A., *Business & Society: Ethics and Stakeholder Management* (6th Edition, International Student Edition, Thomson South-Western, 2006) pp. 174–175; DeGeorge, R., *Business Ethics*, (4th Edition, Prentice Hall, 1995) pp. 20–21. Note: for many people, their ethical first principles are provided by the dictates of religious belief, tradition and instruction (*divine command ethics*). The focus in moral philosophy, however, is on ethical theories grounded in reason rather than in faith.

Normative ethical theories provide a basis for guiding, directing and supporting people in formulating moral norms, in moral reasoning, in justifying moral claims and in assessing the moral adequacy of behaviour, for answering the question 'where is the moral line?' by clarifying what is good and what makes an action right.[29] Furthermore, normative ethical theories seek to clarify the ultimate ends we ought to choose and to pursue, and the fundamental moral principles that should govern our choices and pursuits.[30]

2.3.5.1 Consequentialist vs. Non-consequentialist Ethical Theories

Secular ethical theories can be broadly classified into those that adopt a consequentialist (*teleological,* 'ends logic') approach and those with a non-consequentialist (*deontological,* 'duty logic') approach to morality. The classification reflects differing foundational premises for addressing *why* particular actions *should be* judged moral or immoral, good or bad, right or wrong.

For consequentialists, the morality of conduct (its goodness/rightness or badness/wrongness) depends entirely on its consequences in terms of some underlying *end value*: for example, in terms of its consequences for individual pleasure, human happiness, societal welfare or the common good. Consequentialists start with a concept of the good that should be sought, and this serves as the criterion for judging whether conduct is right or wrong. For example, stealing or torture might be considered morally acceptable by a consequentialist if they result in good outcomes. Conduct that brings good consequences is right and moral; conduct that brings bad consequences is wrong and immoral. The test of whether an action is right or wrong is whether it causes good or harm.[31]

For consequentialists, morality is a calculation based on predicted outcomes in terms of some defined good. For example, the act of stealing is not considered to be *inherently* right or wrong. It will depend on the circumstance. An action is only considered to be wrong if it has harmful consequences in the particular context in which it is undertaken. The same action may, however, be considered morally acceptable in a different context if it produced beneficial consequences. For consequentialists, the end value justifies the means.

---

[29] Benn, P., *Ethics* (Fundamentals of Philosophy Series, UCL Press, 1998) p. 60.
[30] Audi, R. (General Editor), *op. cit.* above, n. 3, p. 285.
[31] Driver, J., *Ethics: The Fundamentals* (Blackwell Publishing, 2007) p. 40; Chryssides, G. and Kaler, J., *op. cit.* above, n. 15, p. 88.

> "Consequentialists start not with moral rules but with goals. They assess actions by the extent to which they further these goals. The best known, though not the only, consequentialist theory is utilitarianism."[32]

For non-consequentialists, the value and moral adequacy of an act (its goodness/rightness or badness/wrongness) is inherent in the act itself and in the actor's *intention*. It does not depend on anything outside the act in itself. The consequences of the act are of no relevance; the act has intrinsic value; it will be right because it is intrinsically right, or wrong because it is intrinsically wrong. The means is an end in itself. Non-consequentialists start not with desirable end values, but with moral principles or rules of action that one has a duty to observe irrespective of circumstance. What the principles or rules are will depend on the particular non-consequentialist moral theory in question.[33] The best known non-consequentialist theory is Kant's duty ethics (see **Section 2.4.2** below).

Faced with an ethical dilemma, consequentialists calculate and weigh up the outcome value in terms of benefits and harms resulting. For any proposed action, they will ask whether good will come from it. For non-consequentialists, the issue is not about calculation of consequence, but whether the action is *intrinsically* right or wrong. For any proposed action, they will ask whether it accords with the principles that define one's duty. In many situations, the approaches are likely to arrive at the same judgement about the moral adequacy of an action. The difference between them is in terms of the underlying reason *why* they do so. For example, both approaches might agree that 'stealing is wrong', but they will have arrived at this conclusion for different reasons. The distinction centres on their differing tests for moral adequacy. For a consequentialist, the moral response to an issue can vary with the circumstances: it is a situational, contingent morality. The consequentialist may, in different context, conclude that 'stealing is not wrong'. For the non-consequentialist, the circumstances make no difference: if 'stealing is wrong', then it is always wrong.

> "The division between consequentialists and non-consequentialists is also likely to manifest itself in their respective responses to moral issues; they have a radically different conception of the nature of the problem and therefore radically different approaches to its solution. ... Adherence to principle is the basis of the non-consequentialist approach, pragmatic flexibility that of the consequentialist."[34]

---

[32] Singer, P., *op. cit.* above, n. 25, p. 3.

[33] Harris, C., *Applying Moral Theories,* (5th Edition, Thomson Wadsworth, 2007) p. 12.

[34] Chryssides, G. and Kaler, J., *op. cit.* above, n. 15, p. 90.

A brief overview of the main normative ethical theories is provided below in **Section 2.4**.

2.4 Normative Ethical Theories

There are four dominant normative ethical theories, each of which is outlined below:

- classical utilitarianism;
- Kantian duty ethics;
- virtue ethics; and
- Rawls' justice ethics.

2.4.1 Classical Utilitarianism: 'The Happiness Theory'

The best-known consequentialist ethical theory is classical utilitarianism.[35] Utilitarianism provides a clear and universally applicable criterion as a basis for judging whether behaviour should be considered right or wrong; for determining moral obligation and specifying how people ought to behave; for determining whether and why acts are morally defensible.

The theory was first formulated by Jeremy Bentham (1748–1832) and developed further by John Stuart Mill (1803–1873). For Bentham and Mill, what is good is *happiness*. Seeking happiness is the ultimate end purpose of human activity, the ultimate end value, the thing that all people desire and seek for its own sake. In the words of Mill:

> "The utilitarian doctrine is, that happiness is desirable, and the only thing desirable, as an end; all other things being only desirable as means to that end."[36]

Utility means 'usefulness': it is the usefulness of actions in producing good end consequences, in engendering happiness, that is the fundamental basis for determining their moral worth. The right thing to do is that which is likely to promote *the greatest happiness* for everyone affected by an action. In utilitarian reasoning, the end goal is happiness for all; actions are morally justifiable if they contribute to the realisation of this end goal; right if they augment or promote the happiness of those affected, wrong if they diminish or oppose that happiness. The production of happiness and the reduction of unhappiness:

---

[35] For a highly readable explanation of classical utilitarianism, see Sandel, M., *Justice: What's the Right Thing to Do?* (Allen Lane, 2009) Chapter 2.

[36] Mill, J.S., *Utilitarianism, op. cit.* above, n. 27, p. 288.

"should be the standard by which actions are judged right or wrong and by which the rules of morality, laws, public policies, and social institutions are to be critically evaluated".[37]

What then is 'happiness'? For Bentham, happiness is a balance of *pleasure* (which is good) and *pain* (which is bad). According to Bentham:

> "Nature has placed mankind under the governance of two sovereign masters, pain and pleasure. It is for them alone to point out what we ought to do, as well as to determine what we shall do. On the one hand the standard of right and wrong, on the other the chain of causes and effects, are fastened to their throne. They govern us in all we do, in all we say, in all we think: ... The principle of utility recognises this subjection, and assumes it for the foundation of that system, the object of which is to rear the fabric of felicity by the hands of reason and of law." [38]

The utility of an action depends on whether it increases pleasure and/or diminishes suffering, and so adds to the sum of human happiness. In the words of John Stuart Mill:

> "The creed which accepts as the foundation of morals, Utility, or the Greatest Happiness Principle, holds that actions are right in proportion as they tend to promote happiness, wrong as they tend to produce the reverse of happiness. By happiness is intended pleasure, and the absence of pain; by unhappiness, pain and the privation of pleasure."[39]

For the utilitarian, the general happiness principle is the basis for the moral evaluation of behaviour. Morality is based on a *calculation* of the consequences of behaviour in terms of its aggregate impact on the pleasure and pain experienced by all parties affected. For Bentham this was a practical proposition: pleasure and pain, he suggested, should and could be measured using seven parameters: intensity, duration, certainty or uncertainty, propinquity or remoteness, fecundity, purity and extent. Everyone's happiness should be measured as the same and in the same way; there should be no privileged persons and no privileged pleasures or suffering. Morality is, in effect, a form of applied-mathematical egalitarian benefit/cost analysis; a *felicific calculus*.

---

[37] West, H.R., *An Introduction to Mill's Utilitarian Ethics* (Cambridge University Press, 2004), p. 1.

[38] Bentham, J., *An Introduction to the Principles of Morals and Legislation* (1789), Section 1.1. Reprinted in Engelmann, S.G. (Ed.), *Jeremy Bentham, Selected Writings* (Yale University Press, 2011).

[39] Mill, J.S., *Utilitarianism, op. cit.* above, n. 27, p. 257.

Mill suggested a rethinking of Bentham's theory. One of his concerns was with Bentham's view that all pleasures are essentially the same; that there is no qualitative difference between the pleasures of the opera, theatre or symphony, and the more sensual indulgences of the music hall or pub. This led to the dismissive characterisation of utilitarianism as a 'hedonic calculus' and a 'swine morality'. Mill argued that pleasures differ *qualitatively* as well as quantitatively; that the more demanding pleasures of the intellect, feelings and imagination are of a higher order, have a greater intrinsic value, and are more desirable than the self-indulgent, transient, shallower animalistic pleasures of the body. This difference in the quality of pleasures, Mill suggested, should be considered in the calculation of overall aggregate happiness.

> "It is better to be a human being dissatisfied than a pig satisfied; better to be Socrates dissatisfied than a fool satisfied. And if the fool, or the pig, are of a different opinion, it is because they only know their own side of the question. The other party to the comparison knows both sides."[40]

Mill also allowed for the possibility of a further modification to Bentham's *act utilitarian* approach called *rule utilitarianism*. Rather than evaluate each action on a case-by-case basis, general rules of conduct can be formulated and evaluated in terms of their long-term consequence for the overall happiness of society. The focus is on the *social utility* of the general rule rather than the utility of individual acts. The general rule should be applied consistently even if its application in some particular instance might not add to the aggregate happiness of all affected in the short term. For example, the application of the rule 'innocent until proven guilty' carries the risk that a person who committed a crime may go free for lack of sufficient proof. But it also means that there is less likelihood of an innocent person being wrongly convicted. On balance, the consistent application of the rule results in greater human happiness over the long term and it is for this reason that the rule should be adhered to.

Rule utilitarianism addresses criticisms leveled at Bentham's act utilitarianism, that it did not consider the distribution of happiness among people and the question of social justice. A focus on the long-term social utility of observing rules of behaviour to apply in all cases, rather than on the utility of individual acts each assessed separately and disconnectedly, allows for the incorporation into the analysis of consequences of considerations of the distribution of outcomes and of social justice. For example, people may add to their own happiness by causing harm to others (even if as unavoidable 'collateral damage' rather than directly intentional). This act could be

40 *Ibid.* p. 260.

morally justifiable in the particular case. Observance of the rule that 'people should not cause harm to others', by contrast, is consistent with the idea of justice as fairness for all, respecting everyone equally and thereby adding to overall human happiness in the long run. Social utility underpins Mill's argument for liberalism, advocating, as a rule, maximum freedom for the individual to act as they choose restricted only by the obligation not to harm others.[41] Michael Sandel summarises Mill's view as follows:

> "Mill thinks we should maximize utility, not case by case, but in the long run. And over time, he argues, respecting individual liberty will lead to the greatest human happiness. Allowing the majority to silence dissenters or censor free-thinkers might maximize utility today, but it will make society worse-off – less happy – in the long run."[42]

In an example of the contemporary relevance of Mill's views, they were directly and strongly echoed in an editorial in *The Irish Times* (occasioned by the newly crowned Rose of Tralee), supporting the then proposed constitutional referendum on marriage equality:

> "One of the hallmarks of a free society is that every citizen should be able to pursue whatever lifestyle choice he or she prefers, free from discrimination, once those choices do not impinge on the rights of others."[43]

2.4.1.1   Utilitarianism: Arguments For and Against

Utilitarianism provides a readily understandable and practical approach to moral reasoning. Its recognition of the central importance of happiness to people has a powerful instinctual appeal that accords with observable human behaviour.

> "It seems reasonable that morality, if it is to guide conduct, should have something to do with happiness. It seems natural to seek pleasure and to avoid pain and distress, but it also seems sensible to balance these against each other, to put up with a certain amount of pain in order to achieve a quantity of pleasure that outweighs it. In taking the general happiness as the standard of right action this proposal seems to satisfy at once the presumptions that moral action should be unselfish and that moral principle should be fair. It seems to provide a coherent system of conduct".[44]

---

[41] Mill, J.S., *On Liberty* (1859; Himmelfarb, G. (Ed.), Penguin Books, 1985).

[42] Sandel, M., *op. cit.* above, n. 35, p. 50.

[43] "The Rose of Tralee 2014: Lovely, Fair and Gay", *The Irish Times*, Editorial, 30 August 2014.

[44] Mackie, J.L., *op. cit.* above, n. 9, p. 126.

People are naturally inclined towards goal-directed behaviour, seeking meaning in purpose. Utilitarianism highlights the importance that consideration of consequence plays in decision-making. It provides a clear and definite first principle, that of human well-being, as the criterion for guiding individual and collective behaviour, a standard for morality that is universally applicable. In evaluating the moral adequacy of individual behaviour, of general rules of action and of collective social arrangements, utilitarianism requires that the happiness of all persons affected should be considered impartially and objectively. Everyone's well-being is considered equally and the best interests of the individual are necessarily balanced with, and constrained by, the best interests of all. Utilitarianism also provides for the possibility of incorporating consideration of the happiness of animals, as sentient creatures capable of experiencing pleasure and pain.[45]

Utilitarianism recognises that morality should serve humanity and not vice versa; that morality is a means towards the end of making the world a better place for all who live in it. It is the good that determines the right. The right thing to do is that which is demonstrably good; this is utilitarianism's essential guide for moral direction. And although it is a universal theory, it is pragmatic, flexible and situational; it can be applied to all aspects of living and can be adopted to take into account the contingencies and sensitivities of particular circumstances. Peter Singer argues that one of its strengths is in providing a useful minimal *first basis* for evaluating and resolving controversial moral dilemmas that require a social, political and institutional policy response.[46]

Critics of utilitarianism (and of consequentialist ethics more generally) argue that its underlying premise is fundamentally flawed. In asserting that morality is a calculation of end consequence in terms of aggregate human happiness, and that it is only the outcome that ultimately matters, the dignity and rights of individuals may be overridden by the demands of social and political expediency. Utilitarianism, it is argued, lacks an inherent concept of human rights and of social justice. People are not valued and respected intrinsically and essentially. Arguably, utilitarianism accords no inalienable rights to the individual at all. The well-being of the individual may be treated as secondary to the well-being of the collective. It incorporates a potential for unfairness in the treatment of individuals. Its flexibility and adaptability suggests that it can be used to justify almost anything (including, for example, cheating, stealing, torture, war, killing, dictatorship, slavery, apartheid, child labour and corporal punishment).

---

[45] According to Bentham: "The question is not, can they *reason?* nor can they *talk?* but, *can they suffer?*". Bentham, J., *An Introduction to the Principles of Morals and Legislation, op. cit.* above, n. 38, Chapter xvii, section 1.

[46] Singer, P., *op. cit.* above, n. 25, Chapter 1.

There are also inherent difficulties in its practical application. The notions that aggregate happiness is measureable in an objective manner, or that the outcomes of actions are reliably predictable, are flawed. Also, utilitarianism implies that the moral adequacy of behaviour will only be known after the event when it may be too late to make amends for what, in retrospect, were mistakes of judgement.

Utilitarianism requires that people be capable of committing any act that serves the interests of promoting the aggregate happiness of the collective without suffering any personal consequence in terms of a disturbed conscience. However, this does not accord with the felt experience of many people, who may suffer pangs of conscience even though they acted for the greater good. For example, telling lies does not always come easy to people, even when they reason that it is better to do so. And utilitarianism is relentless in its moral demands on the individual: no matter what one does, there is always something else that one could and should have done that would have added more to the overall sum of human happiness. For example, how can we enjoy a special treat of a meal in a restaurant knowing that the money we spend could be better used to alleviate the suffering of famine victims reported on the news earlier in the day?

2.4.2 Kantianism: An Ethic of Duty

Immanuel Kant (1724–1804) is the great philosopher of the Enlightenment and of the centrality of human reason to our understanding of the world. He sought to ground ethics in reason alone. For Kant, the basis for morality is not consequence; rather, it is to act for the sake of a universal *duty* or *moral law*, which one can discover and know through the use of one's reason. The duty or moral law must apply *universally* irrespective of the consequence of acting in accordance with it in any particular context or circumstance. It is only when one acts for the sake of this duty or moral law that one acts from a *good will*, and that one's behaviour can be considered to be right and good.

For example, if you stop to help someone change a flat tyre on their car, and do so because you think that you would like someone to do the same for you someday, essentially, your actions are motivated by self-interest, by an instrumental motive, i.e. seeing others as having only instrumental value. For Kant, your actions cannot be considered moral as you were not acting from a sense of universal duty and so you were not acting with a *good will*:

> "It is impossible to conceive anything at all in the world, or even out of it, which can be taken as good without qualification, except a *good will*."[47]

---

[47] Kant, I. and Paton, H.J. (Translator), *The Moral Law: Or, Kant's Groundwork of the Metaphysic of Morals*, Analysis and Notes by Paton, H.J. (Routledge Classics, 2005) p. 63.

Universal duties or moral laws are commands that one gives oneself. They are not imposed by any outside authority or based in social convention; each person is their own moralist (the author of their own moral law) and must discover and know their duty for themselves through the use of reason. Kant requires that one should do the right thing because it is inherently right without qualification. In direct contrast to utilitarianism, that which is good is that which is right; what is good is determined by, and is indistinguishable from, what is right. The purposes and intentions of people's behaviour (*ends*) are morally inseparable from their way of behaving (*means*); to will an end is to will the means to that end. The test of morality is whether one's actions are motivated from a universal duty or moral law that is in itself inherently right and good; again, it is the *intention* or *motive* of the moral actor that matters.[48] As Paul Smith explains:

> "Kantian ethics and utilitarianism relate the concepts of the good and the right in opposite ways. Utilitarianism starts from a conception of the good … and uses it to try and work out the right. Kantianism, in contrast, starts from a conception of the right, of morality, which enables us to identify which ends and means are permissible, prohibited or obligatory. It denies that the good can be conceived independently of the right."[49]

People, according to Kant, are *natural beings* with desires, inclinations and feelings. However, it is the capacity to act from reason that distinguishes us as *moral beings*. It is this capacity for free choice, autonomous action, self-reflection and self-governance grounded in reason that gives human life its intrinsic dignity and value. We can reflect on and choose the principles that underlie our actions. We can ask and reflect on questions 'why ought I to do that?' or 'why did I do that?' It is this capacity that enables us to act from a *good will* in accordance with a duty/moral law that we have given ourselves. It is only by doing so that our actions have moral worth and can be considered morally adequate.

2.4.2.1 The 'Categorical Imperative'

Kant does not tell us what our moral duty is or provide us with a list of moral laws to be obeyed. Rather, he provides us with a guiding criterion that enables us to know our duty. Kant explains that moral duty is the necessity to act in conformance with a *categorical imperative*, which is the supreme principle of morality. The test of the morality of a contemplated

---

[48] See Sandel, M., *op. cit.* above, n. 35, Chapter 5, "What Matters is the Motive".
[49] Smith, P., *Moral and Political Philosophy: Key Issues, Concepts and Theories* (Palgrave Macmillan, 2008) pp. 167–168.

action is whether the principle on which it is based is absolute, unconditional and unqualified, that it applies necessarily and regardless of one's desires or inclinations, of the circumstances and of the consequences. Only actions motivated from a categorical imperative are morally right and good.

Kant provided a number of explanations of what he meant by the 'categorical imperative'. His first formulation (known as 'the formula of universal law') is as follows:

> "Act only on that maxim through which you can at the same time will that it should become a universal law."[50]

The maxim (principle) on which one acts should, with logical consistency, be universalisable: it should be a principle of action that one would want everyone to adopt as a moral law and to act on always, without exception, as a duty. For example, 'promises should always be kept' is a maxim that can be universalised. In contrast, the maxim 'promises may or may not be kept' cannot be universalised; it is logically inconsistent. Something cannot be a moral duty that cannot be a duty for everyone always. The question we must ask in evaluating the morality of behaviour is 'can I will that everyone should do that all the time?'

> "Principles that cannot serve for a plurality of agents are to be rejected: the thought is that nothing could be a moral principle which cannot be a principle for all. Morality begins with the rejection on non-universalizable principles."[51]

Kant's second formulation of the categorical imperative (known as 'the formula of the end in itself' or as 'the formula of humanity') is as follows:

> "Act in such a way that you always treat humanity, whether in your own person or in the person of any other, never simply as a means, but always at the same time as an end."[52]

This formulation of the categorical imperative places humanity, as manifest in each individual person, at the centre of moral deliberations. It recognises that human beings have an intrinsic, unconditional and absolute value. People are not mere objects with instrumental value (recall the 'instrumental motive' of our tyre-changing Samaritan above). To act morally in accordance with a

---

[50] Kant I., *Groundwork of the Metaphysic of Morals.*, *op. cit.* above, n. 47, p. 97.
[51] O'Neill, O., "Kantian Ethics" in Singer, P. (Ed.), *A Companion to Ethics* (Blackwell Publishing, 1993) p. 177.
[52] Kant I., *Groundwork of the Metaphysic of Morals.*, *op. cit.* above, n. 47, p. 107.

categorical imperative requires that we act always with respect for persons as autonomous beings, with respect for the inviolable dignity of the human person. We should never treat people (including ourselves) as mere means to an end, but always and primarily as ends in themselves.

2.4.2.2 Kantian Ethics: Arguments For and Against

Kantian ethics underpins, informs and permeates much of contemporary discourse about morality and its practical manifestation in our moral intuitions and public policy frameworks. His ideas about the autonomy of moral agents, human dignity and the obligation to show 'respect for persons' are well understood and central to modern perceptions of human worth and of universal human rights.[53] They are "the most influential attempt to vindicate universal moral principles without reference to preferences or to a theological framework".[54]

There are aspects of Kant's approach that are intuitively appealing. The notion of acting selflessly and authentically, motivated only by a universally shared duty, grounded in pure reason has an almost mystical attraction. However, Kant's abstract ideas and language are intellectually challenging and difficult to grasp. He offers little practical guidance about what one ought to do or how one ought to live. It seems implausible that people have the capacity to reason their way to a categorical imperative, and to act accordingly free from the influence of sentiment and of their natural selves. Or that they would even choose to do so: reason is not the only capacity that distinguishes us as human and gives dignity to human life. The categorical imperative is a rigid, inflexible and impossible standard to live up to. Observed behaviour suggests that context and consequence do matter to people, and that they adapt the application of moral principles in response to the contingencies of circumstance. As Kenan Malik explains:

> "Context matters because we live in an an imperfect world. It is that imperfection, of the world and of human nature, that creates the very need for morality. It is also the reason that such morality cannot be categorical."[55]

2.4.3 Virtue Ethics

Virtue ethics is the oldest tradition in Western moral philosophy, primarily associated with classical Greek philosophy and with Aristotle (381–322 BC) in particular. Rather than basing morality on considerations of how we

[53] Malik, K., *The Quest for a Moral Compass: A Global History of Ethics* (Atlantic Books, 2014) p. 207.
[54] O'Neill, O., *op. cit.* above, n. 51, p. 184.
[55] Malik, K., *op. cit.* above, n. 53, p. 207.

ought to *act,* virtue ethics focuses on how we ought to *be* in the world, on the type of person we ought to seek to become. Virtues are traits of character manifest in the mind, heart and soul of a person. Morality is grounded in the character of the moral agent; a virtuous person will act morally. What is right and good is what a virtuous person will do.

Aristotle explains that to be a good human being is to realise one's natural purpose by fulfilling one's potential as a person; to be the best one can be.[56] This is what is intended by nature and what people ought to strive for. The supreme good, the end that people ought to desire for itself, is a state of *eudaimonia,* usually translated as *happiness* or *flourishing* – a state of living well and doing well in the context of one's community. A good life is *a life of happiness*; virtue is the means to this end. Happiness requires actions that are motivated by and accord with virtue. There are two categories of virtue: intellectual virtues (qualities of the mind); and moral virtues (qualities of character). The latter dispose us to act well, and can be identified and understood through reason and self-reflection. They can be learned and cultivated through education and habit-forming practice, and by following the example of virtuous role models.

Aristotle suggests that the moral virtues provide a middle way of moderation (a 'Golden Mean') between the vices of excess and of deficiency. He identifies 12 moral virtues: courage, modesty, pride, temperance, righteous indignation, generosity, magnificence, magnanimity, patience, honesty, wittiness and friendliness. *Courage,* for example, is the mean between cowardice and rashness; *modesty* between shyness and shamelessness; *pride* between vanity and humility; *temperance* between gluttony and abstinence; *righteous indignation* between envy and spitefulness.

A virtuous person will have the instinct and capacity to know the right thing to do, at the right time, in the right way, in any given context. Good and right acts are the kind that a virtuous person performs. Ethical decisions and moral behaviour are a manifestation of the *practical wisdom* of a virtuous character. "Virtue makes us aim at the right target; and practical wisdom makes us use the right means."[57]

2.4.3.1 Virtue Ethics: Arguments For and Against

Virtue ethics highlights the importance of the character of the moral agent in promoting moral behaviour. The cultivation of virtuous traits

---

[56] Aristotle, *The Nicomachean Ethics,* translated by D. Ross, revised by J.L. Ackrill and J.O. Urmson (The World's Classics, Oxford University Press, 1980).
[57] Aristotle, as quoted by Audi, R. in *op. cit.* above, n. 5, p. 6.

and habits of virtue predisposes people to know and to do what is good and right, as does the inspirational example and demonstrated excellence of virtuous exemplars. And virtue is at the core of what it means to be a professional: the nurturing and cultivation of virtuous traits and of practical wisdom is critical to the development of professional excellence.

However, virtue ethics seems incomplete as a theory. Virtue is as virtue does: it is only apparent after the event; and an understanding of *being* requires an understanding of *doing* (otherwise, as W.B. Yeats asks: "how can we know the dancer from the dance?"[58]). How does the virtuous character choose what to do? To suggest that the practical wisdom of a virtuous person is a manifestation of natural instinct, of training or of replication of previous good example, is to deny the potential role of reason and creative imagination in evaluating options for action and in resolving moral dilemmas. If what is good and right is simply what a virtuous person does, then morality can be arbitrary; if, however, a virtuous person does what is good and right, then there is something more fundamental than virtue. The position is well summarised by Frankena: "Traits without principles are blind, but principles without traits are impotent."[59]

Virtue is also an unreliable guide to morality. It seems unlikely that there will be complete consensus among people of virtue about what is the right thing to do in any particular situation. There is no definitive list of virtues or of the priority to be accorded each. What is considered virtuous depends on the social context and can change over time, as personal and social circumstance change. What is virtue in the young can seem folly in the old, and vice versa.[60] There may be a thin psychological line between virtue and vice; virtue can, over time and almost unnoticed, transmute into myopia, hubris and a predisposition towards conformity and inaction. Past virtue is not a reliable predictor of future behaviour. To paraphrase the closing lines from Sophocles' play *Oedipus Rex*: call no person virtuous until after they are dead. The fall from grace of Aung San Suu Kyi in 2017 is a case in point: "She is proving to be the wrong person at the wrong time for Myanmar."[61]

Virtue does not appear to be essential to feeling happy and fulfilled, or to self-respect and enjoying the respect of others, or to be considered exemplary. The assumption that virtuous people get more from life is flawed.

---

[58] Yeats, W.B., "Among School Children" published in *The Tower* (1928).
[59] Frankena, W., *Ethics* (2nd Edition, Prentice Hall, 1973) pp. 63–71, quoted in Pojman, L. and Fieser, J., *Ethics: Discovering Right from Wrong*, (6th Edition, Cengage Learning, 2009) p. 160.
[60] For example, read Turgenev's novel, *Fathers and Sons*.
[61] Phil Robertson of Human Rights Watch, quoted in the *Financial Times*, 24/25 February 2018.

Reason can suggest behaviour that is not accepted as virtuous as the path to happiness. Flourishing physically, emotionally, economically and socially does not necessarily depend on acting in accordance with accepted virtue. Dishonesty, self-promotion and disloyalty can bring rewards. Acting contrary to conventional ideas of virtue, or using virtue as a means towards self-serving ends that are not necessarily in society's immediate best interests can bring personal fulfilment; and can be sanctioned by society retrospectively. It can be good for oneself and for society that one lacks virtue.[62] Virtue may come at a high personal price, which does not necessarily lead to personal flourishing; for example, patriotism may be considered a virtue, but whether one can flourish by acting in accordance with the advice that *dulce et decorum est pro patria mori* is questionable.

2.4.4 *Rawls' Ethics of Justice*

Social contract theory is an approach to ethics associated with political philosophy, and in particular with the writings of Thomas Hobbes (1588–1679), John Locke (1632–1704) and Jean-Jacques Rousseau (1712–1778). It is based on the idea that rational, self-interested people will agree to cooperate voluntarily for long-term mutual benefit. The basis for cooperation is an implicitly agreed 'social contract' that underpins social and political institutions, including government and law. The social contract sets out the terms for cooperation that are acceptable to all participants. It provides a basis for balancing and regulating the competing demands of self-interested individuals to ensure that everyone ends up better off than they otherwise would have been, promoting the collective common good as a consequence.

Of course, the social contract is not an actual, written contract kept in a vault somewhere; it is hypothetical, a metaphor. There are many variations of the social contract theory, but most theorists start with a thought experiment, asking what life would be like in an *original state of nature* (before the existence of any social or political or civil order or institutions). They then ask what social and political arrangements people in this state would voluntarily agree to. Everyone gives something, by sacrificing an element

---

[62] Refer to the speech given by the character Harry Lime (played by Orson Wells) in the 1949 film *The Third Man*:

> "You know what the fellow said – in Italy, for 30 years under the Borgias, they had warfare, terror, murder and bloodshed, but they produced Michelangelo, Leonardo da Vinci and the Renaissance. In Switzerland, they had brotherly love, they had five hundred years of democracy and peace – and what did that produce? The cuckoo clock."

of their immediate short-term interest, but everyone ends up better off over the long term. Morality is the set of rights, duties and obligations that arise from the implied social contract: what people in a social context require from each other, what they should expect from each other and what is accepted as just and fair in order to live harmoniously and beneficially together.

Following in this tradition, the American philosopher John Rawls (1921–2002) proposed a set of principles grounded in justice that people would voluntarily accept and agree to as the basis for a social contract, and that would provide a foundation for the regulation of a just society.[63] To direct his theory, Rawls draws on the Kantian principle of respect for persons as ends in themselves and on the related principle of the equality of autonomous, rational moral agents. Every individual has absolute inviolable rights grounded in justice. According to Rawls:

> "Justice is the first virtue of social institutions, as truth is of systems of thought. A theory however elegant and economical must be rejected or revised if it is untrue; likewise laws and institutions no matter how efficient and well-arranged must be reformed or abolished if they are unjust. Each person possesses an inviolability founded on justice that even the welfare of society as a whole cannot override.[64]

For Rawls, justice is about fairness in terms of assigned social rights and responsibilities, and in terms of the distribution of social goods (including income, wealth, power, opportunity, privilege, liberties, respect and status). People would only voluntarily agree to a social contract that they considered was fair in these regards. However, one's view on what is fair is subject to personal bias and prejudice, depending on who you are and on your social situation and status. To avoid such prejudice and bias, Rawls proposes a thought experiment, providing for the negotiation of the social contract from *an original position of equality*.

Rawls argues that the way to think about justice as fairness is to ask: what *principles* would people agree to in an 'original position of equality'? He asks: what principles would be acceptable to everyone as the basis of a hypothetical social contract, and as such, should govern the ordering of our collective social and economic life? Rawls assumes that people are rational, self-interested actors, essentially uninterested in one another's well-being. Each person is out to get the best result for themselves. To achieve the original position of equality in this context, Rawls proposes the idea of each individual party to the social contract (the contractors) choosing from behind a *veil of ignorance*,

---

[63] Rawls, J., *A Theory of Justice* (The Belknap Press of Harvard University Press, 1971).

[64] *Ibid.*

a hypothetical viewpoint from which each person (each contractor) knows nothing of themselves (gender, nationality, race, ethnic group, etc.) or their social position. What would you want, and what would you decide to do, if you did not know who you were? Rawls proposes that the principles self-interested, rational people would choose from behind such a veil of ignorance will be fair and just; it will ensure each person acts from an impartial view-point, rather than on the basis of who they are, what they own, their personal tastes, etc. Asking people in these circumstances to decide what is best for themselves has the same consequence as asking them to decide what is best for everyone in society. The contractors will adopt an impartial, empathic and altruistic perspective, albeit one grounded in self-interest.

Choosing from behind a veil of ignorance ensures an original position of equality that is fair. Contractors will choose principles for a just society under these conditions, agreeing voluntarily to a contract that is beneficial to all. Acceptance and enforcement of the contract does not involve coercion or deception. It is based on equality of position and knowledge on the part of all of the contractors, ensuring the contract is fair and just.

Rawls suggests *two principles of justice* that all rational, self-interested people should be willing to agree to voluntarily from behind the veil of ignorance, because everybody in society will benefit from adherence to them. These principles will be the foundation of the hypothetical social contract.

The first is the *liberty* principle. Each person in society should have as much basic liberty as possible, as long as everyone is granted the same liberties. At a minimum, Rawls proposes that everyone has the right to a range of basic freedoms including freedom of belief, freedom of speech, freedom from threat to personal safety, security of property and the satisfaction of basic needs. These basic freedoms are always protected and they take priority over any considerations of social utility. They cannot be restricted to benefit the general welfare of the majority. As Michael Sandel explains, we "would not sacrifice our fundamental rights and liberties for social and economic benefits".[65]

The second principle of justice is the *difference* principle. Social and economic differences or inequalities are acceptable, but only on two conditions that render them fair and just:

1. they must be available to everyone equally – there should be equality of opportunity and access; and
2. they must work to the advantage of everyone. (For example, inequality in income is acceptable if it harnesses and incentivises the talented individual to work in the service of all and for the common good.)[66]

---

[65] Sandel, M., *op. cit.* above, n. 35, p. 151.
[66] Consider whether this is as an adequate justification for economic inequality, pay differentials and bankers' bonuses.

Paul Smith summarises Rawls' position as follows:

"Rawls proposes two principles of justice: first, reasonable people with conflicting interests and values could nevertheless agree on the principle that each citizen ought to have equal basic rights and liberties; second, inequalities of income and wealth can be acceptable as just to all reasonable citizens if there is genuine equality of opportunity and if the social system makes the worst-off group as well off as possible. A society founded in these principles would be one without oppression or exploitation."[67]

2.4.4.1 Rawls' Ethics of Justice: Arguments For and Against

Rawls creates a foundation for a social contract that is just and fair, and that respects people equally. The two principles of justice are the starting point. He provides a powerful vision of social equality, but one that recognises the importance of individual freedom and difference; one that does not require the equal distribution of income and of wealth. It is a view grounded in equality of opportunity rather than equality of outcome, providing that the inequality of outcome is good for society. He suggests a theory of distributive justice in which inequality is not arbitrary, but is so arranged that it works for the good of the less fortunate and the overall common good.

However, there are questions about the practicality of Rawls' thought experiment. Deciding from Rawls' original position of equality (from behind a 'veil of ignorance' about one's self) requires an act of imagination that may be beyond the capacities of most people. It is unrealistic to suggest that we can ever hope to escape from the knowledge of who we are, even if we consciously try to do so. We are subject to deep-seated, unconscious and inescapable prejudices and biases that inevitably distort our thinking and perspectives. Rawls' theory, it is argued, and the fundamental principles he suggests contractors would choose, reflects his own prejudice and bias as a privileged member of an already rich and liberal democratic society.

Furthermore, even if we could achieve the original position of equality, people might not choose the two principles Rawls envisages as the basis for a social contract. Some people might gamble that they will belong to an elite group and accordingly advocate for a set of less egalitarian principles. Some might not agree to the liberty principle, favouring restrictions on the fundamental rights and liberties of individuals in the interests of promoting social order and faster economic development. Others might advocate for a strict egalitarianism, rejecting the difference principle on the basis that it allows for inequalities in social and economic outcome which

---

[67] Smith, P., *op. cit.* above, n. 49, p. 186.

they consider to be inherently unjust under any circumstance. Still others might advocate for a libertarian position, rejecting the difference principle on the grounds that social and economic inequality is inherently just as a reflection of the natural order; those naturally endowed with special talents, they argue, are deserving of all the economic rewards they can command (particularly as they have to work hard, make personal sacrifices and take risks to hone their talents in order to realise these rewards).

Rawls' hypothetical contract provides a basic structural framework for the long-term development of a just society, but it may prove difficult and contentious in its application as a guide to the formulation of generally acceptable economic and social policies and practices. It does not provide ready answers for many contentious contemporary moral issues, including, for example: is positive discrimination in politics and in the workplace, on the grounds of gender, race or disability, just?; is it just to tax corporate profits at a relatively low rate on the basis that this promotes economic development to the greater benefit of society?; is reducing the tax rate on high income earners (and thereby increasing relative inequality) justifiable on the basis that doing so promotes the expansion of the economy (of the overall 'economic pie'), leaving everyone better off in absolute terms?; is the level of senior corporate executive pay and perquisites, both in absolute and relative terms, just?

2.5 Approaches to Resolving Moral Problems

The moral problems that are most challenging, controversial and intractable do not generally involve issues of 'good versus bad' or 'right versus wrong'; rather, they involve issues of 'good versus other good' or 'right versus other right'; issues of competing moral obligation and of perspective on what is good and what is right, and why this is the case. The difficulty in reaching a resolution is that the competing arguments are being made from different conceptions of the 'good' and the 'right', from different theoretical perspectives and from different ethical first principles. Essentially, the competing arguments are based on different fundamental premises.

As discussed in **Sections 2.3.5** and **2.4**, normative ethical theories provide us with ways of looking, ways of seeing and ways of thinking that should help us reach justifiable resolutions to moral problems (even if they do not always lead to a consensus view). They provide us with frameworks for the interrogation of conscience through critical thinking, analysis and evaluation, providing a framework of criteria for testing the validity of moral perspectives and prescriptions, and for guiding their practical application in real situations. Such ethical theories should not be seen as 'either/or' alternatives, but rather as complementary and enriching (as 'both/and') approaches to moral reasoning. No single theory seems sufficiently comprehensive to embody all factors of importance to the resolution of problems; each, however, can provide unique insights that are important in the analysis and evaluation process.

The potential role and importance of normative ethical theory in moral reasoning is illustrated in **Figure 2.1** below.

FIGURE 2.1: THE ETHICAL REASONING PROCESS[68]

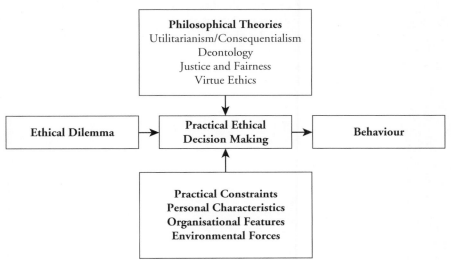

Difficulties in resolving moral problems may also arise because of knowledge gaps, disagreement about factual issues, and disagreements about the meaning of concepts and about whether the concept is appropriately applicable in the particular context (for example, consider the difference of meaning of 'bribery', 'facilitation payments' and 'dig outs', particularly if 'no favours were asked or apparently given'). Moral problems are generally complex, multi-faceted, ambiguous and unstructured. We approach them with incomplete and unreliable knowledge and understanding, and a great deal of uncertainty. They may also be difficult to resolve because of the 'bounded rationality' and personal circumstances of the moral agent.

Approaching resolution in a structured systematic manner and addressing each of the potential sources of disagreement is more likely to bring a morally justifiable and generally acceptable resolution. Implementing the steps in **Table 2.1** (as a minimum) may prove helpful in this regard:

[68] Brooks, L. and Dunn, P., *Business & Professional Ethics for Directors, Executives & Accountants* (7th Edition, Cengage Learning, 2015) Figure 3.1, p. 129.

TABLE 2.1: STEPS IN RESOLVING MORAL PROBLEMS

1. State the facts of the situation, identifying any knowledge gaps.
2. Identify and tease out the meaning of the behaviour.
3. Identify the range of possible options for resolution.
4. Test for welfare: predict and evaluate the consequences of each proposed option for everyone affected in terms of desirable end-values (e.g. in terms of happiness).
5. Test for justice and fairness of outcome: is anyone harmed?
6. Test for duty: identify the principle of action underlying each proposed option and test it as a 'categorical imperative'.
7. Test for virtue: for each of the options, ask whether it is what a virtuous person would do.
8. Test for conscience: what option can you best live with?

Chapter 3

Business Ethics

Hugh McBride

3.1 Introduction

Business ethics[1] is an area of applied ethics involving critical enquiry into the moral dimensions of business activities and behaviour. It is concerned with inquiring into *whether* and *why* the end purposes of business activities, and the means of behaviour deployed in pursuit of those ends, should be judged to be ethically good or bad, right or wrong. Business ethics is "the study of practices and policies in business, to determine which are ethically defensible and which are not".[2]

Business ethics has both descriptive and normative aspects (see **Chapter 2**). It involves inquiry into the values, attitudes, principles and norms that are evident and prevalent in contemporary business practice. It is an enquiry into *'what is'*. More importantly, however, it is also an inquiry into *'what ought to be'*, into the values, attitudes, principles and norms that should underpin and govern business behaviour, including questioning whether actual business practices are morally justifiable and legitimate when tested against normative standards.

Normative ethical theories (see **Chapter 2**, **Section 2.3.5**) provide conceptual frames of reference and criteria for determining what behaviour in business ought to be, and for assessing the moral adequacy of the manner in which business is actually conducted.[3]

---

[1] There are many fine texts on the subject of business ethics, for example: Frederick, R.E. (Ed.), *A Companion to Business Ethics* (Blackwell Publishers, 1999); DesJardins, J.R and McCall J.J., *Contemporary Issues in Business Ethics* (6th Edition, Cengage Learning, 2014); Shaw, W.H. and Barry, V., *Moral Issues in Business* (12th Edition, Cengage Learning, 2013).

[2] Jackson, J., *An Introduction to Business Ethics* (Blackwell Publishers, 1996) p. 1.

[3] For a view on the relevance of ethical theory to management practice, see, for example, Collins J.W., "Is Business Ethics an Oxymoron?" (1994) *Business Horizons*, Vol. 37 No. 5, 1–8.

Consequentialist theories such as utilitarianism focus attention on business purposes, on the impact that business activities and behaviour have on the well-being of society, and on the contribution of business towards enhancing the common good. They raise fundamental questions about the values that underpin business activities, about who and what business should be for, and about the nature of its social responsibility.

Deontological theories focus attention on the duties and obligations of people and organisations, acting individually and collectively, in their conduct of business. They raise fundamental questions about the manner in which business should be conducted to engender trust among all stakeholders, applying the imperatives of universalisability, of respect for persons and of justice.

Virtue ethics focuses attention on the character and behaviour patterns of people working in business, and on the culture and ethical climate that this reflects and cultivates. It raises questions about the character traits and habits that should be considered virtuous in business to exemplify professional excellence, and the manner in which such traits and habits can be nurtured and encouraged.

Meta-ethical theories provide frames of reference for analysing and evaluating perspectives on business activities and behaviour that are grounded in moral relativism or moral pluralism.

Moral psychology provides frames of reference for understanding and interpreting the behaviour of moral agents acting in a business context, the manner in which they respond to moral challenges, and how they approach the resolution of moral dilemmas.

3.1.1 The Purpose and Value of Business Ethics

Business ethics provides *ways of looking, ways of seeing* and *ways of thinking* as a basis for enhanced moral reasoning, judgement and action in a business context. It is not about formulating and promulgating a particular set of prescriptive rules for purported proper behaviour in business; nor does it involve moralising or proselytising for a particular notion of what is good and right conduct. Rather, it is about the application of concepts drawn from moral philosophy as a basis for analysing, understanding and critically appraising the moral dimensions and implications of business activities and behaviour. Its value as a field of study is primarily in:

- stimulating awareness and sensitising us to moral issues in business;
- elucidating the responsibilities, duties and obligations of business people and organisations from a moral perspective;

- enhancing our capacity to analyse and evaluate contentious moral issues in business and present the moral case for and against proposed actions;
- enabling us to make better-informed choices;
- helping us to resolve dilemmas of conduct in business that raise moral concerns.

Despite the value it can bring, however, business ethics as a subject remains somewhat peripheral in mainstream business education programmes, not generally enjoying the recognition, platform and prominence it deserves. For many people both inside and outside of business, ethics and business are considered inimical, and the concept of *business ethics* is considered to be an oxymoron.[4] They do not consider that ethics has any relevance to business practice, other than as an element of public relations 'spin'; mere soothing rhetoric deployed to soften and enhance image and reputation, and to whitewash over the reality of necessary, albeit exploitative and opportunistic, practices. At best, 'ethics' is considered to be a costly and unnecessary decorative frill.

This view of business ethics implies a judgement about the reality of business behaviour and a perception of the nature of its underlying morality. Human behaviour is always and inescapably a manifestation of some moral perspective, of some particular set of values and principles that underpin judgement and choice of action. Care needs be taken, however, not to confuse 'what conduct ought to be' with 'what conduct is'; to confuse business ethics with a perception of a particular kind of morality evident in some contemporary business conduct. For example, any suggestion that current business practices are morally dubious is, in itself, an ethical evaluation of 'what is'. But it does not necessarily imply that business must or should be conducted in this manner: that 'business ethics' is an oxymoron. Furthermore, it seems unlikely that most people consider business to be an inherently immoral form of human activity. Why would people consider business to be a legitimate and justifiable activity, or why would people choose to work in business, if it was inevitably and unavoidably immoral?

There is nothing new or recent about interest in business ethics. It has a long history. The Roman jurist, statesman and writer Cicero (106–43 BC), for example, was interested in what should be considered a fair price for grain during a famine (see below). The same concerns about *just pricing* are evident in the controversy over the pricing of anti-retroviral drugs for AIDS sufferers in developing countries in the early 2000s, and more generally, in the on-going debate about the pricing of pharmaceutical products protected

---

[4] See, for example, Crane, A. and Matten D., *Business Ethics: A European Perspective* (Oxford University Press, 2004) pp. 7–14; Chryssides, G.D. and Kaler, J.H., *An Introduction to Business Ethics* (Cengage Learning, 1993) pp. 2–35.

by intellectual property rights. Michael Sandel in his book, *Justice: What's the Right Thing to Do?*,[5] discusses allegations of price gouging in selling water in Florida following a hurricane in 2004, rehearsing the same arguments about just pricing that Cicero had outlined over 2,000 years earlier.

Marcus Tullius Cicero (106–43 BC), the Roman jurist, statesman and writer posed the following dilemmas as test cases for teasing out moral issues in business in 44 BC.[6]

Suppose there is a food shortage and famine in Rhodes and the price of corn is extremely high. An honest man has brought the people of Rhodes a large stock of corn from Alexandria. He is aware that a number of other traders are on their way from Alexandria – he has seen their ships making for Rhodes, with substantial cargoes of grain. Should he tell the Rhodians this? Or should he say nothing and sell his stock at the best price he can get?

Or suppose that an honest man wants to sell a house because of certain defects of which he alone is aware. For example, the building may appear to be quite healthy, but is in fact insanitary; or it is badly built and in danger of falling apart but this is not apparent. Suppose the owner does not disclose these facts to the purchasers, and sells the house for much more than he expected. Has he behaved ethically?

Is there any unfairness and dishonesty involved in a seller not fully revealing the facts as he knows them to the potential buyers? Is the seller obliged to fully inform the potential buyer? Is 'not revealing' the same as 'concealing'?

3.1.2 The Relevance of Business Ethics

Concern for ethics is inescapable and is applicable to all human activities. Business does not exist in a vacuum. It derives its legitimacy and moral justification from its social context. The expectations and demands of society define the ethical environment for business and the terms of the implied *social contract* which it is obliged to observe (see **Chapter 2**). Business must serve human welfare in its purposes and activities, acting in accordance with prevailing values and moral principles. Business decision-making is inseparable from, and systemically connected with, ethical considerations.

---

[5] Sandel, M., *Justice: What's the Right Thing to Do?* (Allen Lane, 2009) pp. 3–5.
[6] Cicero, *De Officiis* (On Duties), Book III, from *Selected Works*, translated by Michael Grant, (Penguin Books, 1960).

Business ethics is critically important in view of the central role of business activity in promoting and fostering human welfare, and its potential impact on the lives of individuals as well as on overall social development. Yet, while business is expected to be a force for social good, it also has the capacity to cause significant harm to people and to the planet. Inquiry into business ethics is necessary to help business to 'get it right morally' so that it can understand and fulfil its responsibilities and obligations to society. The need for attention to ethical considerations in business activity is particularly important given the growth in size, scope and power of global corporate organisations and their significant influence in shaping the modern world.

Success in business over the long term is not possible without trust and honest dealing. There are sound reasons based in prudence and economic self-interest for business to act ethically. Far from getting in the way, ethical behaviour enhances long-term profit-making in an environment of business stakeholder interdependence.[7] A business can strengthen its competitive position and enhance shareholder value by maintaining high ethical standards.

> "Many students ask, "Is ethics really relevant?" ... First, although business errors can be forgiven, ethical errors tend to end careers and terminate future opportunities. Why? Because, unethical behaviour eliminates trust, and without trust, business cannot interact. Second, the most damaging event a business can experience is a loss of the public's confidence in its ethical standards."[8]

Interest in business ethics has been growing in recent years and decades for a number of reasons, including:

- changing expectations and increasing moral sensitivity in wealthier societies;
- a realisation that there are environmental limits to economic growth;
- concern about an evolving global political-economic order, dominated by powerful and largely democratically unaccountable global corporations;
- an increasingly active role by an intrusive media (including social media) rendering business practices and corporate behaviour more visible and exposed, with corresponding demands for improved transparency and public accountability;
- a seemingly never-ending litany of business scandals involving unethical conduct causing significant harm;

[7] Collins, J.W., *op. cit.* above, n. 3.
[8] Keown, A., Martin, J., Petty, J. and Scott, D., *Foundations of Finance* (4th Edition, Prentice Hall, 2003) p. 22.

- the rapid development of new technologies (e.g. artificial intelligence) giving rise to new ethical challenges in their application;
- the recognition of *management* as a distinct professional occupation, characterised by mastery of a body of expert knowledge and a commitment to ethical behaviour;
- the looming threat to business and corporations of ever increasing regulation unless they act voluntarily to improve their behaviour.

Today, most business is conducted by corporate entities, such as private companies limited by shares (Ltds) or public limited companies (Plcs). For convenience, we shall assume this to be the case (unless otherwise stated). We shall treat 'business activity' as synonymous with 'corporate activity', and will use the terms 'business ethics' and 'corporate ethics' interchangeably. The term 'business' is also widely used in everyday discourse to include the activities of non-commercial, not-for-profit entities operating in the voluntary, community and public sectors. Aspects of business ethics also apply to the activities and behaviour of these types of organisation.

There are three levels at which it is necessary to consider business ethics.[9] First, it is necessary to consider the ethics of the **free-market system** that provides the context for corporate activity. Secondly, it is necessary to consider the ethics of **corporate behaviour** within a market context. Thirdly, it is necessary to consider ethics as it relates to the **behaviour of individuals** acting within a corporate context. It is with this three-level approach to business ethics that we have structured our discussion in the rest of this chapter.

3.2 The Ethics of the Free-market System

"… free markets are the best way to make the world richer, healthier and happier over the long term".[10]

Markets have been part of human society since earliest times, an essential economic and social institution. A market is a forum (a *place,* or nowadays, a *space*) for exchange through trade, for buying and selling goods

---

[9] This accords with the three levels suggested by Robert Solomon: the macro, the molar and the micro level. See Solomon R.C., "Business Ethics" in Singer P. (Ed.), *A Companion to Ethics* (Blackwell Publishing, 1993) pp. 354–365.

[10] Somerset Webb, M., "Required Reading for Socialists this Christmas", Investing, *Financial Times*, 16 December 2017.

and services.[11] This is the central characteristic and function of all markets, whether the colourful street markets that we visit on our holidays to experience authentic local produce and culture, or the global financial markets of barely imaginable scale and scope that exist in the virtual reality of cyberspace and that play such an influential role in the political economy that contextualises our lives.

The free-market economy has long been one of the defining features of the 'Western capitalist free world' and today we seem to be living ever more in thrall to 'the market'. The extent of contemporary near blind faith in the virtues of the unfettered market is such, however, that it has become, almost by default, the presumed regulator not only of economic life but also of political, cultural and social life more generally.[12] The prevalence of market ideology, market thinking, market values and the language of the market in all spheres of social activity is such that we seem to be living not only in a free-market *economy* but in a free-market *society*.

> "The great missing debate in contemporary politics is about the role and reach of markets. Do we want a market economy or a market society?"[13]

It is pertinent then to consider *why* the free market has become such an important and influential institution in contemporary life. What is the basis for its legitimacy? It is also pertinent to consider whether free-market capitalism is a moral system, ethically justifiable and defensible. The market to a great extent defines the context for the conduct of business, creating the conditions for survival and success. Any inquiry into business ethics requires an understanding of the market context. What behaviour should be expected, and considered morally justifiable, by business and its agents acting within free markets?

3.2.1 Adam Smith: Social Prosperity from Self-interest

The theoretical and moral justification for markets was first provided by Adam Smith (1723–1790), a Scottish philosopher, appointed to the Chair of Moral Philosophy at the University of Glasgow in 1752. His first major work was *The Theory of Moral Sentiments* (1759) but he is mainly remembered and celebrated for his seminal work on political economy, *An Inquiry into the Nature and Causes of the Wealth of Nations* (1776). The ideas therein, grounded in shrewd observation and empirical evidence, have helped to

---

[11] For a history of the impact of trade and global commerce, see Bernstein, W., *A Splendid Exchange: How Trade Shaped the World* (Atlantic Books, 2009).

[12] See, for example, Judt, T., *Ill Fares the Land: A Treatise on our Present Discontents* (Allen Lane, 2010).

[13] Sandel, M., *What Money Can't Buy: The Moral Limits of Markets* (Penguin Books, 2013) p. 11.

define and shape the modern world and continue to resonate strongly and inform contemporary thinking and public policy.[14] Smith sought to uncover *causal laws* that explain how nations increase their wealth. He attempted to explain how and why markets increase the wealth of nations and work for the overall benefit of society.

Adam Smith identified two key interdependent elements as the engines of economic growth and the underlying source of wealth generation: the division of labour (specialisation) and the possibility of trading for mutual benefit. By dividing up and specialising tasks, labour productivity and output can be greatly increased, which generates surpluses that are available for exchange, enabling people to trade and to supply one another with the products and services that they need and want. The alternative to trade is self-sufficiency: without trade, people would have to meet all their needs themselves. Trade enables people to specialise, harnessing the diversity of human capacities, preferences and talents to more individually efficient and collectively productive use. This establishes a potentially virtuous circle of specialisation, productivity, surplus and trade, leading to specialisation.

> "Trade encourages specialisation, which brings prosperity".[15]

The virtuous circle is driven by the prospect of mutual benefit and a gain for each party to the trade. According to Smith, people have a natural propensity to "truck, barter, and exchange one thing for another". They also have a natural propensity to seek to improve their lot. As such, people are naturally inclined to trade and are prepared to specialise because each perceives a benefit for themselves in so doing. Everyone potentially ends up better off and the overall prosperity and well-being of society is increased as a consequence. It is in this manner that the market harnesses human nature and the diversity of human talents to promoting voluntary cooperation among people in providing each other with the things they need and desire for living well, to the overall long-term benefit of society.

People, according to Smith, are naturally inclined to seek their own advantage. An exchange that appeals to someone's self-interest is a much stronger

---

[14] In evaluating Adam Smith, and his contemporary relevance, it is important to keep in mind the times in which he lived. He was writing during what is now known as the period of the Enlightenment and at the start of the Industrial Revolution. This was a time of great change in modes of production and commerce, fuelled by technological and organisational innovation. For example: the emergence of the factory system; growth in banking, in international trade and imperialism; innovations in transport, navigation and in time-telling; population growth, drift from the land and urbanisation. It was also a time of great political change, manifest most notably in the American Declaration of Independence (1776), which laid the basis for modern liberal democracy.

[15] *The Economist,* Leader Article, 7 February 2009.

motivating force for promoting voluntary cooperation with others than is reliance on any inclinations of benevolence. This is the appeal of exchange through trade. In Smith's words:

> "Give me what I want, and you shall have this which you want, is the meaning of every such offer; and it is in this manner that we obtain from one another the far greater part of those good offices which we stand in need of. It is not from the benevolence of the butcher, the brewer, or the baker, that we expect our dinner, but from their regard to their own interest. We address ourselves, not to their humanity but to their self-love, and never talk to them of our own necessities but of their advantages."[16]

Smith is not suggesting that people are motivated *only* by self-interest (by *self-love*), as is clear from the opening sentence in *The Theory of Moral Sentiment*:

> "How selfish soever man may be supposed, there are evidently some principles in his nature, which interest him in the fortune of others, and render their happiness necessary to him, though he derives nothing from it except the pleasure of seeing it."[17]

Rather, he suggests that self-interest can motivate more powerfully and more consistently than altruistic inclinations of kindness, sympathy or self-sacrifice. The self-interest motive is a natural resource that should and can be harnessed and applied to promote the prosperity and welfare of society.[18]

Trade, driven by the '*trucking disposition*' and the self-interest of each participant, promotes and rewards specialisation, hard work and human ingenuity to the extent that it is applied in the service of others. Everyone has potentially something to offer and there is a potential role for the diverse talents of all.

> "Among men ... the most dissimilar geniuses are of use to one another; the different produces of their respective talents, by the general disposition to truck, barter, and exchange, being brought, as it were, into a common stock, where every man may purchase whatever part of the produce of other men's talents he has occasion for."[19]

---

[16] Smith, A., *An Inquiry into the Nature and Causes of the Wealth of Nations* (1776; Wordsworth Editions Ltd, 2012), Book I, Chapter 2, p. 19.

[17] Smith, A., *The Theory of Moral Sentiments* (1759; Penguin Books, 2009) p. 1.

[18] Buchholz T., *New Ideas from Dead Economists* (Penguin Books, 1999) p. 21.

[19] Smith, A. *An Inquiry into the Nature and Causes of the Wealth of Nations*, *op. cit.* above, n. 16, Book I, Chapter 2, p. 21.

For Smith, the market facilitates and enables people to develop their particular talents, motivated by self-interest, by applying them to the service of others. The market potentially works for everyone's benefit: the common man as well as the merchant and prince will prosper, giving rise to "that universal opulence which extends itself to the lowest ranks of the people".[20]

The wealth of a society will grow with the development and expansion of trade and markets. Without the possibility of trade, there will be limited motivation or opportunity for specialisation, and the potential benefits it can confer on individuals and society will not be realised. Smith identified this as the reason why industrial development first happened along the coast or on the banks of navigable rivers, highlighting the importance and impact of innovation in transport to economic growth. Africa's economic under-development, he explained, was due to the lack of maritime inlets and navigable rivers which created barriers to trade.[21]

3.2.2 The Invisible Hand

The question remains, however, as to how trading is regulated to ensure it serves the best interests of society. How, for example, is it decided which products get made? How is it decided what resources should be allocated to what activities? How does it happen that the 'right' products are produced in the 'right' amount and are available to the people who need and want them at the 'right' places and at the 'right' time? The problem is illustrated by a story (perhaps apocryphal) about a new ambassador from the communist USSR arriving in London in the early 1960s and asking the British Foreign Secretary "who organises the bread for London?" "No-one does and no one needs to; the invisible hand of the free market takes care of it", he was answered.

The *invisible hand* is Adam Smith's metaphor for the manner in which the market spontaneously and autonomously orchestrates, regulates and transmutes voluntary conduct motivated by individual self-interest into the long-term collective best interests of society. Individuals will continually try to find activities and trading opportunities that will be to their own economic advantage. This necessarily requires that they consider what other people desire and value. In seeking to intentionally serve their own self-interest by trading in free, fair and competitive markets, they will necessarily and

---

[20] Smith, A., *An Inquiry into the Nature and Causes of the Wealth of Nations*, *op. cit.* above, n. 16, Book I, Chapter 1, p. 15.

[21] *Ibid.*, Book I, Chapter 3. Smith's views on Africa continue to have relevance. They are echoed by Jeffrey Sachs, who explains Africa's failure to develop economically as partly a function of geography, which creates barriers to trade: Sachs, J.D., *The End of Poverty* (Penguin Books, 2005).

paradoxically be directed to serve the overall best interests of society even though this is unintentional.

> "[The individual] neither intends to promote the public interest, nor knows how much he is promoting it ... he intends only his own gain, and he is in this, as in many other cases, led by an invisible hand to promote an end which was no part of his intention. Nor is it always the worse for the society that it was no part of it. By pursuing his own interest he frequently promotes that of the society more effectually than when he really intends to promote it. I have never known much good done by those who affected to trade for the public good. It is an affectation, indeed, not very common among merchants, and very few words need to be employed in dissuading them from it."[22]

The *invisible hand* is a manifestation of the competitive activities of market participants driven by self-interest to serve the preferences and judgements of society. The combined forces of individual freedom, self-interest, human ingenuity, enterprise and hard work, channelled through open and fair competition in markets, ensure that societal resources are allocated to their most efficacious use and in accordance with people's freely enacted choices. By ensuring the efficient provision of the goods and services that people desire and freely choose, the market inherently promotes human welfare and serves the common good. Society's resources will be allocated in accordance with what people individually and collectively value. Each individual's effort in supplying the market is rewarded in a fair and just manner, in accordance with how it is applied to serve others and in accordance with how others value it.[23] Prices play a critical role in regulating the demand and supply of products and services, and it is the buyer in the market who ultimately reigns supreme. Smith's key insight, according to the economist Milton Friedman, is misleadingly simple:

> "Adam Smith's flash of genius was his recognition that the prices that emerged from voluntary transactions between buyers and sellers – for short, in a free market – could coordinate the activity of millions of people, each seeking his own interest, in such a way as to make everyone better off. It was a startling idea then, and it remains one today, that economic order can emerge as the unintended consequence of the actions of many people, each seeking his own interest."[24]

---

[22] Smith, A. *An Inquiry into the Nature and Causes of the Wealth of Nations, op. cit.* above, n. 16, Book IV, Chapter 2, p. 445.

[23] Wolf, M., *Why Globalisation Works* (Yale Nota Bene, 2004).

[24] Friedman, M., *Free to Choose* (Pelican Books, 1980) p. 32.

3.2.3 The Role of the State

Market self-regulation by the invisible hand is insufficient, however, as the sole basis for promoting and ensuring the prosperity and well-being of society. The state also has a key role to play. First, there are certain essential activities that, either through necessity or preference, are best carried out by the state and financed through taxation. Adam Smith, for example, identified defence of the realm, essential public institutions and infrastructure, education, the administration of justice (of the rule of law) and the protection of citizens' rights (including property rights) as falling within this category. Secondly, the state has a critically important role in regulating markets to ensure that, in an imperfect world, the conditions necessary for a vibrant and orderly free market (including, for example, the protection of property rights and certainty of contract) are in place and are enforced.[25] The free market should not mean a 'free-for-all' market; in particular, the market should not be subject to exploitation or manipulation by powerful vested interests. Adam Smith's warning is memorable in this regard: "People of the same trade seldom meet together, even for merriment and diversion, but the conversation ends in a conspiracy against the public, or in some contrivance to raise prices".[26]

The state has a key role to play in protecting the integrity of markets, ensuring the invisible hand is enabled to work its magic in the public interest. Paradoxically, free-market self-regulation by the invisible hand works best within a supporting and enabling framework of state regulation legal certainty. However, striking the appropriate regulatory balance between the invisible hand of the market and the guiding hand of the state remains a contentious issue.

In the 30-year period 1945–1975, political-economy and public policy formulation was dominated by social democratic thinking, characterised by an actively interventionist state and highly regulated markets, guided by the thinking of J.M. Keynes. In the 1970s, there was a revival of what might well be described as free-market fundamentalism, characterised by a belief in *laissez-faire* economics and the power of lightly regulated free markets to create a better world. Following the collapse of communism in 1989, this kind of *neo liberal* thinking, in tandem with the globalisation of markets, became the prevailing ideology of the times. Since then, 'free up markets to work their magic, sans frontiers' has been the basic tenet and

---

[25] The characteristics of a perfect free market include: openness and competitiveness; fairness; fully informed buyers and sellers; protection for direct participants and for third parties; credible and trustworthy participants (requiring ethical behaviour on their part). However, these conditions are rarely met in practice, whether in products/services markets, labour markets or financial markets.

[26] Smith A. *An Inquiry into the Nature and Causes of the Wealth of Nations, op. cit.* above, n. 16, Book I, Chapter 10, p. 134.

conventional wisdom of political-economy. It has given rise to what has been described as *turbo-charged super-capitalism*.[27] It is an orthodoxy that is now subject to vigorous challenge, including by nationalist populism that seeks to restrict trade and market globalisation, for example through imposing tariffs and protectionism.

3.2.4 The Moral Case for and against Free-market Capitalism

Free-market capitalism is considered by advocates to be an inherently moral political-economic system. The invisible hand of self-regulating competitive markets, supplemented by state regulation, necessitates profit-seeking and legitimises it as socially responsible and ethical behaviour. A business can only be profitable over the long term by bringing products and services to the market that people choose to buy, and by doing so at least as, if not more, efficiently than its competitors. Profit is a manifestation of the extent to which a business has served the interests of others; it is a reward for the value-added its products or services provide. The 'creative destruction' of competitive markets ensures that only the good and the best will survive and thrive. The market system driven by self-interest is paradoxically a moral system, serving society's best long-term interests, although this is not actually intended by the individual market actors. Profit maximisation in the context of free markets provides *a normative ethical framework* for business activity.[28]

This does not mean, however, that all profit-making behaviour is necessarily legitimate and ethically justifiable. In their pursuit of profits, businesses may engage in dishonest behaviour, in deception, manipulation, exploitation, with a disregard for any collateral harm caused to others or to the natural environment. The invisible hand, supported by state regulation, will ensure such behaviour is not rewarded. While it may be possible for a business to make profits in the short term by 'getting away with' behaviour that does not accord with the expectations and moral norms of society, because of imperfections in the market that slow its in-built self-regulatory corrective mechanism, this will not be possible or permissible over the longer term. Ethical behaviour is expected by participants in the market in their pursuit of profits. The achievement of the end purpose of profit does not necessarily justify the means deployed.

---

[27] See, for example: Reich, R., *Supercapitalism: The Battle for Democracy in an Age of Big Business* (Icon Books, 2008); Bogle, J.C., *The Battle for the Soul of Capitalism* (Yale University Press, 2005).

[28] For an extreme view on this perspective, refer to the writings of Ayn Rand.

The moral case for markets[29] is based on both consequentialist and non-consequentialist grounds (see **Chapter 2**). The market promotes the overall wealth and welfare of society, it serves the common good, it respects the freedom and autonomy of individuals, it provides for equality of opportunity, and it is fair and just in the distribution of rewards. Advocates of the free market consider it a system of natural liberty, a form of economic liberalism aligned and in harmony with the political liberalism of modern democracy. It provides a basis for voluntary human cooperation grounded in individual freedom, ensuring that scarce resources are used effectively and efficiently, in accordance with the aggregate of individual choices. Proponents of the free market argue that it is has provided us with the world we enjoy, which, even if it is not perfect, is better than any alternative to date at promoting human well-being.

> "Capitalism is not perfect. No economic system ever can be, and the quest for utopia has produced rivers of blood and tears. But if we accept human imperfection, as we must, a free market economy is as good as it gets."[30]

The moral arguments for markets are persuasive, particularly in the context of the apparent high standard of living people in the rich part of the world seem to enjoy. Despite this, however, the moral claims made for markets are also strongly contested. The capitalist market system, it is argued, has inherent ethical shortcomings and in particular the neoliberal form of it that has been dominant for the last quarter century. The *invisible hand* of free markets is an unreliable and inadequate regulatory mechanism for promoting social and ecological well-being. It does little to prevent lasting harm being done to people and the planet by traders in the ruthless pursuit of profit, and provides an inadequate mechanism for correcting these harms once inflicted. The model of a natural and self-adjusting economy working providentially for the best good of all is, according to the English historian E.P. Thompson, a mere 'superstition'.[31]

The free market system seduces people into a Faustian bargain,[32] promising material abundance; it is material abundance, however, that comes at a potentially high cost to the human soul by unleashing some of the darkest elements of human nature and encouraging them to run riot. It is

---

[29] See, for example: Sandel, M., *op. cit.* above, n. 5, Chapter 4; Sandel, M., *op. cit.* above, n. 13.
[30] Robinson, F.S., "Capitalism and Human Values" (2011) *Philosophy Now*, Issue 83, 28–31.
[31] Thompson, E.P., *Customs in Common*, (Penguin Books, 1993) p. 203.
[32] Skidelsky, R. and Skidelsky, E., *How Much is Enough? Money and the Good Life* (Penguin Books, 2013) p. 43.

predicated on a narrow concept of human progress and development in which money is the only measure of value.

> "Capitalism is a two-edged sword. On the one hand, it has made possible vast improvements in material conditions. On the other, it has elevated some of the most reviled human characteristics, such as greed, envy and avarice."[33]

Capitalism, it is further argued, is an insatiable system that is ultimately senseless,[34] addressing shallow wants rather than deep-seated human needs, and is dependent for its perpetuation on individuals' dissatisfaction with their lot. It promotes egregious inequalities within and between nations, concentrating wealth in ever fewer hands. It treats social solidarity and compassion as hindrances to economic progress. The collective, public realm is not valued, giving rise to private affluence amid public squalor.[35] This is contrary to the demands of justice and fairness, resulting in social fragmentation and the shattering of human fraternity. Capitalism is an unjust and unstable system, increasingly representing not the triumph *of* the individual but a triumph *over* the individual.[36]

The free-market system ignores the true social and environmental costs of economic activity and of the harm caused to people and the planet in the pursuit of profit, giving rise to an economic system and a social order that is socially and ecologically destructive and unsustainable. It is an economy of 'unpaid costs'[37] in which the egregious harms caused to people and to the planet are not counted. Markets are ultimately a mechanism for promoting and channelling individual desire into long-term collective human and ecological disadvantage.

> "The perpetual quest for economic growth has turned humankind into an agent of extinction, through a systematic undervaluing of the ecosystemic services that keep our Earth alive."[38]

Contemporary markets, again, it can be argued, are dominated by powerful corporate providers that treat people and nature as instrumental objects to be manipulated and exploited as means to an end. Markets dominated by such corporations are neither free nor fair; they are neither economically efficient nor socially responsible. The market system has

---

[33] *Ibid.* p. 3.
[34] *Ibid.*
[35] Galbraith, J.K., *The Affluent Society* (Hamish Hamilton, 1958).
[36] Bowles, P., *Capitalism* (Pearson Education, 2007) p. 55.
[37] Kapp, K.W., *The Social Costs of Private Enterprise* (Harvard University Press, 1950) p. 231.
[38] Patel, R., *The Value of Nothing* (Portobello Books, 2009) p. 20.

not created a society that is happy, just, democratic, egalitarian and green; a society organised as if the long-term welfare of people and of the planet really mattered.[39]

In conclusion, the question remains whether it is possible to design and organise a free-market system that serves the best long-term interests of humanity and of nature. John Maynard Keynes suggested that:

> "The political problem of mankind is to combine three things: economic efficiency, social justice and individual liberty."[40]

It is arguable that contemporary corporate capitalism falls short on all three criteria. However, terrible and all as it may be, it is also arguable that it is better than any other system devised to date. The challenge is to reform corporate free-market capitalism by rebalancing excessive but unwarranted faith in the *invisible hand* with enhanced regulation by the state, by the active vigilance by civic society and by market actors behaving ethically.

3.3 The Corporation and the Ethics of Corporate Behaviour

The corporation is the dominant actor in contemporary free markets. Arguably, it is also the dominant institution of the modern world. It is certainly one of the most significant and influential economic and social institutional innovations in the last 200 years; the manifestation of an idea that actively shapes how we work, how we live, how we relate to each other, and how we relate to and impact on the natural environment.[41]

The success of the corporate form of organisation is due, in the first instance, to its nature and core characteristics. It is recognised in law as an artificial legal person, enjoying an independent existence and a potentially unlimited lifespan. It can merge with other similar entities, sub-divide in an amoeba-like fashion, morph and shape-shift and re-create itself, transforming its structure, purpose and function. Ownership of this entity is vested in transferable shares, and the owners of the shares (the *shareholders*) generally enjoy limited liability. Share ownership imposes no obligation to participate in the management of the entity; effective managerial control is separable from ownership.

---

[39] See, for example, Schumacher, E.F., *Small is Beautiful: A Study of Economics as if People Mattered* (1973; Vintage Books, 1993).

[40] Keynes, J.M., *Liberalism and Labour* (1926) in Johnson E. and Moggridge D. (Eds.), *The Collected Writings of John Maynard Keynes* (Royal Economic Society, 1978) pp. 307–312.

[41] For a history of the corporation, see Micklethwait, J. and Wooldridge, A., *The Company: A Short History of a Revolutionary Idea* (Weidenfeld & Nicolson, 2003).

The nature and characteristics of the corporate form has enabled the mobilisation of the financial capital needed for the development of industry, promoting innovation and entrepreneurship, and giving rise to material and technological progress that enriches society. Investors can participate, each according to their means, with limited risk of liability, and without the necessity of active involvement in running the organisation. Provision can be made for the control of the corporation by expert and professional management, with a clear remit to act in the best long-term interests of the company, which in a business context is considered synonymous with maximising profit-making for the shareholders over the long term.

By the 1930s, the professionally managed corporation had already become the most significant form of business organisation operating within national boundaries. Today, hugely powerful corporations operating on a global scale dominate markets worldwide, supplying most of the products and services used by people in their everyday lives.

> "Limited-liability, privately owned joint-stock companies are the core institutions of modern capitalism. These entities are largely responsible for organising the production and distribution of goods and services across the globe. Their role is both cause and consequence of the revolution in the scale and diversity of economic activity that has taken place over the past two centuries."[42]

Market capitalism has been transformed into a system of giant transnational corporations[43] enjoying a ubiquitous existence that is not limited by boundaries of geography, history, nationality or culture. The power to control most of these giant corporations is effectively in the hands of managerial corporate-bureaucrats rather than distant and dispersed shareholders. 'Ownership capitalism' has been transformed into 'corporate capitalism'.[44]

There are three inter-related areas of ethical concern about corporations *as* corporations:

- concerns about the nature of the corporate personality and moral agency;
- concerns about the social responsibility of corporations; and
- concerns about corporate governance.

[42] Wolf, M., "Thinking through how to run companies", *Irish Times*, 27 August 2014.
[43] Chang, Ha-Joon, *23 Things They Don't Tell you about Capitalism* (Penguin Books, 2011).
[44] J.K. Galbraith has suggested that the use of the bland and more apparently benign term 'the market system' rather than 'capitalism' or 'the corporate system', to name the modern economic system is an example of a "not wholly innocent fraud". Galbraith J.K., *The Economics of Innocent Fraud* (Penguin Books, 2004).

3.3.1 Ethical Concerns about Corporate Personality and Moral Agency

There is a widely held view that the corporation, as an artificial legal person, has no moral agency.[45] The company or corporation is an instrument mandated by law, compelled by its competitive market habitat, and programmed by conscious design to act only in a self-interested manner, in a calculating and relentless pursuit of financial gain. In theory, corporations can live forever, but most die young, victims of the *creative destruction* of a demanding, harsh and unforgiving free-market environment.[46] The corporations that survive, grow and thrive over the long term, and that are held to be exemplary, are those that are most successful in the competitive market in maximising shareholder value. This must, of necessity, be the focus and duty of the company's managerial employee agents in fulfilling the obligations of their contractual corporate role.

Joel Bakan[47] has characterised the corporation as 'psychopathic' by design, necessarily and ruthlessly single-minded in its coldly rational pursuit of competitive advantage in money-making: a predatory, voracious and exploitative entity, incapable by its nature and context of sympathy, empathy or compassion; an unfeeling, misanthropic machine, without moral responsibility, moral obligation, moral conscience or moral culpability.[48]

> "Only people have moral obligations. Corporations can no more be said to have moral obligations than does a building, and organization chart, or a contract."[49]

For Joel Bakan and other critics of the modern corporation, it will inevitably and inescapably behave without moral restraint causing collateral harm to people and to the planet, using its power to influence regulation in its favour, whether regulation by the invisible hand of the market or by the visible hand of the law and the state. As entities having "neither bodies to be punished, nor souls to be condemned",[50] therefore doing as they

---

[45] For a comprehensive discussion of the issue of corporate moral agency, see, for example: Wolgast, E., *Ethics of an Artificial Person: Lost Responsibility in Professions and Organisations* (Stanford University Press, 1992); and Danley, J., "Corporate Moral Agency", in Frederick, R.E (Ed.), *A Companion to Business Ethics* (Blackwell Publishers, 1999).

[46] See "The last Kodak moment", *The Economist*, 14 January 2012.

[47] Bakan, J., *The Corporation: The Pathological Pursuit of Profit and Power* (Constable, 2004).

[48] In this context, *The Economist*'s portrayal of Facebook is noteworthy: "Its culture melds a ruthless pursuit of profit with a Panglossian and narcissistic belief in its own virtue." *The Economist*, Leader Article, 22 March 2018.

[49] Easterbrook, F. and Fishel, D., "Antitrust Suits by Targets of Tender Offers" (1982) *Michigan Law Review* 80: 1177, quoted in Bakan, J., *op. cit.* above, n. 47, p. 79.

[50] Remarks attributed to Edward Thurlow (1731–1806), Lord Chancellor of England. Quoted in Poynder J., *Literary Extracts* (1844) Vol. 1, p. 268.

like, these amoral corporate psychopaths, created to generate economic wealth and prosperity for their shareholders (and to thereby paradoxically benefit society) have become social and ecological wrecking balls, destructive Frankenstein monsters urgently in need of reform.[51] According to Eric Schlosser:

> "The history of the twentieth century was dominated by the struggle against totalitarian systems of state power. The twenty-first will no doubt be marked by a struggle to curtail excessive corporate power."[52]

There is, however, an alternative perspective: that corporate entities are capable of moral reasoning and should be held morally responsible and accountable as fully-fledged moral agents.

"A corporation can and should have a conscience. The language of ethics does have a place in the vocabulary of an organization .... . Organizational agents such as corporations should be no more or no less morally responsible (rational, self-interested, altruistic) than ordinary persons."[53]

The corporate form does not imply, nor does it legitimise, the 'rule of nobody'. Corporations can only behave the way that the people who own and control them behave. People remain people in a corporate context, and are not excused moral agency, or absolved from moral obligation and responsibility by virtue of their role in a collective endeavour. Corporations act through an internal decision structure,[54] a hierarchical network of managerial agents organised into a formal system for coordinated and integrated decision-making. A corporation's moral character and moral agency is embedded in and expressed through this structure, which equates to a coherent collective 'directing mind' for corporate conduct. Responsibility for corporate behaviour is dispersed, partial, fragmented and not reducible to the actions of any one individual. However, this does not exculpate individual managers from moral responsibility for actions undertaken in their corporate role. The responsibility of people for the behaviour and moral agency of the corporation is proportional to the position and power they hold in the managerial hierarchy. The board of directors, in particular, has a critical governance role in ensuring that the internal decision structure engenders a moral climate conducive to enabling the corporation to fulfil

---

[51] Bakan, J., *op. cit.* above, n. 47. See quote from an interview with Robert Monks, p. 71.

[52] Schlosser, E., *Fast Food Nation* (Penguin, 2001) pp. 260–261.

[53] Goodpaster, K.E. and Matthews, J.B., "Can a corporation have a conscience?" (1982) *Harvard Business Review* January–February, quoted in Chryssides, G. and Kaler, J., *op. cit. above*, n. 15, p. 267.

[54] This is a viewpoint articulated in many publications by Peter French. For example, in "The Corporation as a Moral Person", (1979) *American Philosophical Quarterly*, July, 207–215.

its moral obligations and duties. According to the *UK Corporate Governance Code* (see **Chapter 1**):

> "One of the key roles for the board includes establishing the culture, values and ethics of the company."[55]

Shareholders, as owners and beneficiaries of corporate activities, are not absolved from moral responsibility for the behaviour of the instrument that acts in their name.[56] They too have a critical role in forming corporate (moral) personality and in underpinning and enhancing its moral agency.

Furthermore, corporations can and will be punished for ethical failure, for example by: public approbation; long-term reputational damage; loss of stakeholder trust and respect; damage to their competitiveness; financial penalties such as fines; increased regulation; the removal of corporate privilege.

The recognition of corporate moral agency, the critical role of the board in its manifestation and the potential threats posed by ethical lapse are inherent in public declarations by corporations, business leaders and professional bodies of their commitment to incorporating ethical considerations into decision-making. For example:

> "Ethics are pivotal in determining the success or failure of an organisation. … A failure to do the right thing can cause social, economic and environmental damage, undermining a company's long-term reputation and prospects in the process. … Ethics must be embedded in business models, organisational strategy and decision making processes.
>
> Senior managers and business leaders must demonstrate an ethical approach by example."[57]

3.3.2 The Social Responsibility of Corporations

It is generally agreed that business corporations should be responsible to society and that they should behave ethically. There is an on-going debate, however, about what this should mean in practice in the context of a global capitalist economy. What should be the responsibility and obligations of business corporations to society in a contemporary free-market context?

---

[55] Financial Reporting Council, *The UK Corporate Governance Code* (FRC, 2016) Preface, p. 2.

[56] For an example of shareholder ethical activism, refer to *The Economist*, 14 April 2018, "Voting with your pocket: Activists are using shareholder votes to promote social agendas".

[57] CIMA, *Incorporating ethics into strategy: developing sustainable business models*, Discussion Paper (2010).

How should this be reflected in corporate purposes (*ends*) and in corporate behaviour (*means*), including in the behaviour of corporate management and all other employees?

Consideration of the social responsibility of a business corporation is an *ethical* issue, in that it is concerned with the type of corporate behaviour that will promote human welfare and that, as a minimum, will respect all stakeholders and not cause harm to people or the environment. What kind of corporate behaviour should be considered morally adequate and socially acceptable? What kind of corporate behaviour should be judged good and right? The social legitimacy of the corporation is based on how well it fulfils its ethical obligations.

Broadly speaking, the debate about the social responsibility of corporations centres on two divergent perspectives:

- the **traditional** '*profits for shareholders*' perspective; and
- the '*corporate social responsibility*' (**CSR**) perspective.

The traditional model of corporate social responsibility was articulated by Milton Friedman in an article published in 1970: "The Social Responsibility of Business is to Increase its Profits".[58] The role and responsibility of corporate management in a free-market economy is to make profits for shareholders, acting within the law and in accordance with ethical custom.

> "… there is one and only one social responsibility of business – to use its resources and engage in activities designed to increase its profits so long as it stays within the rules of the game, which is to say, engages in open and free competition without deception or fraud."[59]

Milton Friedman argues that the best way for business to promote human welfare is through the honest pursuit of profits in open and competitive markets, guided by the invisible hand, state regulation and societal expectations. Corporations are instruments established for this purpose and are mandated by law to behave accordingly. Corporate management are agents of the corporation and its shareholders; they have an overriding duty and obligation arising from their role to seek to maximise long-term corporate profits. It is their success in doing so that legitimises the corporation.

In Friedman's view, the pursuit of profit through free markets is inherently good and right, providing a *normative ethical principle* to guide

---

[58] Friedman, M., "The Social Responsibility of Business is to Increase its Profits", *The New York Times Magazine*, 13 September 1970.
[59] *Ibid.*

business behaviour.[60] Profits are a just reward for serving society's best long-term interests as guided by the market. Behaviour directed towards profit-making will lead to the most efficient use of scarce resources in accordance with the wishes and free choices of free people. The pursuit of profit respects the autonomy, equality and rights of individuals, and, in the context of free competitive markets, will result in a fair and just distribution of rewards. It will promote individual and overall societal welfare over the long term, serving the common good and bringing the greatest happiness to the greatest number. The essential argument is that free-market corporate capitalism is a moral political-economic system. There is no conflict between profit-seeking and overall societal welfare; on the contrary, the former promotes the latter. In the words of *The Economist* magazine:

> "The goal of a well-run company may be to make profits for its share-holders, but merely in doing that – provided it faces competition in its markets, behaves honestly and obeys the law – the company, without even trying, is doing good works. ... There is no need for self-less sacrifice when it comes to stakeholders. It goes with the territory. Thus, the selfish pursuit of profit serves a social purpose."[61]

The alternative, corporate social responsibility (CSR) perspective remains a relatively ill-defined, vague and somewhat arbitrary concept. Generally, CSR is understood to mean that corporate purposes should be broader than mere 'profit-making for shareholders within the law', and that corporations should behave responsibly towards all their stakeholders in their pursuit of profits. However, within this broad notion of *'profit-making plus'*, there are many shades of differing opinion among its advocates about what CSR should mean in practice.

The debate about the need for a broader understanding of the social responsibility of corporations than that suggested by the traditional 'profits-for-shareholders' model arises in the context of:

- a critical questioning of the growing power and influence of huge corporations operating on a global scale;
- the significant and often detrimental impact corporations have on the natural environment and on the welfare of stakeholders, giving rise to concerns about ecological and social sustainability;
- significant market and regulatory failure in preventing harm and abuse of power by largely unaccountable corporations and their management;

---

[60] Refer, for example, to DesJardins, J.R. and MacCall J.J., *op. cit.* above, n. 1, pp. 1–23.
[61] "Capitalism and Ethics: The Good Company", *The Economist*, Leader Article, 20 January 2005.

- a loss of faith in the efficacy of the *invisible hand* of markets and of state regulation;
- changing societal expectations about what constitutes legitimate and morally acceptable corporate and managerial behaviour, rendering 'business as usual' to be no longer an acceptable option.

Generally, the CSR perspective recognises that corporations have a broad and multi-faceted set of responsibilities and obligations to a wide range of stakeholders. Corporate management should aim to balance these stakeholder interests in their decision-making. Corporate strategies should, for example, incorporate consideration of economic, ecological and broader social ends; they should seek to balance concerns about the long-term impact of the corporation on profit, planet and people. Advocates of CSR take the view (to a lesser or greater extent) that business corporations should be expected to play a role in promoting public policy objectives by actively seeking to solve society's problems and to making the world a better place.[62] For example, this viewpoint was clearly and succinctly expressed by the petrochemical company BP as follows:

> "A good business should be both competitively successful and a force for good."[63]

The CSR perspective looks beyond the invisible hand of the market regulated by the state to the *visible hand of management* as an adjunct mechanism for regulating the interaction between corporations and society. CSR provides a mechanism for reforming corporate capitalism on a voluntary, bottom-up basis so that it will better promote human welfare and serve the greater good of society. The debate *within* the CSR perspective centres on the extent to which various stakeholder concerns should be made integral to corporate strategic goals, and on the basis for resolving trade-offs among competing and conflicting stakeholder interests.

Both the traditional and the CSR perspectives recognise and accept the virtues of competitive free-markets as the preferred driver of economic growth and prosperity. It is the nature of corporate behaviour within this market context that is in question; whether it should and can be reformed and improved. The debate centres on the legitimacy of corporate *ends* and of the *means* deployed in pursuit of these ends in a market context.

---

[62] Refer Henderson, D., *The Case against Corporate Social Responsibility* (2001) *Policy*, Vol. 17 No. 2, 28–32.
[63] BP, *What We Stand For*, Statement of Business Policies (2002).

3.3.2.1 The Business Case for CSR

One of the main arguments made for adopting the CSR perspective is based on enlightened self-interest. Essentially, that there is a strong business case for embracing CSR as it can enhance a company's ability to make profits for its shareholders over the long term. Incorporating a CSR perspective into its strategy potentially provides a boost to a corporation's image and reputation. This will be rewarded in the product/services market by customers and in the financial markets by investors. It will give rise to potential labour market benefits by facilitating employee recruitment, commitment and retention. It potentially generates cost savings and increased productivity through, for example, eco-efficient processes, a more satisfied and productive workforce operating in a safer and healthier workplace, and the diminution of health & safety risks and of potentially costly accidents. CSR is a long-term investment in enhanced stakeholder relationships thereby, creating an improved and stable context in which to do business and to make profits. Furthermore, it is argued, corporations perceived as not embracing CSR will be punished in the markets. Adopting a CSR perspective will also serve to forestall increased regulation by the state, preserving corporate autonomy and avoiding higher regulatory costs and imposed inflexibility.

The 'business case' argument for CSR is, however, simply a restatement of the traditional Friedman 'profits for shareholders' model. CSR, justified with the business case outlined above, is a positioning strategy, driven by a consequentialist calculation of economic self-interest and is fully consistent and aligned with the traditional profit-making model of corporate responsibility. CSR is necessary and good because it is necessary and good for profits. The resulting CSR practices are, arguably, the modern manifestation of the invisible hand of contemporary markets at work in corporate business decision-making.

> "CSR that is not profit-maximising might silence the critics but is, in fact, unethical."[64]

For Friedman and others, CSR that is not about profit-making is fundamentally subversive and unethical. For management to sacrifice profits in pursuit of broader social objectives is not only unnecessary, it is an act of folly that is economically, democratically and ethically irresponsible. It is contrary to their *duty* and moral obligations as corporate agents. It is akin to management imposing a tax on shareholders, which is wrong in principle and in consequence.[65] Friedman goes as far as to suggest that any such non-profit

---

[64] "Corporate social responsibility: Two-faced capitalism", *The Economist*, 22 January 2004.
[65] For a critical evaluation of Friedman's arguments, see, for example, DesJardins, J.R. and MacCall J.J., *op. cit.* above, n. 60, pp. 1–23.

focused activity on management's part is a form of theft. If they want to 'do good works', they should do so as private citizens and at their own expense. Corporate management are not democratically accountable and they lack the competence to make public policy choices. CSR that is not a strategy for profit-making involves corporate management in an unwarranted intrusion into the political realm in which they have no legitimate authority and in which they constitute a threat to democratic freedom by undermining the basis of a free society. It is the responsibility of democratically accountable politicians to decide on public policy priorities and on resource distribution towards broad social ends, not the managers of corporations.

Aneel Karnani has warned that CSR may even present a danger for society, explaining that:

> "The idea that companies have a duty to address social ills is not just flawed, it also makes it more likely that we'll ignore the real solutions to these problems."[66]

Karnani argues that when CSR and profit-making are aligned, the idea of CSR is irrelevant. In circumstances in which profits and social welfare are in direct opposition, an appeal to CSR will almost always be ineffective, because executives are unlikely to act voluntarily in the public interest and against shareholders' interests. Nor should they, for to do so is contrary to the movement for better corporate governance which, according to Karani, demands that managers fulfill their fiduciary duty to act in the shareholders' interest or be relieved of their responsibilities. More importantly, however, there is a danger that a focus on CSR will delay, discourage or divert attention from more effective solutions to striking a balance between profits and the public good. These include government regulation, active advocacy by civil society watchdogs, and self-control by corporations emphasising transparency and accountability.

3.3.2.2 CSR: A Continuing Debate

The view one takes on the social responsibility of corporations depends to a great extent on one's trust in the efficacy of the invisible hand of the market, in state regulation and in the inherent honesty of business behaviour. Arguably, earning profits in a modern context requires that corporations respect all stakeholder interests and that they do not intentionally cause harm to people or the environment. More than ever, transparency is demanded by stakeholders and corporations are challenged to account for their social and environmental impact. (Despite this, however, it can be

---

[66] Karnani, A., "The Case against Corporate Social Responsibility", *The Wall Street Journal*, 22 August 2010.

difficult to treat the claims of some corporations, that they are committed to social responsibility, with other than cynicism in the context of their aggressive corporate tax avoidance strategies.)

Muhammad Yunus suggests that although CSR may be grounded in good intentions, it generally ends up as little more that 'window dressing'. The bottom line remains financial gain.

> "By their nature, corporations are not equipped to deal with social prob-
> lems. It's not because business executives are selfish, greedy, or bad. The
> problem lies with the very nature of business. Even more profoundly,
> it lies with the concept of business that is at the centre of capitalism."[67]

There is a third, perhaps more radical, perspective on corporate social responsibility grounded in the idea of a radical root-and-branch reform of the concept of the corporation, giving rise to a new type of entity. The traditional shareholder-oriented corporation has outlived its value to society and a new type of corporate institution is now needed, more suited to meeting contemporary social and environmental needs. The rules of the game need to be changed, including a rebalancing of the relationship between the state and the markets. Charles Handy,[68] for example, has suggested that the company is a community of stakeholders, a hexagonal ring comprising financiers, employees, customers, suppliers, environment and community. If such a stakeholder corporation is to exist it needs to be created and recognised in law because asking management to behave other than in accordance with the rule book is unfair and unrealisable. This, Handy suggests, is needed because otherwise our future is endangered.

3.3.3 Corporate Governance

Corporate Governance that has not been fertilised by Ethics is simply a sterile instrument without any substance.[69]

Corporate governance is perhaps the most widely used and abused phrase in the contemporary organisational lexicon. It remains an ill-defined, broad, multi-faceted and contested concept: "an enormous umbrella term that everything gets chucked into".[70] In broad, general terms (discussed in

---

[67] Yunus, M., *Creating a World without Poverty: Social Business and the Future of Capitalism* (Public Affairs, 2007) p. 17.

[68] Handy, C., *Beyond Certainty: The Changing Worlds of Organizations* (Harvard Business School Press, 1996) Chapter 4, "What is a Company For?", pp. 57–85.

[69] Barker, P., "Corporate Governance – A Virgin Birth!", Chartered Accountants Ireland, *Corporate Governance News*, 16 January 2014.

[70] A remark made by Prof. Noel Hyndman of Queen's University Belfast at the Irish Accounting and Finance Association (IAFA) Conference, Dublin City University, May 2006.

detail in **Chapter 1**), corporate governance involves the manner in which corporate entities are *governed* and *run*; in which they are *directed, steered* and *led*. It is concerned with: the end purposes of corporate conduct and the means deployed in pursuit of those ends; the responsibilities and obligations of corporations; balancing competing stakeholder interests; and with ensuring the legitimacy of corporate behaviour in pursuit of its ends. Corporate governance is concerned with both corporate *performance* and *conformance*[71]: with who corporations are for, what they do, how they do it, and how well they do it, in accordance with the requirements of law, regulatory agencies and society.

Improving corporate governance has been a central focus of regulatory attention since the late 1980s. Despite significant efforts in this regard, however, concerns about significant weaknesses in corporate governance remain, fuelled by a litany of high-profile corporate scandals (including organisations in the voluntary sector and the public sector), and by an increasingly intrusive and critical media questioning the legitimacy of management, of corporations and of markets.

Concerns relate to weaknesses in both performance and conformance aspects of governance. For example, that:

- the interests of shareholder and of other stakeholders are not being adequately served;
- there is poor stewardship of resources by corporate management;
- corporate behaviour is lacking in openness, transparency and accountability;
- corporate financial reporting lacks credibility;
- the regulatory agencies are failing to hold corporations to account.

Corporate behaviour often appears excessively focused on boosting short-term financial results, with poor or even reckless risk management compromising the long-term viability of the corporation, and with little evident concern for the social costs of externalities or for fulfilling corporate obligations and responsibilities to society.

Criticism of standards of corporate governance reflects a loss of trust in corporations and markets. The most virulent criticism is often from disappointed advocates of the free-market system and strong supporters of the legitimacy of the corporation as a vital social institution. For many of these critics, the root cause of the weaknesses in corporate governance is

---

[71] IFAC and CIMA, *Enterprise Governance: Getting the Balance Right* (Professional Accountants in Business Committee (PAIB) of IFAC, 2004). Available at http://www.cimaglobal.com/Documents/ImportedDocuments/tech_execrep_enterprise_governance_getting_the_balance_right_feb_2004.pdf (accessed July 2018).

unethical self-serving behaviour by managerial agents, abusing their power to 'feather their own nests' rather than acting in the best, long-term interests of the corporation and its shareholders.[72]

J.K. Galbraith[73] argues convincingly that corporate managers are incentivised and likely to act in their own self-interest, abusing their powers for self-enrichment, and giving themselves rewards "that can verge on larceny". Martin Wolf writes of the "chronic vulnerability of the corporation to managerial incompetence, self-seeking, deceit or downright malfeasance".[74]

John C. Bogle[75] suggests that something went badly wrong with capitalism in the late 20th century: that there was a gradual shift (a 'pathological mutation') from owner's capitalism to manager's capitalism. As a consequence, corporations are run by managers *for* managers with adverse consequences for shareholders and for society in general. Commenting on corporate governance, Alan Greenspan, Chair of the US Federal Reserve from 1987 to 2006, has observed:

> "Democratic corporate governance has morphed into a type of authoritarianism … [and] as with authoritarianism everywhere, the lack of adequate accountability in corporate management has spawned abuse."[76]

It should, perhaps, be no surprise that there will be problems of managerial moral agency in corporate entities. Adam Smith warned long ago that:

> "directors of [joint stock] companies … being the managers rather of other people's money than their own, it cannot well be expected that they should watch over it with the same anxious vigilance with which the partners in a private copartnery frequently watch over their own."[77]

The efforts made to date to improve corporate governance have mainly been focused on enhancing regulation (in its broadest sense), including legal reform. But regulation, whether principles-based or rules-based, has

---

[72] See, for example, Hutton, W., "Let's end this rotten culture that only rewards rogues", *The Observer*, 30 June 2012: "The Barclays rate-rigging scandal has once again exposed a world where men and women with little skill and no moral compass can become very rich very fast."

[73] Arguments presented in Galbraith, J.K., *The Economics of Innocent Fraud*, op. cit. above, n. 44, and in Galbraith, J.K, *The Culture of Contentment* (Penguin Books, 1992). The direct quote is taken from the former, p. 29.

[74] Wolf, M., "A Manager's Real Responsibility", *The Financial Times*, 30 January 2002.

[75] Bogle J.C., *The Battle for the Soul of Capitalism* (Yale University Press, 2005).

[76] Greenspan, A., *The Age of Turbulence* (Penguin Books, 2008) p. 425.

[77] Smith, A., *An Inquiry into the Nature and Causes of the Wealth of Nations*, op. cit. above, n. 16, Book V, Chapter 1, p. 741.

so far proven costly and inadequate as an approach to resolving governance problems and preventing managerial abuse. The fundamental problems are arguably a consequence of ethical lapse at senior managerial level, particularly in the boardroom. Regulation alone will not provide the basis for fostering the ethical culture that is necessary to underpin good and right behaviour. The board and the executive management team are the de facto conscience of the corporation, responsible for embedding ethics in decision-making and behaviour throughout the organisation and in all its activities. Promoting good governance requires what Lyne Paine calls "moral thinking in management".[78]

Ethical behaviour is necessary to ensure the long-term economic success and social legitimacy of corporations, including avoiding the risks and costs of bad governance as arising from unethical behaviour. Long-term business success is not possible without stakeholder trust and honest dealing. This cannot be imposed effectively from the outside; it must originate internally in the corporation. The moral tone must be set by the board of directors and top management (particularly by the 'one at the top'). The ethical compass of the board and of executive management, reinforced by the corporation's external professional advisors, is critical in ensuring and enhancing good governance.[79]

In summary, ethical behaviour by management and boards is a requirement for good corporate governance. Ethics should be a core part of management and director education.

> "Good corporate governance ... requires business ethics at several levels: individual decision making, corporate culture and an overall understanding of a collective business purpose that balances different interests and values."[80]

3.4 The Individual in Business

People working in business encounter ethical dilemmas through the role they perform and as agents of the corporate organisation. The particular

[78] Paine, L.S., "Moral Thinking in Management: An Essential Capability" in Rhode, D. (Ed.), *Ethics in Practice: Lawyers' Roles, Responsibilities and Regulation* (Oxford University Press, 2000).

[79] See also, O'Shea, R., *Leading with Integrity: A Practical Guide to Business Ethics* (Chartered Accountants Ireland, 2016), Chapter 1, "The Case for Ethical Leadership", pp. 3–25, and Chapter 6, "Ethical Corporate Governance", pp. 181–207.

[80] Orts, E., "Law is never enough to guarantee fair practice: The collapse of Enron has important lessons for managers and boards about running a business ethically and responsibly". *The Financial Times*, 23 August 2002.

nature, scope and complexity of the moral issues arising will vary depending on:

- the nature of the industry (e.g. financial services, manufacturing, healthcare, fashion);
- the disciplinary and functional area of work (e.g. finance, production, human resources, marketing);
- the socio-cultural context (e.g. national or international, mono-cultural or multi-cultural);
- the level of responsibility in the corporate organisational hierarchy (e.g. an owner of the business, an employee or professional advisor, a senior manager or front-line supervisor).

It is possible, however, to identify a number of common themes across the wide and varied range of moral dilemmas encountered. Generally, the dilemmas involve one or all of the following:

- tension and conflict between the individual's values, the expectations of their job/role and the demands of the organisation;
- tension and conflict between the individual's self-interest, the interests of colleagues, the interests of the organisation and the interests of various other stakeholders (both proximate and distant);
- tension and conflict arising from competing responsibilities, loyalties and moral obligations;
- tension and conflict between the competing demands of principled behaviour (of duty), of pragmatism (of likely consequences) and of the individual's conscience (what one can live with) – between the individual doing 'the right thing' or doing 'what would be best for all concerned in the context'.

Specific ethical issues encountered may relate to how the organisation treats its employees, how employees treat the organisation, and how the organisation interacts with its customers, suppliers, financiers, the state, the local community, the public more generally and the natural environment, including, for example:

- unfair practices in recruitment, promotion and reward, including discrimination on the basis of gender, race or ethnicity;
- inadequate safety and security in the workplace;
- dishonesty and unprofessional behaviour;
- covering-up known malpractice and attempting to silence dissent;
- turning a blind eye to exploitative practices in the supply-chain;
- colluding with competitors, price-fixing and profiteering;
- aggressive advertising to children;
- misrepresenting and selling unsafe products and services, and not providing for customer protection;

- seeking to exert covert political influence;
- bribery;
- knowingly endangering the local community;
- not adequately providing for the protection of the natural environment.

Business ethics is concerned with inquiry into how people *ought to* act and with how they *do* act when they are faced with ethical dilemmas requiring moral judgement in a corporate work context (see **Section 3.1** above). People do not stop being people in the workplace; they are not excused their moral agency or moral obligations by virtue of assigned duties arising from a job or role. Individuals have no special exemption licence that permits behaviour that would be judged unethical in other spheres of living.

However, it is important to recognise and acknowledge that the capacity of individuals to influence events in a particular organisational circumstance may be limited, that doing the right thing can come at a high personal cost and also at a cost to others. For example, it may be difficult for an individual to act in accordance with a perceived personal moral obligation if to do so is contrary to what 'everyone else is doing'. Considerations of futility (no impact), perversity (making things worse) and jeopardy (danger of high cost to the individual)[81] are inescapable and will influence an individual's judgement and behaviour. This highlights the critical importance of the senior management responsibility for nurturing and promoting an ethical organisational culture, giving people working in and for the organisation confidence and trust that ethical behaviour is expected, valued and supported. Senior management, in their decision-making and behaviour have a vital role in setting the ethical 'tone from the top', and in providing the infrastructure and resourcing necessary to foster and support people in behaving ethically.

The reality for many people encountering ethical issues through their job is that their concerns are not taken seriously, respected or acted on by their superiors in the managerial hierarchy. They find little active support among their peers. Their experience is often negative, their concerns effectively dismissed, and they feel themselves warned off from pursuing the issues further. This has driven some people – those who "cannot tolerate the violation of morality or the public trust"[82] and who feel obliged to do something about it – to speak up and become 'whistle-blowers', often at great personal cost and sacrifice. Society owes a debt of gratitude to such whistle-blowers as it is often only thanks to their fortitude, tenacity and strength of

---

[81] See Power, S., *'A Problem from Hell': America and the Age of Genocide* (Flamingo, 2003), Preface, p. xviii.

[82] Solomon, R.C., "Business Ethics" in Singer, P. (Ed.), *op. cit.* above, n. 9, p. 364.

character that we know about bad behaviour by and in corporations, and have been able to act to prevent it continuing and to mitigate its impacts.

The scale, scope and frequency of corporate scandals in recent times suggest that unethical behaviour is commonplace, but that it is increasingly difficult to hide. Surveys indicate that many employees feel under pressure to act unethically. For example, a 2015 study of UK executives reported a greater number feeling pressure to compromise their organisation's ethical standards than in 2012 (rising from 18% to 30%).[83] On the positive side, however, changing societal expectations about morally acceptable corporate behaviour appear to have stimulated a publicly espoused commitment by corporations to ethical improvement. The hope is that the rhetoric will become the reality.

[83] *Managing Responsible Business 2015 Edition: The ethical challenges organisations must navigate to succeed in a connected world* (CGMA, 2015). Available at https://www.cimaglobal.com/Research--Insight/Managing-responsible-business/ (accessed July 2018)

PART II

CASES

In Part I of this book, we introduced the concepts of corporate governance and ethics. As outlined in the Introduction, our goal here is not to present a comprehensive review of these areas and we encourage interested readers to also study some of the other sources that we have referenced along the way to get further background and insight. However, we believe that what we have produced should provide readers with a practical grounding in both corporate governance and ethics and equip them with the knowledge to address practical scenarios in an informed and thoughtful manner.

Part II provides readers with opportunities to apply this knowledge (and knowledge from other sources) as they tease out issues and seek to develop workable solutions to problems and situations, compliment or critique practices and suitably advise stakeholders in a 'safe', fictitious environment. As you know, and will see, the world of ethics and corporate governance – like business in general – is not 'black and white'; in this book, we have tried to help you to see through, or even around, the 'grey'. Therefore, while it is valuable to use the knowledge contained in Part I, and elsewhere, when addressing the forthcoming case studies, do not forget to apply common sense as well, a skill that is essential for a modern-day effective accountant, professional advisor, manager, leader and business person.

Case 1

Astorma Plc

Clare Kearney and Rosemarie Kelly, Waterford Institute of Technology

Astorma Plc is a pharmaceutical company listed on a recognised stock exchange. The company has recently issued its annual report to shareholders. Detailed information relating to the company's corporate governance has been extracted from the annual report and is presented below.

Statement from the Directors' Report

"The directors of Astorma Plc support high standards of corporate governance that are critical to business integrity and to maintaining trust in the company. For the financial year, the directors confirm that the company has complied with the provisions of the *UK Corporate Governance Code* and the "Irish Corporate Governance Annex".

Board of Directors

Director	Position	Number of full years on board	Meeting attendance in last financial year
O. Mann	Chair	16	6/6
L. Childe	Chief executive officer	8	6/6
T. Potts	Finance director	5	5/6
P. Grace	Production director	3	6/6
L. Boyd	Marketing director	4	6/6
S. Jones	Non-executive director	7	4/6
A. Lone	Non-executive director	2	2/6

Re-appointment of Directors

All directors are automatically re-elected at the end of each year.

Remuneration Committee

The remuneration of executive directors is determined by the remuneration committee, which consists of T. Potts, A. Lone and S. Jones.

Chief Executive Officer

L. Childe, who is married to S. Jones, has been the chief executive officer of the company for eight years and will become chair when O. Mann retires at the end of the year.

Other Directorships

P. Grace and L. Boyd hold a number of non-executive directorships in other companies. In addition, P. Grace is the chair of the board of another, unrelated company, Rascott Plc.

Audit Committee

The membership of the audit committee comprises L. Childe, P. Grace and L. Boyd. This committee meets each year in March to discuss the conduct of, and findings arising from, the external audit.

Internal Control System

During the year, T. Potts conducted a review of the company's internal control system and concluded that it was operating effectively. A report on this matter has been prepared and this is available to shareholders on the company website.

Required

Based on the information provided, evaluate corporate governance at Astorma plc:

(a) Consider the accuracy of the statement from the Directors' Report.
(b) Describe any areas of non-compliance with the *UK Corporate Governance Code* and the "Irish Corporate Governance Annex".
(c) Provide recommendations to bring the company's corporate governance in line with best practice.

Case 2

Wonderous Stay Hotel Group Plc

Rosemarie Kelly, Collette Kirwan, and Richard Burke, Waterford Institute of Technology

The Wonderous Stay Hotel Group Plc is listed on the London Stock Exchange. Each year the group prepares its consolidated financial statements for the year ended 31 October. The following information has been extracted from the corporate governance section of the 2017 annual report of the group.

ANNUAL REPORT 2017 – CORPORATE GOVERNANCE SECTION (EXTRACT)

Board Member	Position on the Board of Directors	Appointed to the Board	Committee Membership
Jack Hickey	Chair	March 2006	Audit committee
Albert Maher	Chief executive officer (CEO)	September 2008	Remuneration committee, Risk committee
Sid Foley	Finance director	May 2016	Nomination committee
Ann Roberts	IT & communications director	January 2017	Remuneration committee
Mary Clancy	Marketing director	October 2017	Audit committee
Jim Camron	Human resources director	November 2016	Nomination committee
David Riches	Senior non-executive director	February 2013	Risk committee
Mark Lane	Non-executive director	September 2009	Remuneration committee, Risk committee
Yvonne Scott	Non-executive director	November 2016	Nomination committee, Risk committee

The chairs of the four board committees are as follows:

• Audit committee	Jack Hickey
• Nomination committee	Sid Foley
• Remuneration committee	Mark Lane
• Risk committee	Yvonne Scott

Additional Information

In addition to the information disclosed in the annual report, the following information is provided (which does not appear in the annual report):

- In January 2019, Jack Hickey will step down as chair of the board due to family commitments. Albert Maher will succeed Jack Hickey, taking up the role of chair in January 2019. To assist with their search for a new CEO, the board of directors recently engaged the services of an executive recruitment firm. If an appropriate CEO is not identified by January 2019, Albert Maher will stay on as an interim CEO until a replacement is found.
- Mark Lane was the first non-executive director to be appointed to the board. Mark Lane and Albert Maher were the joint founders and owners (each owning 50% of the share capital) of a successful hotel group in the United States. In 2007, both Mark and Albert sold their shares in the hotel group. Shortly after selling his shares, Albert Maher was headhunted for the position of CEO of Wonderous Stay Hotel Group Plc. He is renowned for his strong knowledge of the hotel sector.
- Yvonne Scott joined the board as a non-executive director immediately after she retired from the position of finance director of the Wonderous Stay Hotel Group. Sid Foley a tourism marketing expert succeeded Yvonne as finance director, a position that Yvonne had held for seven years. Yvonne is also a non-executive director on the board of an Irish semi-state tourism agency and the chair of the board of a FTSE 250 entity. Given her extensive experience, Yvonne was the obvious candidate to chair the risk committee.
- On 1 November 2017, Wonderous Stay Hotel Group introduced a share option scheme, under which executive directors have the option of exercising their share options from 31 October 2019.

Required

Comment on the corporate governance disclosures provided by Wonderous Stay Hotel Group Plc by reference to recognised good corporate governance practices.

Case 3

Great Homes Forever Ltd

Rosemarie Kelly,
Waterford Institute of Technology

Great Homes Forever Ltd is a retailer of furniture and homewares. The company was established in Dublin in 1990 by two brothers, Gary and Hugh Fox. In the early days, the company operated from one shop based in Rathmines and had few employees. Consequently, the brothers were very involved in the day-to-day operations of the business. Today, the company has six stores in Ireland and one in London, and employs over 100 staff.

When the company was established, Gary and Hugh were the only shareholders and directors, each owning 50% of the ordinary shares. They both contributed €100,000 to the company and also became guarantors for a substantial bank loan. At that time, the company did not have a board or hold any formal board meetings as the brothers discussed all company matters on a daily basis and considered that a formal board meeting would be "a waste of time as we know what's happening anyway".

By 2000, the company had three stores in Ireland and employed 30 staff. To meet the surge in demand for furniture and homewares, the company needed finance for expansion and two new shareholders were admitted in February 2001: Future Horizons Dac, an investment company, provided €100,000 for a shareholding of 20%; and Philip Gavin, a retired director of a major homewares company based in the UK, also contributed €100,000 for 20% of the ordinary shares. When the new shareholders asked about attending board meetings they were informed by Gary Fox that "we haven't established a board and so don't have formal board meetings, but we do have monthly management meetings, which are the same thing really. You're welcome to sit in on any of those meetings if you like."

During the period 2001 to 2008, Great Homes Forever expanded rapidly, opening three more stores in Ireland and one in London. To finance the expansion, the company obtained a substantial bank loan from National Priority Bank Plc. Gary and Hugh were required to give personal guarantees as security for the loan. One of the bank's conditions for providing the finance was that the company would establish a board of directors on which the bank would have representation. It was agreed that the bank would nominate one non-executive director to the board of Great Homes Forever Ltd.

In 2002, a formal structure was established for the board of Great Homes Forever Ltd (see **Table 1** below). Gary and Hugh Fox assumed responsibility for the chair and managing director roles respectively. Hugh's wife, Marie, a chartered accountant and finance director at Great Homes Forever Ltd, and Alan James, the company's logistics director, also joined the board. National Priority Bank Plc nominated Cian O'Brien as their non-executive director representative. It was agreed that there would be two formal board meetings per year, in February and August. The monthly management meetings would continue as before. This board structure and the schedule for board meetings are still the same today.

The company's growth slowed to a halt when the financial crisis occurred in late 2008 and, until recently, it has struggled to maintain sufficient sales and profit to keep its stores open. However, the Irish economy has steadily improved since 2016 and the growth in consumer confidence has resulted in more disposable income available for spending on furniture and homeware.

At the most recent board meeting, Marie Fox, the finance director, highlighted concerns expressed by the external auditors in relation to the company's internal controls, particularly its cash receipts and payments system. The auditors have identified regular bank reconciliation as one of the key internal controls; however, the company has not prepared such a

TABLE 1: BOARD STRUCTURE OF GREAT HOMES FOREVER LTD		
Director	**Position**	**% Shareholding**
Gary Fox	Chair	30%
Hugh Fox	Managing director	30%
Marie Fox	Finance director	–
Alan James	Logistics director	–
Cian O'Brien (nominee of National Priority Bank Plc)	Non-executive director	–

reconciliation for six months. In response, Gary Fox said that "this issue should be addressed at a management meeting not at a board meeting. It's up to you to deal with this, Marie."

Another issue was raised by Hugh Fox at the same board meeting: a letter had been received from one of the other shareholders, Philip Gavin, requesting that he be appointed as a non-executive director of Great Homes Forever Ltd so that he can attend its board meetings. In his letter, Philip added that his experience and expertise would be extremely useful in developing the company's strategy. Gary Fox responded to this, saying: "I don't think that the board should be any larger; it would be too difficult to make decisions. And as for developing strategy, well that clearly is the responsibility of the management team – they have the best knowledge and experience to do this."

Required

Evaluate corporate governance at Great Homes Forever Ltd.

Case 4

Keane Manufacturing Ltd

Margaret Cullen,
University College Dublin, Centre for Corporate
Governance

Keane Manufacturing Ltd is a medium-sized Irish manufacturing company. It was founded in 1993 by Dermot Keane who, for 23 years until 2016, was managing director of the company. In November 2016, Dermot's son, Brian Keane, was appointed managing director of Keane Manufacturing. Prior to Brian's appointment, the board of Keane Manufacturing Ltd consisted of:

- Dermot Keane (managing director and chair);
- Margaret Keane (wife of Dermot Keane); and
- Bill O'Connor (lifelong friend of Dermot and legal counsel to Keane Manufacturing Ltd).

When Dermot was managing director and chair, board meetings tended to be ad hoc and quite informal. In fact, many of the board meetings were held over dinner at the Keane family home. Needless to say, minutes of these meetings were not maintained. Dermot did not believe in employing a full-time Company Secretary, so any legal formalities were completed by Bill O'Connor.

It was from experiencing these informal board meetings at home and through daily family discussions that the next generation of Keanes learned about the business that Dermot had built.

Brian Keane began working for his father's company in 2004 when he was straight out of college and eager to learn. Dermot was keen that Brian learn the ropes of the business, so for the next 12 years, Brian worked on the factory floor as a general operative, progressed to marketing and then to finance prior to his appointment as managing director. Between 2012 and

2014, Brian completed a part-time MBA, though his father believed it was a waste of time, often bemoaning the cost and the time wasted studying, adding comments such as "I didn't need any fancy qualifications" or "there's little you can learn in a classroom about running a company". Brian, however, believed that he had learned much from the MBA course that was useful and could be applied to the running and development of the business.

In 2016, Dermot somewhat reluctantly decided to step down as managing director and pass on the reins to his son. He had attended a breakfast briefing, delivered by a large accountancy firm, on the topic of family business succession and planning. At the breakfast briefing, Dermot met a number of founders who had successfully passed on businesses to sons, daughters and/or non-family managers. Around this time, Dermot was also coming under increased pressure from his wife to take a step back from the business so they could travel and spend more time together in their "twilight years".

However, Dermot was not ready to "be put out to pasture" completely and decided to stay on as chair of the board. His semi-retirement did not last very long. Within two weeks, he was back spending almost every day in the office, a situation Brian and other members of the management team found very frustrating. Dermot began to interfere constantly with the running of the business, frequently ringing suppliers and key customers, often contradicting decisions made by Brian and the other managers. Staff at the company found this confusing: who was the real boss?

Having been in the managing director role for six months, Brian has decided it is time to put his own stamp on the governance of the company. He has great ambitions for Keane Manufacturing and is keen to put a board of directors together that will assist in driving his vision for the company forward.

Brian wants to appoint Karl Curran, the head of finance, to the board of the company. Karl has been with Keane Manufacturing for over 10 years and Brian trusts him as a colleague. Like Brian, Karl 'cut his teeth' at the company and knows it inside-out. Prior to Brian's appointment, Karl, like many other senior employees, had been kept at arm's-length from decision-making by Dermot. The company has lost some good people as a result.

Karl also sees the potential in the company and is ready and willing to support Brian. He is not convinced, however, that Dermot will agree with Brian's strategic vision for the company or his plans to restructure its governance. Staff are constantly expressing frustration at receiving conflicting instructions from Brian and Dermot. While they may be extremely loyal to Dermot, even blindly so, they prefer Brian's style and approach. Karl intends to give it one more year. If Dermot is still hanging on, he plans to begin looking for a new role.

To strengthen the board of directors, Brian also wants to replace his mother, Margaret, and Bill O'Connor with two independent non-executive directors. Brian particularly wants to engage an individual with experience in marketing products globally (the company has always concentrated on the Irish, UK and mainland European markets) and another individual with a very strong understanding of best practice in corporate governance.

Although Dermot very reluctantly agrees to Karl Curran's appointment to the board, he insists that his good friend Bill must remain. Margaret Keane steps down willingly.

To start with, Brian proposes that Catherine Walsh, a former partner of an accountancy firm and a fellow MBA graduate, be appointed to the board as an independent non-executive director. Brian believes that Catherine will bring significant corporate governance expertise and SME-sector experience to the company. ("Catherine has a strong personality", Brian thinks. "She will be well able for my father and his pal Bill O'Connor.")

Dermot Keane agrees to Catherine Walsh's appointment as non-executive director. Catherine is delighted to be offered a position on the board of Keane Manufacturing. She first met Brian in college and thinks he's a great guy. She knew he had exciting plans for the company but was being constrained by his father. Catherine is somewhat concerned that she did not have a formal interview for the non-executive director position. Brian just called her one afternoon to ask her if she would be interested. They subsequently had lunch, when Brian explained that he wanted her to help him in formalising the governance structure of the company, including having at least four board meetings per year. They agreed a non-executive director fee of €15,000 per annum. Catherine has not yet met Dermot or Bill, though she had a coffee with Karl after she accepted the position. To Catherine, Karl seems very competent and level-headed – a good ally to Brian without being overly deferential.

The new board, comprising Dermot Keane, Brian Keane, Bill O'Connor, Karl Curran and Catherine Walsh is due to have its first meeting next week and the main item on the agenda is how to grow the business over the next five years. Brian wonders how his father will deal with the new governance culture he is trying to create at the company. He is hopeful that Catherine's appointment, in conjunction with Karl's, will provide a powerful counter to the dominant force that is his father and Bill.

Brian is proud of the business his father has built and grown organically since its foundation. However, Brian wants now to take it to the next level, growing the company by acquiring complementary businesses, both domestically and internationally. In doing so, he is confident that Karl Curran will keep him and the company on track financially, advising him against making any crazy decisions. Brian understands that his father, Dermot, is risk averse and very reluctant to follow such a strategy. If he could get his father to buy in to the acquisition strategy, he would really value his input and support. Dermot's depth of knowledge of the industry is immense. However, he is biased towards maintaining the status quo and it will be hard to change his mind.

Dermot Keane has no intention of allowing his son and the two new directors to change what he regards as a governance process that has worked very well at the company for many years. He asks the advice of his friend, Bill O'Connor, who explains that as chair, he is responsible for running the board and can influence board discussion and outcomes as a result. As such, according to Bill, he can be disruptive to the company's board meeting process. Bill promises that he "has his back".

Dermot is proud of his son, but Brian would not be where he is if it were not for Dermot's hard work over more than 20 years. He feels let down that Brian wants to change things and perceives these changes as an indictment of his years at the helm. He does not see the need for formalising the company's board meetings nor why it is necessary to pay Catherine Walsh €15,000 annually when Bill O'Connor has offered his services *pro bono* to date.

Bill O'Connor is managing partner of a successful law firm and is very comfortable financially. He does not like to see his old friend so upset at the changes his son is looking to implement at his company. Bill thinks that Brian is "getting too big for his boots". He has heard about the new director, Catherine, and cannot imagine that she will add much to the board as she knows nothing about the industry. He is confident that the informality of the board meeting process has not held the company back. Having heard that Catherine is going to be paid for her director's role, Bill has sent Brian a note expressing an expectation that he will be remunerated going forward on at least equivalent terms.

Prior to accepting the non-executive director role at Keane Manufacturing, Catherine requested that Brian appoint a Company Secretary to help in preparing for board meetings. Brian has outsourced the Company Secretary role and services to A-Back Services Ltd. In advance of the first meeting of the new board, Catherine decides to try to influence proceedings from the outset. She calls the Company Secretary and asks that an open draft agenda be circulated to all directors. She asks the Company Secretary to ensure that the chair signs off on the agenda.

Following input from Karl and Brian, Catherine includes the following on the agenda for the first board meeting:
- ratification of director appointment and the appointment of A-Back Services Ltd for provision of company secretarial services;

- vision, mission and strategy of the company;
- role of the board of directors;
- proposal to establish a risk register;
- risk identification, reporting and monitoring procedures;
- conflicts of interest policies and procedures;
- prior month's management accounts;
- any other business.

The Company Secretary calls Catherine and tells her that Dermot did not add anything to the agenda, only commenting that "it was fine, although all a bit pointless".

Required

(a) Consider the corporate governance environment, procedures and structures in place at Keane Manufacturing Ltd.
(b) Do you think that Brian has approached this situation in the right way? Why?
(c) What would you do if you were Dermot?
(d) What challenges does Catherine face in her new role as an independent non-executive director on the board of Keane Manufacturing Ltd? If you were Catherine, how would you approach these challenges?
(e) If you were engaged as a consultant to assist this company, outline five measures that you would recommend.

Case 5

HYTR Construction Ltd

Collette Kirwan,
Waterford Institute of Technology

Henry Taylor is the founder of HYTR Construction Ltd, a company trading for 15 years. Henry holds 80% of the equity share capital in the company. Denis Buckley, a retired engineer, holds 10% of the equity share capital. Vicky Kenny, a well-known business person, holds the remaining 10% equity share.

Before his retirement, Denis Buckley provided engineering services to HYTR Construction Ltd. When Henry heard about Denis' retirement, he immediately approached Denis and asked him to join the board of HYTR Construction as a non-executive director. By way of compensation, Henry offered Denis a 10% equity share in HYTR Construction Ltd. When Denis joined the board, the net asset value of HYTR Construction Ltd was minimal.

Henry has always admired Denis and the successful engineering business that Denis built. During the five years that Denis has been on the board, a close mentor–mentee relationship has developed between Denis and Henry.

As mentioned above, the reminder of the equity share capital is held by Vicky Kenny, a business person with equity interests in a number of businesses. Vicky also has a large property portfolio. Fourteen months ago, Henry asked Vicky to join the board of HYTR Construction Ltd as a non-executive director. Denis thought that Vicky's knowledge of the property market would help him plan for his eventual retirement. (Henry hopes to retire early and to fund his retirement from rental income.) To keep the two non-executive directors on a level standing, Henry also offered Vicky 10% equity in HYTR Construction Ltd. However, Vicky paid full value for her equity holding.

Recently, Vicky met Henry at a race meeting where Henry made a point of introducing Vicky to his partner, Martina Blake. This surprised Vicky because, despite Henry's introduction, Vicky had already met Martina in a business capacity: Martina's firm, Blake & Associates, provides architectural services to HYTR Construction Ltd. During a brief conversation with Martina, Vicky learnt that Henry and Martina had bought a house together within the past few months, and that the house had required major refurbishment work.

A few days later Vicky met with Denis to discuss the upcoming annual general meeting (AGM) of HYTR Construction Ltd. A few weeks previously, the financial statements of HYTR Construction Ltd had been circulated to the board of directors, along with the agenda for the AGM. During her meeting with Denis, Vicky recounted how she had 'bumped into' Henry and Martina, and how Henry had introduced Martina as his partner. Denis also knew Martina as managing partner of Blake & Associates, but neither Vicky nor Denis were aware that Martina and Henry were in a relationship. Denis then raised with Vicky his concerns that the level of architectural fees paid by HYTR Construction Ltd to Martina's firm had increased significantly during the past few months. They agreed that they would raise their concerns about this with Henry at the forthcoming AGM.

The AGM of HYTR Construction Ltd commenced like previous AGMs of the company: Henry welcomed Vicky and Denis to the meeting and provided a brief overview of the company's performance for the last 12 months. Then the financial statements were presented. At this point, Denis raised his concerns regarding the level of architectural fees being paid by the company. Henry answered with a detailed justification of the fees, explaining that they were linked to the activities of the business, specifically to the increase in the number of tenders the company had submitted. Denis asked why these tenders had not translated into new contracts, to which Henry responded: "increased competition". Denis and Vicky carefully listened to Henry's explanation, which seemed reasonable, even convincing. Henry, who was chairing the meeting, moved onto the next item on the agenda.

Required

(a)   Discuss the potential issues in relation to the provisions of services by Martina's firm.

(b)   What course of action should Denis and Vicky take?

Case 6

A Company at the Crossroads: Preparing for the Future

Chris O'Riordan,
Waterford Institute of Technology

Paul and Michelle Joyce are twins (47 years old). Both are 50% shareholders in Joyce Chemicals Ltd, a manufacturer of chemical materials used in the production of industrial cleaning products. While the company does produce some generic materials, the significant majority of its income comes from the production of patented chemicals that it has developed itself. Currently, 570 people are employed at its two factories in County Louth; the company employs a further 100 staff throughout Europe and the US in sales and marketing roles.

Joyce Chemicals weathered the storm of the financial crisis and has since delivered consistently increasing profits, largely due to the success of two products, DC101 and DC555, both of which are market leaders in the industry. The patents for these two products were developed over a number of years by Paul and Michelle's father, Gerry, an internationally renowned industrial chemist. Gerry Joyce died two years ago, aged 73. Until his death, Gerry was an active member of the board of directors, serving in the role of research director. Gerry was also the majority shareholder in the company (80%), while Paul and Michelle each held 10%. Gerry's will decreed that both Paul and Michelle would receive his shareholding in equal parts as they were his only surviving relatives (his wife had passed away 10 years previously). Paul has worked in the company since completing a science degree in 1994. Michelle joined the company on a full-time basis in 2010, having completed undergraduate and postgraduate degrees in marketing and worked as an advertising executive in London.

The company's financial controller, Mark Williams, has recently raised some concerns about the future of Joyce Chemicals Ltd. In 18 months, the patents for both DC101 and DC555 will expire, which will allow competitors to produce generic versions of the chemicals. As a result, both the sales price and sales volumes of these products will fall drastically, reducing Joyce Chemicals' profits to minimal and unsustainable levels over, at best, a two-to-three-year period. Both Paul and Michelle are very worried about this, though they are also encouraged by reports from the company's research and development division about four new chemical products that are in various stages of testing. The indications are that at least three of these products should be suitable for the market and, if put into production, will be even more profitable than DC101 and DC555.

To bring these new products to market, however, the company will need a capital injection of €110 million. This is vastly in excess of the resources available to the company's two shareholders, Paul and Michelle. While they both are wealthy on the back of the company's success, their assets are not particularly liquid and they are reluctant to 'put all their eggs in one basket'. They would each be willing to personally commit up to €5 million, but cannot go beyond this. They have spoken with a number of banks and understand that debt finance of €10 to €20 million is obtainable, though the banks are reluctant to lend more, as the company is currently running a substantial overdraft. While Paul and Michelle have, quietly, put out inquiries to see if there would be individual investors interested in buying into the equity of the company, this has been inconclusive. As a result, they are both in agreement that now is the time to pursue an IPO (initial public offering) on the Alternative Investment Market (AIM).

Currently, there are three directors on the board of Joyce Chemicals. Paul is the CEO, a role he has held since he joined the company. Michelle is the sales director and is also the Company Secretary. In addition to the two executive directors, Joseph Nolan is a non-executive director and – on paper at least – the chair of the board. Joseph is an old friend of Gerry and was appointed to the board 10 years ago (by Gerry) to give "an outside, alternative perspective" to decisions and as a support to Paul and Michelle when Gerry finally stepped down from the board. Now in his mid-sixties, Joseph lives in Sweden, to where he retired last year after finishing his full-time job as a senior executive in an international bank based in Dublin. As the non-executive director/chair, Joseph is paid a nominal annual fee plus expenses. He remains committed to his role with Joyce Chemicals because of his friendship with Gerry, though he has also acknowledged that traveling to Ireland for board meetings is becoming more difficult.

Largely because of this, and given that Paul and Michelle are both on site all of the time, the board of Joyce Chemicals has not met in over 10 months. Paul does send the occasional e-mail to Joseph, as a matter of courtesy, to let him know what decisions they have made, while Michelle sends him documents to sign when needed. Joseph does not seem to be concerned about any of this and is happy to work away on this basis. Recently, Joseph suggested to Paul that Catherine Nolan – Joseph's daughter – be brought on to the board as a further non-executive director. Catherine is 25 years old. She is completing a training contract as a legal professional at an international law firm in Dublin. Catherine is interested in the non-executive director role as she feels that it would enhance her CV and she has indicated that she would attend board meetings when she has the time. In addition, Catherine would like to gain experience in industry and had discussed this with Michelle. Therefore, it is decided that Catherine will join the company in two capacities; as a non-executive director and assisting Michelle with the Company Secretary role.

Paul Joyce is quite happy with how the company is being run at present: he is close to the action, there is a lack of interference with his decisions and everything operates efficiently. Michelle openly admits that she does not have much interest in the management or administration of the business – her talent is for marketing and as long as she is focusing on this area, she is content to go along with Paul's wishes. Going forward, while Michelle and Paul acknowledge that they may need to change the company's structure to some degree if it is to evolve, they want to keep such change to a minimum – the simpler and more streamlined the better, as this was the approach that brought their father success.

Required

Paul and Michelle have asked for your insights and suggestions.

Case 7

'Bob's Place': Doing Good the Right Way

Chris O'Riordan,
Waterford Institute of Technology

In late 2016, three friends – Pat Maher, Maureen O'Rourke, and Amy Brennan – met to mourn the recent passing of their neighbour, Bob Walker. Bob was a solicitor and, while he had a successful practice, he was also well-known in his local community for the help that he gave to people in considerable financial difficulty. This help was in the form of providing people with free advice and representing them in any legal proceedings (at no cost to them) arising from these difficulties. During the financial crisis, which had hit the community very hard, Bob spent most of his time on this *pro bono* work, even while he bravely fought a long-term illness.

Sharing their memories of Bob, Pat, Maureen and Amy agreed that the advice that he had given was hugely valued by those who received it, and that such a support service was still needed by people in the locality. They started to form a plan for a community-based initiative to continue Bob's legacy. A centre would be developed (called 'Bob's Place') where people in financial difficulty could come to speak in confidence with appropriate professional advisors, including solicitors, accountants and counsellors, as the centre would aim to help people in a variety of ways during challenging times in their lives. Professional advice would be offered free-of-charge to anyone who needed it, while the costs of the centre would be covered by fundraising and donations.

Through some of his business contacts, Pat was able to source an unused office space with three separate rooms at no cost for six months. Pat, Maureen and Amy furnished the office with spare tables and chairs from their own houses, and a local business agreed to cover the costs of the centre's utilities for half a year. Within four weeks of Bob's death, the centre opened its doors for the first time. Through local media coverage, posters and door-to-door flyers, the community became aware of 'Bob's Place' and people began to enquire about its services. Both Maureen and Amy, as solicitors, committed to each give up to eight hours a week of their time to the centre for six months, while Pat (a school principal) agreed to handle all the administration and basic book-keeping.

Six months on and 'Bob's Place' is constantly busy. In the *pro bono* hours they each committed to working at the centre, Maureen and Amy are unable to cater for all of the people seeking their assistance. They cannot commit any more of their time for free to the project. As a result, they are now hiring in solicitors – at hourly market rates as required – to work with people. In addition, the centre hires in a qualified accountant and a counsellor – also at hourly market rates as required – to further enhance the service offering at 'Bob's Place' for those who need it. These professional fees and the other running costs of the centre are being paid through fundraising and charitable donations. Pat is increasingly involved in co-ordinating events raising funds on behalf of 'Bob's Place'. He regularly attends these events on behalf of the centre, collecting all cash raised and banking this once a week.

With all of the extra work, the three original founders of the centre decide to bring in more people and establish a management committee. Three new members join the management committee: Martin Redwood (a quantity surveyor, who owns a number of local rental properties); Karen Murphy (an engineering lecturer); and Frank Power (a solicitor, who was already doing paid work for the centre and who also does work for a number of financial institutions). Martin is Amy's brother-in-law, while Karen is Maureen's first cousin and a neighbour of Pat. Other individuals with business backgrounds had indicated their willingness to join the management committee, but Maureen says that she is not in favour of them coming on board. When pressed, she refuses to give her reasons but is adamant that it would be "them or me".

At the first management committee meeting, it is agreed that all professionals (including Maureen and Amy) will be paid for services provided, but at a rate 5% below market rates to reflect that that they are working for a community group. In addition, Pat indicates that the centre needs to employ a part-time administrative assistant, as he has to reduce his day-to-day involvement. Pat agrees to accept the position as chair of the management committee and is unanimously elected to the role. As Pat is already the sole signatory on the centre's bank account (which is in his name), it is expected that this will have no material impact for the centre. Frank advises the management committee that he wants to take responsibility for fundraising co-ordination, as he has some ideas as to how they can generate more revenue, including seeking 50% part-payments from those availing of the service, which would be paid directly to the professional advisor involved. He argues that this will reduce the centre's costs, while still delivering value to service-recipients. A majority of the management committee agree with this proposal, though Pat and Karen vote against it.

After the meeting, Pat and Karen privately discuss the outcome of the vote as they remain dissatisfied. While respecting the views of the majority, they are concerned that the processes followed by the management committee may not be appropriate and sufficiently rigorous. 'Bob's Place' has grown in size and complexity, but its structures and procedures have not. Much of what they have done up until now in terms of governance processes and procedures is very informal, and little is written down. The problem is that Pat and Karen do not know where to start. As an organisation, they had started small and thus wanted to take small, gradual and realistic steps in making improvements, but with the goal also to future-proof and protect the centre.

Required

Your firm has been approached by Pat and Karen to give appropriate and relevant professional advice on the governance structures and procedures at 'Bob's Place', with an emphasis on prioritising actions that they need to take. They have also asked you to extend your advice, where you see fit, into other areas of importance.

Case 8

Zaba Plc

Anthony Burke and Richard Burke,
Waterford Institute of Technology

Zaba Plc is a large European event management company. Its main business is organising destination weddings for people across Europe. In addition, it arranges international walking tours, retreats and group holidays. Last year, the company organised over 300,000 events predominately in Spain, Portugal and Italy. Recently, Zaba Plc planned weddings in Greece for the very first time. Since commencing trading in 2003, the company has performed well and generated significant wealth for its shareholders. Dividends have grown at an average rate of 5% per annum over the past seven years.

Zaba Plc's board is responsible for choosing which country will host its flagship wedding fair each year, which attracts a large worldwide audience of attendees. Martha Rollings is the current chair of the board. She has been in the role for 15 years, or for five terms, each term in office being three years. In the most recent election for the position of chair, Rollings received 80% of the available votes. She offered holiday vouchers each worth €2,000 to a number of board members prior to the election. In a statement about the matter, Rollings said: "These people are working very hard for our company so the least I can do is provide them with a token of my appreciation for all their dedication and efforts." Rollings believes that her continuity as chair of the board of Zaba Plc is vital for the effective functioning of the company, stating that:

> "Nobody understands wedding functions or holidays better than me, nor do they have the capacity to choose the optimum destination for our clients. I am in the best position to make key decisions regarding the choice of destination weddings and I do not welcome the interference of others in this process."

There are currently 10 members on Zaba Plc's board, including the chair (Rollings), three senior executive directors and five other executive directors. The board currently has only one non-executive director, Tracy Power, who is a former colleague of Rollings and who is paid a large salary each year by the company for undertaking this role. The current composition of the board is provided in **Table 1** below.

Board Member	Job Title	Years on the Board
Martha Rollings	Chair	15
Maria Taylor	Senior marketing executive	3
Laura Silva	Senior finance executive	6
Gloria Walsh	Senior operations executive	9
Harry Roche	Business development executive	6
Kevin Jacobs	Marketing executive	6
Jessica Nolan	HRM executive	12
Kate Hobbs	Purchasing executive	9
Samantha Jackson	Supply chain executive	6
Tracy Power	Non-executive director	9

TABLE 1: THE BOARD OF ZABA PLC

At a recent board meeting it was decided that the 2019 wedding fair should be held in Italy. However, after the meeting, the senior finance executive, Laura Silva, who lives in Southern Portugal, and who worked for a district council in Portugal before joining Zaba Plc, telephones Martha Rollings to argue passionately that the 2019 wedding fair be held again in Portugal. The wedding fair has been held in Portugal for the past six years, despite both Spain and Italy expressing strong interest in hosting the event. Laura argues:

> "There is no need to move the wedding fair away from Portugal, Martha. We get many people there every year for the event and everybody enjoys it. We are making huge profits for our shareholders and as long as we continue to do that they won't really care about where we hold the wedding fair."

Following her telephone discussion with Laura Silva, Rollings reverses the decision of the board to hold the wedding fair in Italy and decides that it will take place in Portugal in 2019.

At the same recent board meeting, it was also decided that Zaba Plc will continue to organise events in Spain, Greece, Portugal and Italy. Two board members tried to introduce some alternative ideas, including the suggestion that they expand into some other countries; however, Rollings did not afford these ideas any time or consideration. Following the meeting, two executive directors approached the senior marketing executive, Maria Taylor, and expressed their dissatisfaction with Rollings. The first of these board members, marketing executive Kevin Jacobs, states that:

> "We feel that Cyprus should be included as one of our wedding destinations as it is a country that has developed rapidly in recent times. However, Martha shut this idea down, telling us that there is little or no interest in Cyprus as a wedding destination."

Human resource management (HRM) executive Jessica Nolan also expresses her concern to Taylor about how her ideas were totally dismissed by Rollings at the meeting:

> "We also believe that there is a need to expand the reach of our business; for us, this could be the Caribbean, even Australia, as people are looking further afield when organising their weddings. Our market research suggests that this would considerably increase the revenue the company generates. However, we were knocked back straight away and told that we don't have a clue about organising destination weddings."

Martha Rollings' stewardship of the company has attracted external attention. A newspaper recently reported that she and two senior executive members on the board accepted gifts of holiday homes from one of Zaba Plc's current suppliers. In response to these revelations, Rollings stated:

> "The gift of the holiday homes was as a result of us bringing extra business to these companies. They just wanted to say thank you, which is nice, as you often end up generating considerable business for suppliers and get little or no thanks."

It has also emerged that Zaba Plc only held three board meetings last year.

Required

Briefly comment on the structure of Zaba Plc's board and comment on the other corporate governance issues raised in the case.

Case 9
Science-Force

Collette Kirwan,
Waterford Institute of Technology

Science-Force is a not-for-profit organisation established in April 2009 by Margo Fitzwilliam. The organisation's mission is to promote and support females to pursue careers in the sciences. The organisation engages with 10 to 18-year-old females through school initiatives, after-school workshops and summer science camps. More recently, Science-Force, in partnership with a number of corporate entities, has arranged summer internships for 16 to 18-year olds who have applied, or are interested in applying, for third-level science courses.

Margo trained as a biotechnologist and worked in the agri-food sector. Her personal experience inspired her to establish Science-Force, particularly her disappointment that relatively few females pursue careers as scientists, and fewer still are promoted to positions of leadership in industry, government agencies and academia.

Six months after establishing Science-Force, Margo persuaded her college friend, Charlotte Watson, a secondary school science teacher, to join her in running things on a voluntary basis and in her spare time. In 2012, Margo left the agri-food industry behind and became the full-time chief executive officer (CEO) of Science-Force. Six-months later, Charlotte joined Science-Force as its full-time chief operating officer (COO). Both executive positions are salaried. Today, in addition to the CEO and the COO, Science-Force employs a further 10 full-time equivalent staff members.

As Science-Force began to grow, Margo needed assistance and expert advice from a wider group of people and, in the year she became full-time CEO, she put together a board of directors to support the mission of the organisation. Today, the board consists of six non-executive directors. Two non-executive directors have been on the board since its inception and both share Margo's passion for the purpose Science-Force was set up. They consider themselves the custodians of the organisation's values and mission. Of the other four non-executive directors, two have been on the board for the last four years, while the other two joined the board two years ago. Collectively, these four, more recent non-executive directors have a mix of experience and expertise including financial, legal, fund-raising and marketing (see **Table 1**).

TABLE 1: BOARD OF DIRECTORS OF SCIENCE-FORCE		
Non-executive directors	**Duration on the board**	**Experience/Expertise**
Alice Green	6 years	Professor of science in an Irish university
Mark Summers	6 years	Medical consultant in a private hospital
Josh Bain	4 years	Accountant and financial controller in a large private entity
Victoria Huse	4 years	Marketing executive and owner of a marketing agency
Liz Baker	2 years	Lawyer in a medium-sized law firm
Karl Stiles	2 years	Fund-raising executive in a large international charity

Alice Green is the chair of the board and Josh Bain is its Secretary. Although Margo and Charlotte are not directors, they attend all board meetings. However, when the board discusses matters pertaining to the performance of Margo and/or Charlotte, both are asked to leave the meeting.

The board's annual strategy meeting is taking place. The main topics for discussion are:

1. the organisation's fund-raising strategy; and
2. the remuneration of Margo Fitzwilliam.

Matter 1: Science-Force's Fund-raising Strategy

A US pharmaceutical company, with significant business interests in Ireland, has offered to provide substantial funding to Science-Force. Karl Stiles informs the board that the level of funding available would allow Science-Force to double its outreach and educational efforts. However, Margo expresses significant concerns about accepting financial support from the US company, which, she informs the board, has recently been publicly criticised for the lack of female representation on its own board (in fact, the US company has no female board members) and the small percentage of senior management positions in the US company held by women.

Moreover, a group of female employees are currently pursuing a legal case against the US company, claiming gender-based pay discrimination. Both Margo and Charlotte express deep concerns that being associated with such a company could damage the reputation of Science-Force.

Karl Stiles replies, arguing that the funding should be viewed simply as a means to a greater end. Josh Bain supports Karl and informs the board that such funding would secure the long-term viability of Science-Force. However, Margo is adamant that Science-Force should not accept funding from the US company and she states that her conscience would not allow her to continue to work for Science-Force if this funding is accepted. Both Alice Green and Mark Summers support Margo. Victoria Huse suggests that, with the right public relations management, any potential reputational damage could be minimised. Liz Baker states that the board must remember why Science-Force was established and that the funding on offer would allow the organisation to achieve its mission to a much greater extent.

Alice, who thinks that the funding discussion is going around in circles, then suggests moving onto the next item on the agenda.

Matter 2: The Remuneration of Margo Fitzwilliam

The next item on the agenda is Margo's remuneration. Therefore, Margo and Charlotte excuse themselves from the room. Alice informs the board that, in accordance with the policy of the organisation, the board is required to approve Margo's remuneration for the forthcoming year. Josh Bain raises a concern he has regarding recent publicity surrounding the remuneration of senior executives, including CEOs of not-for-profit organisations, noting that much of the debate in the media has focused on the appropriateness of financially rewarding senior executives with donations from the public, corporates and/or government. Having listened to the points raised by Josh, both Liz Baker and Karl Stiles express concerns that Margo's remuneration might be viewed as excessive by external parties. However, Alice reminds the board that Margo is the driving force behind the organisation and has taken it to where it is today. Mark Summers remarks that, in the current job market, attracting someone of Margo's capabilities would require remuneration significantly in excess of the amount she is currently paid, adding that he is doubtful anyone else would have the passion and motivation that Margo has for Science-Force and its mission.

Karl Stiles, still annoyed by Margo's resistance to the funding on offer from the US pharmaceutical company, suggests that perhaps the board should hire a recruitment company to search the market for appropriately qualified and experienced CEOs. He argues that the board will never know if a better CEO is out there unless they look and perhaps it is time that the board identifies Margo's successor. Alice, who does not like the direction in which the discussion is heading, intervenes and states that Margo's position as CEO is not on the agenda for today's meeting.

Margo and Charlotte re-join the meeting but, as it is late in the afternoon, Alice suggests that a follow-up special board meeting be convened later in the month. This would allow board members more time to think about the two matters and, hopefully, at the next meeting, agreement can be reached about the appropriate courses of action.

As everyone leaves the room, Mark Summers approaches Margo and informs her about the discussion that took place regarding her remuneration. He also tells Margo that if the board decides to accept funding from the US company, he will resign from the board and report the funding matter to a friend of his, a public-interest journalist with a national newspaper.

As Karl drives home that evening it occurs to him that the resolution of one issue could help resolve the other; he is sure that a new CEO, young, ambitious and even willing to accept a lower salary, could be convinced of the merits of accepting funding from the US company.

Required

(a) Evaluate the contribution and performance of each individual who participated in the board meeting.
(b) Regarding the two outstanding matters, propose how these might be resolved and suggest how (if at all) consensus might be reached.

Case 10

Out with the Old and in with the New

Richard Burke, Chris O Riordan and Collette Kirwan, Waterford Institute of Technology

Pendable Plc is a company listed on the Irish Stock Exchange. It special-
ises in the manufacture of safety equipment used by companies operating
in many different sectors. Pendable Plc has a dispersed shareholder base,
with only a few shareholders having holdings of 3% of equity or more.
Pendable Plc survived the financial recession that began in 2008 relatively
intact. This was largely because of its highly conservative approach to risk
and its substantial cash holdings which, although declining, are not at or
approaching hazardous levels. Shareholders have remained committed to
the company throughout this time and its share price has grown year-on-
year at a steady but not spectacular rate. However, the company has paid
no dividend for a number of years.

In the last six months, the company has experienced some turmoil at board
level. Though the chair of 10 years retired as planned at the start of this
period, the CEO, who was expected to vacate his executive position and
become chair of the board, suddenly resigned after developing an acute and
severe health condition. In addition, the finance director, who was viewed
as the most likely successor to the CEO, also left the company when she
was headhunted by an international competitor. Because she was joining a
competitor, it was mutually agreed that her departure from the company
would be immediate. This all meant that, within the space of a few weeks,
Pendable Plc had lost its chair, CEO and finance director. Worse still, there
were no successors in place.

With the assistance of the remaining board members (four non-executive
directors and two executive directors) as well as the services of an international executive recruitment firm, Pendable Plc have appointed a new chair
and a new CEO. Both of these individuals, fortunately, can commence
work with the company at short notice.

Michael North (56 years old) joins as chair, having previously served as CEO of three listed companies in continental Europe, as well as filling a number of non-executive director roles in the US and Australia. Michael will retain two of these non-executive director roles for the foreseeable future. He has a reputation as someone who believes in the importance of detailed information and, wherever he has worked, he has always sought to be made aware of what is happening day to day. Temperament-wise, Michael is regarded as somewhat abrasive and argumentative. Directors who worked with him previously when he served as a CEO have suggested that he can adopt an autocratic style at management meetings, prioritising issues and items that he views as important without necessarily sharing his reasons. However, he has also been known to be a warm and engaging person in the right environment, someone who is willing to listen to what others have to say and take on board their perspectives.

At the request of Pendable's board, Michael has identified two people he would like to introduce as new non-executive directors: Patrick Smith and Rachel Thomas. Michael previously worked with both individuals and found them to be great sources of support and expertise. About Patrick Smith, he comments:

> "Patrick has worked for over 30 years in the financial services industry and I have known him for 20 years. He has a wealth of financial expertise, which this company is sadly lacking. His appointment will be extremely pertinent in terms of improving the level of financial expertise on the board."

Regarding Rachel Thomas, Michael adds:

> "I've known Rachel for over five years. She married my brother recently and has served on three other boards in high-profile companies. I think it would be crazy if we were to pass up on appointing her to the board. Before we know it, some other company will have snapped her up."

At the same time that Michael North became chair, Kate Lewis (37 years old) was appointed as Pendable's new CEO. Kate has never held a CEO position, though she had been Deputy CEO and Senior Vice President of a UK-based multinational professional services firm. She has also worked as an executive director in two private companies and has some non-executive director experience in a well-known international charity. Quietly spoken, she is known to be a reflective and a strategic thinker who likes to discuss ideas widely and seek consensus. Kate herself acknowledges, however, that delegation is not one of her strengths and that she can struggle to accept the assistance of others, particularly if she feels their input will interfere with her vision.

Kate is a firm believer in the merits of performance-related pay (PRP) and plans to introduce such a scheme for all staff and all executive and non-executive directors of Pendable Plc. She has considered the different models of PRP and holds the view that it might be better to link PRP to sales or profits, rather than the company's share price. In addition, Kate would like the board to reconsider the recent appointment of a new firm of external auditors. She worked in an organisation for which this firm had been the external auditor and, at the time, felt that the service that the audit firm provided was sub-standard. Furthermore, Kate believes that once the company has a strong internal auditor there will be no difficulties regarding the preparation, processing and review of financial statements.

Kate comments:

> "We need to carefully reconsider the appointment of the new external auditor. For the service they offer, they are extremely expensive. My experience is that once you have a strong internal auditor it makes everything plain sailing. There is less bureaucracy and cross-checking, and we can get on with trying to run the business and making money for our shareholders."

Kate also wants to amend the composition of the audit committee, which currently consists of three non-executive directors.

> "One non-executive and two executive directors should be more than sufficient for an effectively functioning audit committee. Like I said, we have a strong internal auditor so there should be very little work for the audit committee. Patrick Smith will also be joining the board and he has a wealth of experience regarding accounting and financial matters. In addition, we have a risk management committee in place, which means that there will be less for the audit committee to worry about."

In appointing the new chair and the new CEO, both the existing board of directors and the recruitment firm fully acknowledge that Michael and Kate each lack experience in the particular roles. However, their track records of success have been exemplary everywhere they have worked and their potential to continue this with Pendable Plc is regarded as being worth the risk.

At the same time, the board are very aware that now is the time to set up their governance correctly and future proof it. Consequently, they have asked your firm of consultants to prepare a short presentation to the entire board of Pendable Plc that will advise them on the roles and responsibilities of the different board members, how they should interact and demarcate these roles and responsibilities individually, and any changes that you recommend being made to the board and its structure. The board are clear that they are not looking for a "generic, stock presentation taken straight out of a textbook" but one that reflects the company's specific needs and, crucially, where they as a board need to improve.

Required

Prepare the presentation as requested by the board and deliver this accordingly to the members.

Case 11

Shun Ltd

Collette Kirwan,
Waterford Institute of Technology

The photograph opposite depicts a meeting of the board of directors of Shun Ltd, a medium-sized electronics company. Starting on the left of the photo and moving clockwise, the first person is Derek, a non-executive director of Shun Ltd and the executive finance director of Bot Ltd, a long-standing customer of Shun Ltd. Next is Jim, the executive finance director of Shun Ltd and sitting beside Jim is Mark, the Company Secretary. The person standing is Bill, the CEO of Shun Ltd. He joined the company five years ago and has grown the business significantly in that time. Rob, sitting at the top of the table, is the non-executive chair of the board of Shun Ltd. He is a partner in a law firm. Next is Jeff, an executive director and the chief risk officer of Shun Ltd. Beside Jeff is Sarah, a non-executive director of Shun Ltd and the owner of a marketing consultancy business. Finally, at the bottom right is Liz, who is also a non-executive director of Shun Ltd and a HR expert.

The board are discussing a recent breach in the company's IT system which allowed the system to be hacked and information on employees, customers and suppliers to be accessed. The breach occurred because the company failed to upgrade its firewall software. Following the breach, immediate action was taken and the firewall software was updated. During the board meeting, the board discussed at length the causes and implications of the breach. Bill, Rob and Mark are debating how the board's discussion of the IT matter should be recorded in the minutes of the meeting. Because the weakness in the IT system is no longer an issue, Bill is recommending that the discussion should be recorded as: "A recent IT system upgrade was noted".

Required

Based on the information provided, both visual and narrative, comment on the boardroom dynamics.

Case 12

Neptune Plc

Rosemarie Kelly,
Waterford Institute of Technology

Neptune Plc, a large company listed on the Irish Stock Exchange, is based in Cork and manufactures luxury bathroom fittings including sinks, baths and shower trays.

The company holds monthly board meetings in its Cork offices. The board of directors of Neptune Plc is structured as shown below:

Director	Board Position
John Murphy	Chair
Peter Browne	Chief executive officer
Maria Smyth	Finance director
Karl Patten	Marketing director
Brendan Flynn	Operations director
David Tully	Non-executive director
Mark Deegan	Non-executive director

At a recent board meeting, two matters arising were discussed at length:

1. Though the company has been very successful over the past five years, Karl Patten, the marketing director, expressed concern about the increasing level of competition in the industry, stating that: "New entrants to the market quickly set up a website that is e-commerce-enabled and which they promote using digital marketing, including social media campaigns. This gives them the advantage of widespread brand recognition. We just about have a website with our contact details. Something must be done soon or we will lose business."

2. The chief executive officer, Peter Browne, noted that at the company's annual general meeting there were a number of requests from shareholders

to add another non-executive director to the board. In response, the nomination committee, comprising John Murphy, David Tully and Mark Deegan, have convened and developed a shortlist of three suitable candidates for the new non-executive director position. Their profiles are provided below.

Candidate 1: Joan Davitt

Aged 55, Joan Davitt lives in Dublin and is currently a partner in the accountancy firm of Lewis & Stone. She intends to retire from the firm in two years and is planning her retirement based on obtaining non-executive director roles. Currently, Joan serves as a non-executive director on the board of four financial services companies: two Irish-listed companies and two listed companies based in the UK.

Candidate 2: Jason Tan

Jason Tan is 63. He is originally from Malaysia and has lived in Cork for the past 30 years. He has been friends with Peter Browne since they were in university together. Last year, due to ill health, he took early retirement from his position as production manager in Bathworks Ltd. However, after treatment and convalescence he has now recovered fully. Bathworks Ltd is also in the bathroom fittings business and is a strong competitor of Neptune Plc. Jason has never served as an executive or non-executive director on the board of a company.

Candidate 3: Richard Smyth

Richard Smyth is the IT director for a large international online retailer and has particular expertise in the area of website development. He is 30 and lives in Galway, though his job requires a substantial amount of travel and on average he spends two months abroad each year. Currently, Richard is also a non-executive director on the board of an Irish publicly listed construction company.

Required

Review the profiles of each candidate and assess their suitability for the new position of non-executive director on the board of Neptune Plc.

Case 13

Viking (WM) Ltd

Collette Kirwan,
Waterford Institute of Technology

Viking (WM) Ltd is a waste management company providing waste collection and recycling services to over 150,000 household customers and 40,000 commercial customers. The company operates three separate divisions in Cork, Limerick and Waterford, and employs 240 people across its three divisions. The company has three shareholders: Mark Hynds (45% shareholder), Tom Brown (35% shareholder) and Paul Matthews (20% shareholder). Mark is married to Tom's sister Linda, who is the Company Secretary. Paul is not related to Mark or Tom. Paul became a shareholder two years ago when Viking (WM) Ltd was in financial difficulties and funds were needed to secure the future viability of the company.

The board of Viking (WM) Ltd consists of the following members:

Mark Hynds	Chief executive officer	Board member since the company's formation
Tom Brown	Chief finance officer	Board member since the company's formation
Eric Marino	Marketing director	Joined the board three years ago
Linda Hynds	Company Secretary	Board member since the company's formation
James Nolan	Non-executive director	Joined the board five years ago
Paul Matthews	Non-executive director	Joined the board two years ago
Tanya Langton*	Non-executive director	Joined the board two years ago

*Business partner of Paul Matthews

The following is the agenda for the board meeting scheduled to take place in two days.

| Board Meeting Agenda | |
| Location: Viking (WM) Ltd Boardroom | |
Agenda Item	Time
1 Distribution of board papers	10:30 am
2 Election of chair for the meeting (Note 1)	10:35 am
3 Apologies	10:40 am
4 Approve minutes from previous meeting	10:45 am
5 Matters arising from minutes of previous meeting	10:50 am
6 Arrangements for staff Christmas party	10:55 am
7 Review and sign-off of chief executive officer's expenses	11:15 am
8 Car parking restrictions at Cork division (Note 2)	11:30 am
9 Proposed acquisition of waste management company in Tipperary	12:00 pm
Review due diligence report	
Review proposed sources of funding	
10 Update on unfair dismissal case (Note 3)	12:30 pm
11 Review and approval of executives' salaries	12:45 pm
11 Review and agree budget for next financial year	12:50 pm
12 Agree arrangements for next board meeting	1:05 pm
13 AOB	1:10 pm
14 Meeting of non-executive directors (Note 4)	1:15 pm
Board meeting concludes	1:30 pm

Note 1: A rotating chair is elected for each board meeting. Therefore, each non-executive director takes turns chairing a meeting.

Note 2: Employees at the Cork division are experiencing parking restrictions due to construction works taking place adjacent to the Cork premises.

Note 3: A former executive director of Viking (WM) Ltd is taking an unfair dismissal case against the company claiming he was unfairly dismissed as a result of false accusations that were made against him by Paul Matthews.

Note 4: Normal practice at the company is that towards the end of board meetings, the non-executive directors have a separate session, without the executive directors being present. If instructed to do so by the chair, the Company Secretary stays to record matters discussed/agreed.

After board meetings conclude, board members convene to a local restaurant for lunch. For convenience, all board meetings are held on a Friday and often lunch continues into the afternoon or evening.

Required

Comment on:
(a)   the structure of Viking (WM) Ltd's board of directors;
(b)   the agenda of the meeting; and
(c)   the board processes described.

Case 14

GRB Ltd

**Margaret Cullen,
University College Dublin, Centre for Corporate**

Governance

GRB Ltd is a commercial semi-state company with a board of 10 members, comprised as follows:

- chief executive officer (CEO);
- finance director;
- chief operating officer (COO);
- three employee representative directors; and
- four independent non-executive directors.

One of the four non-executive directors acts as board chair and one acts as the senior independent director.

The last independent non-executive director joined the board in May 2017. The CEO, the finance director and the COO (the executive directors) are with the company for over 15, 10 and 8 years respectively, with the CEO being in the role for the last five years.

In January 2018, the three employee representative directors and the independent non-executive directors (excluding the chair) arrive at the boardroom for the monthly board meeting to find that the executive directors and the chair are not present. The senior independent director informs the two remaining non-executive directors that she has been asked by the chair to speak to the independent non-executive directors about the performance of the chair over the prior year as part of an internal board assessment. She was directed by the chair to conduct this discussion in the absence of the executive directors, the employee representative directors and the chair.

The two independent non-executive directors are taken aback as they have not been informed in advance that this discussion would take place before the board meeting. The senior independent director confides that it was only that morning that she was asked by the chair to hold this meeting. There is no agenda or terms of reference for the discussion and the senior independent director asks each director to give their opinion on how the chair performed in the previous calendar year. Meanwhile, unbeknown to the non-executive directors, the executive directors and the chair are waiting outside the room for the board meeting to start.

Though the two independent non-executive directors express their overall confidence in the chair, they also express their frustration at the lack of strategic focus at board meetings and the lack of decision-making around key issues. There is a sense that many key decisions are 'kicked down the road' and that the chair could do more to enhance the effectiveness of the board. After a 20-minute discussion, the senior independent director tells the two independent non-executive directors that the chair has been waiting outside, and expresses concern that the chair will be getting nervous if the independent non-executive directors continue to deliberate. She invites the chair to come in. The executive directors remain outside. The employee representative directors join the meeting as well.

Having jokingly acknowledged that he was indeed becoming nervous, the chair then says that he wanted to speak with all the non-executive directors about the performance of the executive directors over the prior year. The employee representative directors say that they are happy with how the board is operating, including the performance of the executive directors. However, the independent non-executive directors, including the senior independent director, raise a number of issues:

- **Issue 1**: The independent non-executive directors feel that they are never allowed time to deliberate or reflect on forthcoming meetings without the executive directors being present. Generally, they believe, the executive directors go out of their way to ensure that this does not happen at both board and board committee level. One independent non-executive director notes: "It's hard for us to get our ducks in a row. Having reviewed the board pack, I enter the board meeting with no idea of the perspectives of my fellow independent non-executive directors on what the board is about to discuss."
- **Issue 2**: In relation to board committees, it is noted with frustration that while membership of the audit committee and the remuneration committee should comprise independent non-executive directors only, employee representative directors and executive directors consistently attend the meetings of these committees, as do other members of staff.

- **Issue 3**: There is also general frustration among the independent non-executive directors that the executive directors are not effective in bringing strategic options or alternatives to the board. There is a sense that the executive directors are not really interested in the views of the independent non-executive directors and that they lack real focus on the challenges (economic and competitive) facing the organisation.
- **Issue 4**: One of the independent non-executive directors then observes that the employee representative directors do not demonstrate much challenge in the boardroom, a comment to which the employee representative directors take exception. The chair quickly states that this is not the forum for discussing such matters, thereby bringing this discussion to a close.

The executive directors enter the boardroom and the board meeting goes ahead.

Following the board meeting, the chair meets with the executive directors and relays the independent non-executive directors' views and feedback. The executive directors are indignant and the chair is forced to calm the situation. He undertakes to summarise the key points made by the independent non-executive directors and to circulate these in writing to the executive directors.

Three days later, the chair forwards a document to the employee representative directors and the independent non-executive directors, which he has already circulated to the executive directors, outlining the four issues raised with him by the independent non-executive directors.

Required

(a) Consider the approach adopted and behaviours displayed by the various parties (i.e. the chair, the senior independent director, the employee representative directors, the other independent non-executive directors and the executive directors).
(b) How could the situation have been managed more effectively?

Case 15

The Board Meeting: Debating the Old and the New

**Chris O'Riordan,
Waterford Institute of Technology**

The following is an extract from a board meeting:

Tom (chair): So, moving on to the re-appointment of our auditors. Smithson & Kearns have indicated that they are willing to stay on. They have indicated some control weaknesses within our company and have asked that these are responded to and addressed as soon as possible. I don't really understand the issues they are raising. Michael, do you have any observations here?

Michael (finance director): Thanks Tom, I do. To be honest, they are making mountains out of molehills here. There is nothing of substance in what they are raising, just more bureaucracy and paper pushing.

Patrick (non-executive director 1): But, didn't they cite some regulations and auditing standards ... whatever they are? They seemed quite adamant that the control issues be addressed. I can't comment in detail on this issue – as you know, my background is in marketing. But I don't think we should dismiss it out of hand.

Karen (CEO): I'm with Michael on this. Those auditors are a nuisance – everything is a checklist, generic questions, more work. I think they just stretch out the job and this stuff on internal controls is part of it. I don't have the time to be reviewing everything that they are asking me to do. I trust Michael, he's with us a lot longer than them and will be around long after they're gone. I mean, one thing they brought up ... the need for my signature to be on all large purchase requisitions. What happens when I'm traveling on business, which is often, or on holidays and we need something now? Michael knows what to do here and, anyway, my PA has a copy of my signature. He can just add it to the document if I'm not around. Call me and I will give it the OK.

Michael (finance director): I've discussed all of this with them – they need to be more practical. Another issue is asset tracking – they want us to put barcode labels on everything so that we can check that each item is here. We know they're here, we can see them! More rubbish and nonsense. And then when they pointed out that the expense rates we are paying to staff exceed the benchmark civil-service rates, I laughed at them. We have our own calculation of what is reasonable and I am not budging on this. There would be serious push-back from the staff; they value their expenses. These are just some of the issues – I could go on …

Tom (chair): From what I'm hearing, it sounds like Smithson & Kearns are a tad pedantic in their approach and that they have burned some of their bridges here. And I'm being generous in saying a *tad* pedantic! George, there is no need to minute any of this discussion!

George (Company Secretary): Don't worry Tom, I have been around long enough to know what to minute and what not to minute.

Tom (chair): Regarding this situation with the current auditors, what do you suggest we do Michael?

Michael (finance director): I want them out, pure and simple. I've had enough. Karen and I have been speaking with another firm. They are local, similar in size and are much more pragmatic. I play squash regularly with one of the partners and Karen went to college with the managing partner. We would be their biggest client by far, so you can be sure that we would get preferential service at a better price than charged by the current lot.

Karen (CEO): I agree, they will be easy to deal with and would like to take us on as it would be a prestigious client for them.

Tom (chair): This sounds good to me. As a soon to be listed company … well, in the next five years anyway … we need to get on with the job of satisfying our many existing and potential shareholders.

Patrick (non-executive director 1): And we would save some money on audit fees that could be funnelled into advertising. We need to do more on promotions.

Tom (chair): I think we are broadly in agreement. Claire, you are new to the board as a non-executive director and I know you have a financial background. Would you like to add anything to the discussion before we vote?

Required

You are Claire (non-executive director 2). What would you like to contribute to the meeting?

Case 16

Santiago Plc

Anthony Burke and Richard Burke, Waterford Institute of Technology

Santiago Plc is a Spanish car manufacturer. It was formed in 1982 and produces a wide range of models, ranging from sports cars to 'people carriers' for families. The car market has become increasingly competitive and this has resulted in Santiago Plc incurring losses of over €10 million per annum over the past three years. Regarding these losses, the CEO of the business has stated:

"The last three years have proven to be difficult due to a slowdown in demand for our existing models. This has meant that we have had to spend a considerable amount of money on research and development as we focus on developing the best family car in the marketplace."

As a result of the company's investment in research and development, its shareholders have received no dividends in the past three years. The company has also had to borrow additional funds and this has resulted in its capital gearing ratio increasing to 74%. This ratio has increased and the company is now primarily financed through loans and preference shares. Due to the high level of debt on its balance sheet, the company has struggled greatly with interest payments over the past five years. Santiago's share price has also begun to suffer and has decreased by 10% per annum over the past four years. At a recent investor conference call following a presentation of the annual results, the CEO stated:

"It is clearly a challenging time for Santiago Plc. What is required is patience and a continued commitment to excellence. We continue to be committed to our shareholders and to maximising wealth for our shareholders."

During the same conference call, referring to Santiago's mission statement, a senior marketing manager within the company added:

"Our long-term strategy is to develop the most competitive motor car in the marketplace for our customers and to become one of the biggest automobile companies in Europe. We remain committed to all our stakeholders with a particular emphasis on maximising the wealth of our shareholders."

To promote and drive sales of its new family car, Santiago Plc will be offering all customers a €6,000 scrappage deal for trading in their current cars for the new family car. It is also considering providing a 0% finance deal to help customers buy the new model.

Despite its poor financial performance in recent years, Santiago Plc has continued to be recognised for its excellent working conditions. In 2014, it built a multi-purpose gym costing €6 million for employees at its main factory in Madrid. It provides heavily subsidised meals in the staff restaurant. Workers' pay packets have also steadily increased at a rate of 4% per annum over the past five years. Staff morale is generally high. Senior management see the retention of key staff as vital for achieving future growth. One senior manager has commented:

"If we don't keep our best employees, what hope have we? They are our knowledge, our human capital and are integral to us attaining our key goals."

In order to boost the profile of Santiago Plc, the company has recently agreed to sponsor the local football team, who play in 'La Liga', the Spanish premier league. The sponsorship deal is expected to cost €24 million over four years, but senior management believe it will boost the profile of Santiago Plc as the company's logo will be displayed on the team's shirt.

In 2015, through a series of cost-cutting measures, Santiago Plc managed to reduce its annual losses by €4 million. For example, it cut the cost of some car components by 8% by sourcing their manufacture from a single supplier in Portugal. Previously, the company had outsourced the manufacturing of these same components to a number of local Spanish companies. Management felt that this was necessary due the losses incurred in recent years: "Although we would like to continue to use our domestic suppliers, it makes more sense to source our components from Portugal. Ultimately, this will result in better value for our shareholders."

Required

Evaluate how Santiago Plc balances the needs of its stakeholders with its shareholders' needs.

Case 17

Saved by the Bungee Jump

John Casey,
Waterford Institute of Technology

Education Print and Media (EPM) offers IT solutions to higher education institutions and provides online education programmes that it develops in-house. The company was founded by its current chief executive officer (CEO), John O'Mahony. It operates from Ireland but is registered and regulated in Malta. EPM was one of the first companies to identify the potential of technology in education and has grown over the past two decades into a large business with over 300 employees. It has been quoted on the Irish Stock Exchange for the past two years. In that period the value of the company has risen steadily and it now has a market capitalisation of €75 million (1,250,000 shares at a value of €60.00 each). (The most recent financial statements for EPM are provided below at Appendix I.) The company has ambitious goals to expand its operations across Europe.

The shareholding structure of EPM is as follows:

- John O'Mahony   25%   (founder and chief executive officer)
- Crystal VC Ltd   10%   (a venture capital, early-round funder)
- Peter Williams   5%   (angel investor, initial investor)
- Other executives   5%   (five current executive managers)
- Other investors   55%   (numerous unconnected institutional investors)

While the business is John O'Mahony's life work, he is keen to ensure that the company can evolve beyond its current structure. As part of a recent strategy 'away day' for the executive management team (the five executives plus John), there was a lively discussion on the longer-term sustainability of the company. A wide variety of views were aired and some of the views were, in John's opinion, irrelevant. He is reviewing the notes that he took during the day and, combined with his recollections of the discussions, he is attempting to bring a memo to the board that will address the governance issues that arose during the strategy away day.

John opened the initial discussion with a review of the history of the company followed by a passionate speech on the future of the business. He was keen to stress that he would not be around forever and that he wanted the 'cult of the personality' to be disentangled from the success of the business. He declared that this was going to be a 'blue-sky' type of session and that he would welcome any issues for discussion and suggestions for consideration.

As it transpired, much of this initial discussion focused on executive remuneration at the company. Mary, the chief technology officer (CTO), pointed out that in EPM the executive management team are paid a basic salary and, beyond a small shareholding, they have very little incentive to "really push the company's performance to the maximum". Similar technology companies use a range of ways to reward high-performing staff. Frank, the HR director, then suggested that there should be a bonus pool put in place that the executives could share among themselves should certain targets be met. Mary agreed, adding that a bonus pool of €7.5 million would not be unreasonable, to be paid out if the market capitalisation of the company doubled in the next five years. This, she noted, was sufficiently far in the future to avoid any 'short-termism' and the payback to the investors would be a company worth €150 million. Mary and Frank's suggestions received widespread approval among the other executives.

As a 25% shareholder in the company, John has seen his personal wealth appreciate considerably and he is aware and that his personal situation is very different to the other executives. Though he noticed that the mood of the room had shifted at the suggestion of the cash bonus pool, he was uncomfortable with the idea.

In an attempt to dampen expectations, John put forward a suggestion of his own. He passed around a copy of the most recent consolidated financial statements of the company (see **Appendix 1**) and turned the discussion towards the issue of the secured shareholder's loan. This loan is a legacy source of finance from the early days of the company. It is money lent to the company by John and it is repayable to John in its entirety. The loan is secured on the property of the company. While there is interest payable on the loan, the rate is lower than the equivalent commercial rate for a company with a similar risk profile. John's suggestion is that the proposed bonus pool would not be directly payable to the executives but would, instead, be converted into a secured loan on similar terms to the existing secured shareholder's loan. The executives would receive an annual 3% interest payment with the principal due to be repaid to the executives in five years' time. It would also, John added with certainty, greatly reduce the impact on the cash flow of the business as well as having much more favourable tax implications.

Edel, the Chief Financial Officer (CFO), who had been quiet up to that point, said that she would need to seek professional advice on the tax implications of such a loan, at which point there were hushed comments among the others. Though he did not write it down at the time, John asked himself: "what is the point of having a professional accountant when they have to get further professional advice on accounting matters?", and the murmurings in the room were along similar lines.

Edel advised caution on the secured loan idea, saying that under soon-to-be-implemented accounting rules, all operating leases will have to appear on the statement of financial position. This, along with the secured loan arising from the bonus pool, could have a materially negative impact on the gearing of the company. A number of side conversations broke out in the room: this was news to some; others simply did not understand what Edel was referring to or its implications.

Finally, John attempted to take back control of the discussion by clarifying that the company leases most of its IT equipment by way of operating lease agreements, under which the company is committed to repaying €12 million in the next four years. These leases are irrevocable and non-cancellable. The only security offered is the equipment itself because legal ownership of the equipment remains with the lessor. John added that this has always been the arrangement for the company and it has never had difficulty meeting the scheduled repayments. It is cheaper than taking out bank finance. He also noted that the company from which the equipment is leased is a specialist IT-leasing company, in which, by the way, his spouse is a 40% shareholder. This last revelation led to some laughter in the room. It was clear that this was new information to the others, but it did lower the liquidity risk of the company, albeit by an unquantifiable amount.[1]

---

[1] Liquidity risk is the risk that the company will not have the cash on hand to be able to meet its financial obligations on time. Liquidity risk is a timing issue – in this case it is a possibility (unquantifiable) that the IT-leasing company will not repossess its equipment as it will have better information on the true financial health of the business.

At this point the discussion was interrupted. It was time for the team bungee jump and while John was nervous at the thought of leaping off a bridge, he was relieved that this part of the strategy day had been cut short.

Required

Reflecting on the day, John realises that it did not all go as planned, but that many important issues did come to the surface. You are a qualified accountant and have acted as a mentor to John for many years. He has contacted you looking for advice on the memo that he is preparing for the board of directors. You have noted that he did not approach Edel for advice.

Appendix 1: Financial Statements of Education Print and Media

Education Print and Media
CONSOLIDATED STATEMENT OF FINANCIAL POSITION
as at 31 December 2017

	2017 €000	2017 €000	2016 €000	2016 €000
Non-current Assets				
Plant, Property and Equipment		6,225		6,600
Intangible Assets – R&D Expenditure		2,827		1,980
Intangible Assets – Goodwill		450		450
Long-term Investment		1,230		1,230
		10,732		10,260
Current Assets				
Inventory	5,925		8,450	
Receivables	5,550		3,210	
Cash	11,245	22,720	5,460	17,120
Total Assets		33,452		27,380
Equity				
Ordinary Share Capital	1,250		1,250	
Share Premium	1,100		1,100	
Revaluation Reserve	650		400	
Revenue Reserves	4,969	7,969	4,100	6,850
Non-controlling Interests		456		300
Total Equity		8,425		7,150

	2017	2017	2016	2016
	€000	€000	€000	€000
Non-current Liabilities				
Secured Shareholder Loan (APR = 3%)	6,880		6,750	
Secured Bank Debt (APR = 8%)	8,385		3,685	
Retirement Benefit Obligations	36	15,301	39	10,474
Current Liabilities				
Payables	7,500		7,441	
Overdraft (APR = 13%)	720		1,100	
Bank Loan (APR = 8%)	1,386		1,125	
Provisions	120	9,726	90	9,756
		33,452		27,380

Education Print and Media
CONSOLIDATED STATEMENT OF COMPREHENSIVE INCOME
for year ended 31 December 2017

	€000	€000
Turnover		10,000
Cost of Sales		(4,500)
Gross Profit		5,500
Distribution Costs	(500)	
Administration Costs	(545)	(1,045)
Operating Profit		4,455
Interest Paid		(1,065)
Profit before Tax		3,390
Taxation		(1,210)
Profit for the Year		2,180
Other Comprehensive Income		
Revaluation of Property		250
Total Comprehensive Income		2,430
Total Comprehensive Income attributable to:		
Equity Holders		2,130
Non-controlling Interests		300
		2,430

Education Print and Media
CONSOLIDATED STATEMENT OF CHANGES IN EQUITY
for year ended 31/12/2017

	Ordinary Share Capital €000	Share Premium €000	Revaluation Reserves €000	Revenue Reserves €000	Total €000	Non Controlling Interests €000	Total €000
Opening Balance	1,250	1,100	400	4,100	6,850	300	7,150
Total Comprehensive Income			250	1,880	2,130	300	2,430
Dividends				(1,011)	(1,011)	(144)	(1,155)
Closing Balance	1,250	1,100	650	4,969	7,969	456	8,425

Case 18

Bridge Return Fund Plc

Margaret Cullen,
University College Dublin, Centre for Corporate Governance

Bridge Return Fund Plc, an Irish domiciled, alternative investment fund, was launched on 1 July 2014. It is a product of Bridge Fund Promoters Ltd, a UK-based fund promoter. (See **Appendix 1** below for a figure describing the various parties to an investment fund.)

There is a performance fee attached to the fund (i.e. a fee payable to the investment manager, which is related to the performance of the fund compared to a specified benchmark), the wording of which is included in the investment fund prospectus. The performance fee is calculated by the fund administrator on an Excel spreadsheet.

Prior to finalising the performance fee wording, the custodian (the entity with regulatory oversight responsibilities for, including safeguarding the assets of, Bridge Return Fund Plc) requested that the administrator (which is responsible for valuing the Bridge Return Fund Plc) devise the performance fee model and that the appointed investment manager, Bridge Fund Managers Ltd, sign off on the following:

1. that the performance fee wording accurately reflects its intent from a performance fee perspective; and
2. that the performance fee model is an accurate reflection of the wording per the prospectus.

This sign-off was received and the wording and model was subsequently signed off by the custodian. The administrator and custodian are subsidiaries of the same economic entity, Investment Fund Services Inc. The fund's year end is 30 June. In January 2017, there was a change in the actual investment manager managing the fund within Bridge Fund Managers Ltd.

The fund did not generate a performance fee in the first two years post launch. However, a performance fee is generated in the year ending 30 June 2017. Per the fund administrator's calculation, the amount due to the investment manager is €1,780,350. On 17 July 2017, the investment manager requests confirmation from the custodian and the administrator of the performance fee payment due. This amount is provided. The audit of the fund is due to commence in mid-August.

On the 19 July, the investment manager reverts to the custodian suggesting that the amount of €1,780,350 is incorrect and that, per her calculations, the actual performance fee is €2,050,100. The incremental amount of €269,750 is immaterial in the context of the value of the fund. The investment manager claims that the model used by the administrator is not an accurate reflection of the performance fee wording and has provided her own model. While the model presented by the new investment manager could be deemed an alternative interpretation of the prospectus wording, the custodian refuses to approve the incremental payment on the basis that the original model was signed off by the original investment manager.

The investment manager has escalated the issue to the board of Bridge Return Fund Plc, which comprises the investment manager herself, one other director from the parent fund promoter organisation (who has been on the fund board since its launch), one non-executive director (who also acts as a lawyer to the fund) and another independent non-executive director who chairs the board. The investment manager has indicated to Investment Fund Services Inc that the administration and custody business will be pulled if the incremental amount is not paid. A board meeting of the fund has been scheduled to discuss the issue.

The chair of the board of Bridge Return Fund Plc is sympathetic to the approach adopted by the custodian and believes it to be the correct course of action. This viewpoint is not shared by the remaining fund board directors. The chair of the board has contacted the other non-executive director, who, while understanding the custodian's standpoint, considers it key that the amount in question is immaterial, and that the custodian should just approve the increased amount. The fund promoter director representing the parent organisation is concerned about upsetting the star investment manager.

Required

What is the conflict of interest issue here and how could it have been avoided? How has the board structure contributed to the complexity of the issue?

Appendix 1: The Various Parties to an Investment Fund and their Interactions

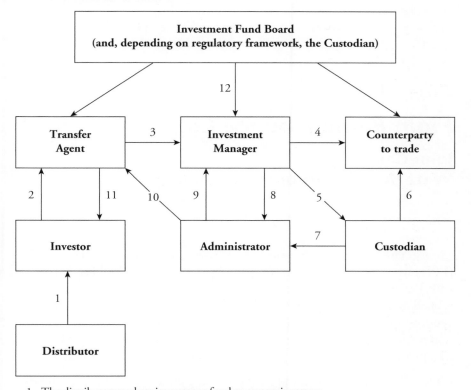

1. The distributor markets investment fund to targets investors.
2. The investor decides to invest in fund and contacts the transfer agent.
3. The transfer agent informs the investment manager of funds available from new investor.
4. The investment manager strikes a deal in the market ('counterparty' in the above figure) based on information received.
5. The investment manager advises the custodian of deals placed.
6. The custodian settles the trade on the market.
7. The custodian advises the administrator of deals placed.
8. The investment manager advises the administrator of deals placed.
9. The administrator agrees the fund valuation (net asset value) with the investment manager.
10. The net asset value is communicated to the transfer agent.
11. The investor is notified of the value of the investment.
12. The board of directors (and potentially the custodian) monitor the process.

Case 19

Plain Plane Finance Ltd

John Casey,
Waterford Institute of Technology

Eimear Power is a recent graduate working for Plain Plane Finance Ltd (PPF Ltd), an aircraft leasing company operating out of Dublin. Currently, PPF Ltd is trying to purchase a significant number of twin-engine, narrow bodied, mid-range jet aircraft and has been negotiating with its two preferred vendors. The total value of the aircraft is expected to be in excess of €500 million, which, while small in industry terms, is a major expansion for PPF Ltd. The finance is in place, and now suitable aircraft need to be sourced.

Eimear Power has been tasked with providing analytical support to the PPF executive responsible for negotiating the deal, Aisling Murphy. However, since the company is quite small, Eimear also becomes a sounding board for Aisling as she attempts to consider all aspects. Given the significant value of the aircraft purchase, she is understandably cautious in the negotiations. Nevertheless, Aisling has reached a decision and her selection is to go to the board of PPF Ltd for approval next week. Though only one of the two preferred vendors will be selected, no indication has been given to either vendor on their likelihood of success.

Work has been hectic. Eimear has spent the last few weeks criss-crossing the globe in an attempt to bring the deal to a conclusion. This morning, out of the blue, she gets a call from a third vendor, Airtrain, which has not been involved in the process up to now.

The caller is an old college friend of Eimear's, Mark Maloney, who is now working for Airtrain. He tells her that due to the recent cancellation of a major order, Airtrain has considerable spare capacity and there is a deal to be done that could be good for both PPF and Airtrain. Eimear points out that the current negotiations are all but complete, with only final board approval remaining. These are lengthy and complex arrangements, involving a large number of people on all sides, Eimear adds, and she and PPF would be reluctant to open up the possibility of a third vendor entering the fray at this late stage.

Mark is nothing if not tenacious and he dons the 'green jersey' saying that unlike the other two vendors, a large part of Airtrain's supply chain uses Irish companies. This deal would have significantly positive effects on these supplier companies, potentially guaranteeing Irish jobs that are currently under threat. This would also reflect well on PPF in political circles.

To Eimear's surprise, Mark offers to pay PPF €3 million to delay its final decision and allow Airtrain two weeks to put in a bid when Airtrain will then fly PPF's decision-makers to their corporate headquarters in Florida to view aircraft and hear more about Airtrain's proposal. In addition, Airtrain will cover any additional expenses associated with delaying the vendor-selection process and evaluating their offer.

Though her eyes light up when she hears Mark's offer, Eimear repeats her reluctance to re-open the bidding process, adding that she needs to spend time with her family, who have been neglected over the past few weeks. Mark immediately offers to fly Eimear's family to Florida to join her after the deal is done, with an option to stay on for a couple of weeks. Noting that it is not her decision, Eimear tells Mark that she will get back to him. She then heads straight for Aisling's office to tell her about the phone call.

Aisling beckons Eimear to come in and close the door, which is unusual, as office doors are usually left open at PPF. She listens impatiently to the details of Eimear's call with Mark, keen to tell Eimear news of her own.

Aisling is seething: she has just come from a senior management team meeting at which it was discussed how the business should manage its financial risks. The finance director (FD) presented a paper advocating a policy of not using financial derivatives to actively manage currency, credit, liquidity and interest rate rises, proposing instead that, where necessary, natural hedges[1] could be put in place. The FD believes that derivatives are too complex and costly, and that in the long run PPF would not gain any real advantage from their use. This approach to managing financial risk would, he argues, expose the company to other risks, which would then also need to be managed.

To put it mildly, Aisling disagrees with the FD and expresses again to Eimear her belief that PPF should take a more active approach to financial

---

[1] For example, matching foreign currency assets with foreign currency liabilities, or ensuring that sales (lease rental income) are euro denominated so as to match with euro-denominated out-goings (mainly salaries and loan repayments).

risk management, involving the use of financial derivatives. Aisling adds half-jokingly: "I mean, this is core to any course in finance or accounting. I sometimes wonder if he ever completed that degree in finance he claims to have."

There is a bit of 'history' between Aisling and the FD. In a previous aircraft-purchasing deal, he took all the credit for arranging a large financing agreement, though it was Aisling that made the contacts and did the work. It especially rankled with Aisling that the FD's annual bonus was greater that year, partly because of that deal. An experienced Chartered Accountant, Aisling is well qualified for the role of finance director at PPF, and she has not made it a secret that she wants the job.

Aisling is adamant that she is not going to let the financial risk management issue rest. She asks Eimear (as one of her direct reports) to prepare a short paper on why a company, in particular a finance company, should use financial derivatives to manage financial risk. Aisling would then take this paper to the senior management team and, if necessary, to the board.

Though Aisling is very capable and has taken an active interest in Eimear's career, Eimear is very uncomfortable with this request, as she feels that Aisling's motivation is her antipathy towards the FD. In addition, she feels that there is some merit in the approach to financial risk management that the FD is proposing.

Required

As she reflects on the various events and conversations of the day, what do you think are Eimear's main concerns? How would you propose addressing these concerns?

Case 20

Explore Plc

Niamh Brennan,
University College Dublin

Explore Plc is an Irish oil and gas exploration company, founded in 2001 and listed on the Irish Stock Exchange since 2008. Unexpectedly, in 2017, Explore Plc announced to the stock market that serious accounting irregularities had been uncovered at the company. To investigate the situation further, an international accounting firm was commissioned to undertake an in-depth review. It was also announced that both the chief executive, Paul Doyle, and the finance director, Ross Holden, were leaving the company with immediate effect. Many staff were relieved to see Paul Doyle leave Explore Plc, as they were afraid of him, finding him to be overly aggressive and unwilling to listen to the opinions of others.

Following the independent review by the international accounting firm, accounting irregularities totalling €75 million were uncovered. The accounting irregularities related to Explore Plc's under-provisioning for future restoration and dismantling costs, provisions required due to the purchase of drilling and exploration equipment.

When the audited financial statements for 2017 were published, they revealed €40 million reduction in profits in 2017, €20 million reduction in profits in 2016 and €15 million relating to prior periods, arising from the accounting irregularities.

Gerry Donovan, an accountant, joined Explore Plc in 2003; since then, Gerry has had a successful career at the company, being regularly promoted, eventually becoming senior finance officer in 2013, 'number two' to the finance director and a member of the senior management team.

In 2015, Gerry Donovan became very concerned about the possible under-provisioning of future restoration and dismantling costs. He regularly raised his concerns at senior management team meetings. However, the CEO, Paul Doyle, would become aggressive with Gerry at these meetings. On more than one occasion, Paul publicly challenged Gerry about his credentials and his loyalty to the company. Other staff were so frightened that they kept quiet, kept their heads down and did not publicly support Gerry, while privately sharing his concerns. In frustration, Gerry Donovan left Explore Plc in 2017, shortly before the accounting irregularities were revealed publicly.

Explore Plc operates a speaking-up ('whistleblowing') policy. This policy is made available to all relevant Explore Plc staff. The policy requires Explore Plc staff to raise concerns regarding inappropriate conduct or breaches of Explore Plc policy.

The whistleblowing policy specifically permits anonymous disclosures to be made by employees. The first paragraph of the whistleblowing policy contains the following highlighted in bold:

> "The objective of this policy is to encourage and enable employees to raise serious concerns within Explore Plc rather than overlooking their concerns or 'blowing the whistle' outside, to provide avenues for employees to raise concerns in confidence."

The whistleblowing policy is readily available to Explore Plc staff, by way of:

(a) a link to the policy on the Explore Plc intranet homepage; and
(b) a link to the policy on the Explore Plc human resources homepage.

Additionally, the whistleblowing policy is regularly emailed to all Explore Plc staff. For example, in an email in 2013, attaching the policy, the CEO explained:

> "Employees are frequently the first individuals to recognise malpractice. However, there is often a reluctance to voice suspicions or speak up for a range of understandable, if possibly misguided, reasons, including fear of disloyalty to colleagues or employer and/or fear of harassment or victimisation arising out of any disclosure.
>
> The aim of our Whistleblowing Policy is to address this reluctance and to encourage you to advise us of any malpractice or wrongdoing within Explore Plc of which you become aware.
>
> We believe that you should feel able to report any incidents of malpractice or wrongdoing without fear of recrimination, provided any such reports are based on genuine concerns and made without malice

or bad faith. This policy is intended to enable you to raise serious concerns, offering such safeguards and support as may be necessary to protect your personal integrity and, where possible, your identity. Please take the time to read the Whistleblowing Policy."

Required

(a)   What are Gerry Donovan's duties to 'blow the whistle'?
(b)   What provisions should be included in Explore Plc's whistleblowing policy?

Case 21
Xten Plc

**Niamh Brennan,
University College Dublin**

Martin Foley is a senior sales executive working for Xten Plc, an Irish company operating in the pharmaceutical sector, which is listed on the London Stock Exchange. One of the leading players in its sector, Xten Plc supplies generic drugs to private healthcare providers, public hospitals and pharmacies across Europe.

Martin reports to the sales director, Tom Taylor. Tom is reputed to be a very dominant character and is known throughout the company for being abrupt and at times aggressive, particularly when dealing with junior members of staff. However, Tom has a very close relationship with the company's chief executive officer. Moreover, the board of directors recognises and admires Tom's ability to negotiate significant contracts with new customers, enter new markets and grow market share. As a result, Tom Taylor's position in the company is considered to be untouchable, notwithstanding his treatment of staff.

During June and July 2018, the Competition and Consumer Protection Commission (CCPC) sends several written requests to Tom Taylor seeking copies of all contracts relating to pricing agreements between Xten Plc and a number of private healthcare providers operating in Europe. Tom becomes concerned about the CCPC's sudden interest in the activities of Xten Plc, especially when he hears from peers working in other pharmaceutical companies that they have also received requests for information from the CCPC.

Tom Taylor is concerned that the CCPC will decide to launch a full investigation and make an unannounced visit to the head office of Xten Plc. He instructs Martin Foley to gather together all documentation relating to contract negotiations between Xten Plc and its customers in the private healthcare sector, and to do so by the following Saturday, arranging to meet him then at the company's head office.

On Saturday at Xten Plc's HQ, under Tom's instruction Martin begins altering certain documents relating to contract negotiations between Xten Plc and its customers. Tom explains to Martin that while the pricing arrangements in place between Xten Plc and certain customers "stretch the boundaries of what's permitted by the pricing agreements set by various governments", he believes that the end result is to customers' benefit:

> "Our customers are paying less for certain drugs, including life-saving drugs, compared to the prices they would have to pay if Xten Plc followed the strict and unfair regulations forced upon the pharmaceutical industry."

A few weeks later, in August 2018, Tom Taylor asks Martin Foley to assist him in making additional alterations to documents. At Tom's request, Martin contacts Sally Burke, a junior sales executive, and asks her to assist him. Martin shows Sally what alternations are required. Moreover, at Tom's request Martin removes certain documents from the company's central files and places them in a safe in Tom's office. Tom reassures Martin that the documents will be returned to the files in due course. Sally is unsure why such documents are being altered and removed. However, her gut feeling is that something is not right.

Required

Describe what you would do if you found yourself in the situation of:
(a) Tom Taylor;
(b) Martin Foley; and
(c) Sally Burke.

Case 22

Shane Nolan

Hugh McBride,
Galway–Mayo Institute of Technology

Shane Nolan is in the third month of his appointment as East Africa logistics manager for the UK multinational corporation, BR Plc. He is based in the port city of Monberri and his responsibilities include the purchase, import and storage of the raw materials, spare parts and equipment required by BR's manufacturing plants in the region. BR is one of the biggest importers through Monberri Port. The logistics operation is crucial to the success of the manufacturing plants.

Shane has just encountered his first serious problem since taking up the post. Normally, it takes four to seven days to process a container through the port, from landing to release. However, the processing of a number of BR containers with vital spare parts has been delayed by the Port Authority. Mr Phiri, the port manager, has indicated that the 'problems' could take up to eight weeks to resolve and in the meantime he cannot guarantee the safety of the consignment. Monberri has a deserved reputation for theft from through-trade and for corrupt practices among port officials. Phiri has told Shane that "ways and means" might be found to speed up the release of the containers but that this would require some "generous good-will gesture" by Shane as "a facilitating mechanism".

Shane discusses the situation with Fr Peter, a Jesuit priest who has lived in Monberri for 17 years, and with whom he has become acquainted since he arrived.

"He is asking for a bribe. Unfortunately, that is the usual way business is done in this country at present. You pay Phiri and all the port officials down the line get a cut. Of course, bribery is officially denounced and it does greatly undermine the potential for long-term development.

But, as they say, in the long term we are all dead. The officials at the port are paid lousy wages and bribery is the only avenue open to them to survive. You would probably do the same in their position."

Prior to leaving London, Shane attended a one-day ethics seminar for BR overseas executives. (The CEO chaired the afternoon session.) BR has a written code of ethics to which management at all levels are required to commit themselves. It specifically prohibits the payment of bribes. However, during a discussion at the seminar, Shane was left with the impression that senior management were equivocal in their attitude. Rather than a clear message of 'simply don't do it', the signal seemed to be that bribery may be unavoidable in some countries but 'don't get caught doing it'. In fact, senior management's primary concern seemed to be avoiding adverse publicity in the UK media.

Shane joined BR Plc after graduating from college and intends having a long-term career with the company. He is considered to be a rising managerial star. His appointment in Monberri is for three years and he can then look forward to a significant promotion. Shane and his wife Ann have settled quickly into the rhythm of life in Monberri. As well as a generous salary and overseas allowance, he is provided with a brand new Toyota Land Cruiser and a substantial, colonial-style house. BR provide for the domestic staff at the house, including a cook and a gardener. The company also pay for Shane and Ann's full membership of the highly exclusive Monberri Lawn Tennis & Polo Club.

Mitch Moore is BR's longest-serving manager in the region and headed up one of the manufacturing facilities. He has advised Shane to pay the bribe:

"That is what everyone else does. That is what London really expects you to do, although they won't say so. It's a normal cost of the business game in these parts. All the guys in power at the port, including Phiri, are members of the ruling ZAFF political party. You pay the bribe by writing a cheque payable to ZAFF. The internal auditors in London rarely pick up on these things, and even if they do it can be passed off as a legitimate political donation. BR's code of ethics doesn't apply out here and everyone understands that. Rumour has it on the corporate grapevine that it might not even apply much in the UK!"

Mitch thinks Shane's suggestion of seeking advice from London is naive:

"They don't want to be bothered with this. They expect you to do the job out here. Look, if those spare parts aren't out of the port in three weeks, operations are going to shut down. The facilities managers are going to be mightily angry if that happens. Apart from the potential impact on our bonuses, we will have to lay off hundreds of workers. Think of the hardship that will cause for them and their families. If you get all 'goody-goody', it could hurt a lot of people. Sure, you could force the issue and refuse to pay the bribe. That may change things for a while and go down well officially and in the media. But it won't do your career prospects any good and it won't solve the problem of corruption."

Shane remains uncertain about what to do. He feels uneasy about compromising himself by paying the bribe. He remembers that BR had threatened to move the logistics operation to South Africa in 2014 in an effort to force a clampdown on corruption at Monberri, which generated a lot of positive publicity for BR at the time. However, Mitch is dismissive of that episode:

"The company could move operations south any time, no problem. But it's cheaper for them to operate out of Monberri, even with the bribes and the theft. What happened in '14 was the kind of public display of corporate moral outrage that happens from time to time. The external auditors were unhappy with the scale of the so-called 'political' donations and began asking questions. The guys in London feigned shock at the discovery. A few managers were scapegoated and hung out to dry. The port authorities cleaned up their act for a while under pressure from the publicity and BR's threat to move. But slowly, over time, normal corrupt practices resumed."

Required:

Discuss the issues arising in this case. What would you advise Shane to do? Explain your reasons.

Case 23

Kilaney Ltd

Hugh McBride,
Galway–Mayo Institute of Technology

Mary Lenihan has been working in the family business, Kilaney Ltd, for the last 10 months. She is 29 years' old and a social science graduate. Following her studies, she worked for two years with a charity organisation in Africa. She then spent two years in Australia working in part-time jobs and travelling. Following this, she moved to London, got married, had two children and worked as an administrator in a support agency for minorities. Eighteen months ago, her grandmother died, leaving Mary a 22% share-ownership in Kilaney Ltd. With the encouragement of her parents and her husband, she decided to move home and take up an executive director role in the business.

Kilaney Ltd was established by Mary's grandfather over 40 years ago. It manufactures chemical compounds and in recent years has specialised in supplying the cosmetics sector with compounds for skin-cream products. It has a mixed base of customers, ranging from multinationals to SMEs. Most of its business is through fixed-term contractual orders. The company is located in Mayo and is the main employer in the local area. Its significance to the local economy has been emphatically emphasised by a number of factory closures in the region over the last two years. The local rate of unemployment is currently estimated at 12%.

Kilaney Ltd has been managed for six years by Mary's two older brothers, Joe and Peter. They both went straight into the business from school and had taken over executive control after the retirement of their father. They each own 20% of the company's shares. Of the remaining shares, 23% are owned by their parents and 15% by a bank. The bank had agreed to convert a loan into shares four years previously following trading difficulties that necessitated a financial restructuring. At that time, a recovery strategy was implemented and this has worked reasonably well. Each of the shareholders has a seat on the board of directors of the company, which also includes two non-shareholding, non-executive directors. One of these is a prominent local merchant and the other is a retired professor of chemistry who was appointed on the recommendation of a state industry-support agency. The board is chaired by Mary's father.

Mary's homecoming has not worked out as she expected. Shortly after the move, her husband was injured in a car accident and is unlikely to return to work in the near future. In the context of her role in the company, Mary quickly realised how little she knew about the business and has faced a steep learning curve. In addition, her relationship with her brothers has steadily worsened. It seems that they resent the fact of her inheritance and her attempt to engage actively in management of the company. Joe's facetious remark, made shortly after her return, to "trust us and leave it to the professionals to do the real work" was, in retrospect, ominous.

The issue now under discussion by the board threatens to cause a major family rift. Mary has expressed concern about the renewal of a contract to supply a customer, Nimh Ltd, with a particular compound for a further period of two years. The difficulty for Mary is that this compound is used by Nimh as a key component in the manufacture of skin-cream products for sale in Africa. These products are used mainly by women as bleaching agents to lighten the colour of their skin and hair, as well as for the treatment of skin ailments and as an antiseptic. Mary wants Kilaney to turn down the contract and her brothers have reacted furiously to the suggestion. Mary's parents have indicated a level of sympathy with her point of view.

Mary explains that there is incontrovertible evidence that the skin-cream products are toxic and that the risks associated with their constant use are significant. They have been described by one health research organisation as a "serious health hazard" possibly causing skin disease, kidney failure, foetal damage and cancer. Following extensive lobbying by development NGOs, a ban on the sale and import of these products within the EU is imminent. At present, some of these products are openly available for sale in ethnic shops around Ireland. Mary argues that the products represent a form of what she calls "commercial racism". The demand for the products, she explains has arisen from an exploitation and manipulation of the deep-seated insecurities of poor black women who are made to feel inadequate in a world that portrays lighter-skinned women with straight blond hair as the role model for female success. "I don't want us to have any part in this type of dirty exploitative business", she declares. "It's indefensible for us to profit from generating misery, for us to be part of the manufacture of products for export to Africa which are deemed unfit for sale in this country."

In response, Peter was incandescent with rage:

"You might not like it, but it is this type of business that has kept this company afloat for the last four years. This contract may be essential for our survival; if we don't take it, we will certainly have to lay off about 30% of the workforce immediately. Will you explain to the workers that your moral scruples are costing them their jobs? Some of them are young and have big mortgages. There isn't anything else for them around here. Some of the older ones might never find work again. Let's get a few facts straight here. First, we are contracting to sell a chemical compound, not a dangerous skin-cream. The logic of your argument is that no one should supply inputs to the tobacco or the armaments or the nuclear industries. What our customers do with the compound is not our responsibility. Secondly, we are doing nothing illegal and neither, incidentally, is Nimh. The ban you refer to relates only to the sale of these creams; it will still be perfectly legal to make these products within the EU for export. And the countries to which these products are exported have not banned them. Thirdly, if we don't take up this contract, our competitors will. We will lose out and it won't change anything. Finally, the state agencies seem to find nothing wrong with this type of business. Both Nimh and ourselves have received generous grants of Irish taxpayers' money and various other supports. Indeed, the trade minister on her recent visit here praised us for continuing to provide jobs in an area where they are desperately needed."

Then Joe spoke:

"Listen Mary, while you were swanning around college and then around the world, Peter and I were here working long hours doing whatever was needed to sustain the business. For the last four years it has been about survival. Our dog-eat-dog industry requires a cut-throat attitude. I really resent an Anita Roddick wannabee, and one with no business experience to boot, trying to tell us how to run our affairs. Business is business and you do what is necessary; if you can't stand the dirt, then don't play in the muck. Business is dirty work sometimes, but you have to be prepared for that if you want to succeed. The campaign against Nimh's products has been funded by manufacturers of so-called 'natural' cosmetics. They are hardly an independent voice, and the research you mention is far from conclusive and its objectivity is questionable. I expect that soon their campaign will be extended to criticising all chemical-based cosmetic

products. And don't you think that you are being somewhat patronis-
ing towards African women? That you are exhibiting a form of subtle
racism? It may interest you to know that Nimh is fully owned by three
African women. As I understand it, the demand for their products
arises because many of Nimh's customers can't afford the more expen-
sive Western brands; so it's these cheap ones or nothing. There is no
alternative for the poor in Africa. And in this regard, I notice you have
nothing to say about their use as an effective and cheap treatment for
skin ailments and as an antiseptic. And just to follow up on one of
Peter's points, the banks and the government have obviously no problem with this type of trade. They have been willing to finance both
Nimh and us. Why should we be expected to apply so-called higher
moral standards than the financial institutions, the government or
anyone else in the industry?"

Mary was taken aback by the vehemence of her brothers' remarks, but
responded:

"Don't try to bully me. This is a board meeting and I remind you that
I am the largest single shareholder and will be treated with respect. We
must recognise an obligation to those affected by our products. Selfish
economic gain should not be our only guide or the only criterion
we apply in our decision-making. How we *behave* in trying to make
profits is important. We have a basic duty to protect and promote the
well-being of others. If we put our heads together, I'm sure we can
identify alternative and viable product markets for the company. And
one further point: it will hardly seem like good business when this
gets into the national media. Bad publicity resulting in a poor image
and reputation will hardly help us in our dealings with the multinationals or in winning new business in future. A piece about Nimh's
products has already been featured in one of the national newspapers
and the story is likely to grow in significance after the EU ban is
implemented."

At this point, one of the non-executive directors, the prominent local merchant, spoke in an avuncular tone:

"Duty is an admirable screen to creep behind when we wish to avoid
doing what ought to be done. Indeed, what must be done? Survival is
the issue here, not gain. There will be plenty of time to worry about
moral niceties when the company is strong again. Meanwhile, we
must continue with this contract."

The representative of the bank and the professor of chemistry both nodded sagely.

Required

Discuss the issues arising in this case. What would you advise:
(a) Mary,
(b) Mary's parents, and
(c) the board,
to do?
Explain your reasons.

Case 24
McEllin Ltd

Hugh McBride,
Galway–Mayo Institute of Technology

McEllin Ltd is a long-established family business involved in the design, manufacture and sale of a wide range of branded children's clothing, including leisurewear, fashion and sportswear. It sells mainly to large retail chains in Ireland and in other countries throughout the European Union. Its customers include prominent high-street retailers that are household names in each of the countries. In recent years, it has faced intense competition in seeking to hold onto its customer base and maintain profitability. However, the company has been successful not only in retaining its existing customers but in adding some new ones, and in extending the range of its product offerings, though margins have grown tighter as operating costs have increased and as customers have used their growing bargaining power to exert downward pressure on prices. McEllin's return on shareholder investment has fallen in recent years and remains just about adequate to provide for the medium-term continuity of the business.

The company attributes its continued success to its ability to 'tune into' its customers' needs, the vibrancy, originality and quirkiness of its designs, the quality of its products, its ability to deliver on its contractual agreements, the persistence of its selling effort and its careful cultivation of customer relationships.

The company was originally established by Joe McEllin in 1952, in Castlekenny, a small town in the West of Ireland. The finance for the start-up was provided by members of Joe's family. The business grew and at one stage, during the mid-1970s, directly employed up to 300 people in the town. At present, Joe remains as the chair of the board of the company and continues to holds a 21% shareholding. The chief executive officer (CEO) of the company is now Joe's daughter, Margaret McEllin, who has a share-holding of 13%. Margaret has worked in the company since she left school.

Joe's son, Peter, is the company's marketing manager. Much of the recent growth in sales is attributed to his flair for sales and ability to build relationships with key customers. He also has a shareholding of 13%.

Most of the remaining shares are held by various family members including Joe's grandson, Tomás, who has a shareholding of 17%. He inherited the shares from his parents who are deceased. Tomás had set up his own business after leaving college. It was successful during the boom years of the 'Celtic Tiger' but ceased to trade in 2009. He then joined McEllin Ltd and has worked since with his uncle Peter in marketing. He is seen by the family as the person to eventually take over as CEO once Margaret decides to retire. Margaret, Peter and Tomás are all members of the company's board.

The company's headquarters remains in Castlekenny, where it employs 85 people in the areas of design, marketing, accounts and administration. However, manufacturing has been outsourced to India since 1998, where McEllin has established a productive contractual relationship with an Indian family business, Patel Pvt Ltd. They make the products in accordance with the designs and specifications supplied by McEllin. Margaret manages the logistics end of the business, including the relationship with Patel. She visits India once a year and members of the Patel family also visit Castlekenny annually. All other communication is by email, telephone and Skype.

Margaret's most recent visit to India was six weeks ago. She had decided that Tomás should accompany her so that he could "get to know all aspects of the business better". Tomás was initially impressed by the Patel family members he met. They were rich, sophisticated, urbane and "really nice, friendly and hospitable people". Some he met were graduates of Harvard and Oxford. However, Tomás was genuinely shocked when he visited one of their factories. Apart from the cramped, unsafe and very unhealthy working conditions, he was taken aback by the general demeanor of the employees, the long hours they worked, the low wages they were paid and the aggressive and threatening tone with which managers and supervisors addressed them. He was reassured by the Patels that all their employees were paid above the legal minimum wage and that employment conditions were among the best locally.

Tomás stays on in India for an additional two weeks on a planned holiday. He spends this time with Clare, an old college friend who has worked in India for a number of years on various development aid projects. She introduces him to a local journalist who was scathing about the Patel family business.

"Their wealth is based on a chain of really dreadful, unregulated, mud-bricked sweatshops operating in the slums of New Delhi that pay starvation wages and use child labour. They are notorious, even in India, for the appalling conditions in which they employ people and the abuses of their workforce including sexual harassment, long hours without a break and lack of toilet facilities. Any workers that protest are immediately sacked and blacklisted. The price of your cheap clothes in Ireland is turning a blind eye to the exploitation and misery of people here."

Upon his return to Ireland, Tomás voices his concerns at a meeting of the board of McEllin Ltd:

"Much as I regret to say it, we are directly implicated in exploitation and in human rights abuses. This could be damaging to us if it became public. Many of our key customers have signed up to fair-trade principles and have promulgated codes that demand ethical practice throughout their supply chain. My real concern, however, is with my conscience. I can't help feeling that we have an obligation to do something about this. I shudder to imagine my own kids in that situation. It may cost us in the short term to act to try and change this but there is an opportunity for us as well. Our customers claim credit for being ethically conscious and an increasing cohort of consumers will pay a premium for clothes that can clearly be identified as coming from a source that respects fair-trade principles and humane labour practices. So apart from the moral aspect, being more demanding on our suppliers could be good for our business."

Margaret is none too impressed.

"We can't be held responsible for the behaviour of our Indian partner. They provide cheap high-quality products, are responsive to our requirements and deliver on time every time. They are perfect suppliers for us and would be damn hard to replace. It's unreasonable to expect that we can or should control our supply chain to the extent you suggest. Even the likes of the big multinational sportswear brands don't seem to be able to do that very well. Anyway, I don't buy this sweatshop exploitation argument. India lags behind us on the development curve and this kind of industrial activity is the only way it can catch up. Cheap labour is its competitive advantage. The workers in the so-called sweatshop at least have a job and are a lot better off than they could be. We don't even know for sure whether Patel are involved in what you suggest. And I don't want to know. The Patels are nice people, and we have found them good and trustworthy to do business with. That's enough for me. Our obligation is to our family and maybe to the local community here in Castlekenny. But that's the extent of it. Our customers' supposed concern for ethical supply chains is just bluff and hypocrisy on their part: they don't really care. You sound like a typical Western liberal, Tomás, with an underlying prejudice against successful Indians that is, I think, bordering on racist. You've already had one business failure – I'm not prepared to see you lead us into another because your distorted conscience is at you. This is a tough business and you better decide whether you have what it takes to run it successfully."

Joe and Peter listen with dismay. Each feels uneasy about what Tomás has reported and think that he has raised an important issue for the future of the company and the legacy of their management and stewardship. But each also recognises the validity of Margaret's perspective and they are unwilling to challenge Margaret as she was the dominant figure within the family and is not to be crossed.

Required

Discuss the ethical issues arising in this case. What would you advise:
(a) Tomás,
(b) Joe, and
(c) the board,
to do?
Make recommendations and explain your reasons.

Case 25

ADC Inc.

Hugh McBride,
Galway–Mayo Institute of Technology

ADC Inc. is a major US food corporation involved in aquaculture and agribusiness on a global scale. It has recently announced plans to develop a super-size salmon farm off the Atlantic coast of Balba. The project has been planned from an early stage in close cooperation with the country's Marine Fisheries Ministry. It has also been approved for substantial grant-aid by the country's Inward Investment Authority. In announcing the project, the corporation's CEO was joined at a press conference in the capital city of Balba by the country's finance minister who was vociferous in her praise of the project and in welcoming the investment.

> "This is just the kind of development we need to underpin our national recovery. It is consistent with our National Development Plan involving a world-leading business making a significant investment in a deprived rural area, utilising our natural resources and creating much needed jobs. It is a significant statement of confidence in Balba's economy going forward."

The finance minister stated that securing the necessary planning and licensing permissions would not be a problem. It was her intention to fast-track the permissions under the recently introduced Important Infrastructure Rapid Approval legislation.

The project involves 'growing' up to 4 million salmon a year in cages on a 460 hectare site in a sheltered bay 2 kilometres offshore from the world-famous Omphin Island. It is estimated that the development will generate revenues of €100 million annually when it reaches full capacity. It will create 400 jobs and provide a direct annual payroll of €21 million into the local economy. The project will include a significant cutting-edge research component involving collaboration with both the region's university and polytechnic, which would prove lucrative and prestigious for all involved. Further economic benefit is envisaged through the development of spin-off, local small-scale businesses servicing the project.

The region in which the salmon farm will be located is an economic black spot with a per capita income well below the national average. As has been the case for generations, many young people have to leave the area in search of work. Even during Balba's boom economy of the previous decade, the region developed relatively little. Its only significant industry is tourism, which is centred on the importance of Omphin Island as an international heritage site, as well as freshwater fishing and the pristine natural environment. Other than this, the local population survive through a combination of subsistence farming, fishing and seasonal work abroad.

Shortly after the announcement of the project, a significant opposition emerges. Protest voices include national environmental protection groups, local hoteliers and other tourism interests, freshwater fishery owners, local fishermen and anglers, and a majority of the Omphin islanders. While each of these groups has their own particular issues, the common unifying basis is opposition to the project because of its scale and potentially adverse impact on the community, tourism, the natural environment and particularly on the already threatened stocks of wild salmon, sea trout and other marine and freshwater life. Local groups are particularly aggrieved about the lack of consultation about such a significant and intrusive development.

A report commissioned by the Balba Fisheries Alliance (BFA) and carried out by a highly regarded international consultancy firm has concluded that there are justified scientific concerns about potential infestations of sea lice that could destroy Balba's prized reputation for wild fish. This would directly endanger an angling industry worth at least €97 million a year and an associated €83 million in annual tourism revenues. The report claims that the environmental impact plans published by ADC Inc. are deeply flawed. It questions the projected jobs numbers, suggesting the figure of 400 is vastly overstated. Many of the jobs, it claims, would go to specialists recruited from outside the region. The report documents ADC's involvement in a range of high-profile environmental failures in various parts of the world, its close linkages with repressive governments involved in proven human-rights abuses and its use of 'generous facilitation payments' to gain influence in some countries in which it operates. "ADC will reap the economic rewards but the local community will carry the risk and pay the social costs", the report concludes.

The Marine Fisheries Ministry responds to the BFA report by re-asserting its and the government's confidence that the project's environmental impact will not be significant. The report, it claims, is self-serving, exaggerated the environmental threat and is unduly alarmist. On a radio programme, the finance minister dismisses the protesters as a "ragtag group of permanently disgruntled naysayers who exude the kind of negativity that stunts our economic recovery and thwart our march to modernity". She again lauds the project for the jobs it will create and the prosperity it will bring. She praises ADC as a world-class organisation which the government are proud to invite into Balba. Despite this, however, at public meetings held on the island and in various towns in the region, it is clear that a sizable cross-section of the local community remain angry, deeply disturbed and concerned about the project.

ADC do not participate in the public debate. However, a few weeks after the publication of the BFA report, a national newspaper runs a story based on an internal ADC document leaked to it by a whistle-blower who, it claims, works at a middle-management level in the corporation. ADC confirms the authenticity of the leaked document as a confidential briefing memo for its senior management team involved in the salmon-farm project. The content of the leaked memo includes the following:

- The primary focus of ADC's strategy is, as always, on maximising profits and value for its shareholders.
- The interests of other stakeholders are costs to be minimised and/or constraints to be overcome.
- ADC operates within the law of the land but should not be expected to do more than this. "It is not in our mandate nor is it our responsibility to be guardians of the environment and of communities; nor are we obliged to apply environmental standards over and above the legal minimum (although we are not precluded from doing so as is clear from our track record)."
- The concerns expressed in the BFA report have some merit. ADC has little experience with the scale of the project proposed and is uncertain about its potential environmental impact. The company is entering "untested waters". This, however, is no different to many other projects in which it has been successfully involved. "We must trust our staff, and be prepared to take risks to generate above average returns. That is why we remain a global leader."
- The allegations about the company's activities in other countries can just be ignored. It is ADC's experience that "national and local economic self-interest is generally powerful enough to override any scruples about previous relatively small-scale failures, alleged human-rights abuses or facilitation payments in faraway places".

The leaked memo also suggests a number of immediate actions to be undertaken by ADC, as follows:

- Employ a public relations officer "to spin our side of the story in the national and local media and to generally promote the project by emphasising the economic benefits for the region".
- Brief key national politicians and local supporters on how to counter, refute and rebut the arguments presented by the opposition groups.
- Establish a 'strategic philanthropy fund' for targeted disbursement in the region "to win hearts and minds. The fund will serve to generate goodwill toward the project and the company, and weaken and split opposition groups."
- Identify and recruit "community opinion influencers, including local sports heroes" as active advocates for the salmon-farm project.
- Recruit key figures at both the university and the polytechnic as advocates for the project.

Required

Discuss the ethical issues arising in this case, drawing conclusions and making recommendations for what should now happen.

Case 26
SCL Ltd

Hugh McBride,
Galway–Mayo Institute of Technology

SCL Ltd publishes a daily national newspaper, *Firinne*. The paper was started in 1951 by Frank Marr with the slogan "the news in the truth". Its tone and content reflected Marr's commitment to nurturing a democratic society that values individual liberty and fairness, and in which the powerful and rich are held publicly accountable by an informed and active citizenship. The paper enjoyed only modest success until the early-1980s when Marr's son Peter took over as editor. Under his inspired leadership, the paper grew rapidly, and by the early 2000s it was established as a leading, influential and respected voice in national and international affairs. During that period, the paper won many awards for the consistently high quality of its content. In particular, its chief news reporter, Charlie George, was recognised and celebrated as one of the 'true greats' of modern Irish journalism.

Over the last 15 years, however, the paper has been in steady decline, with a shrinking and aged readership base and falling advertising revenue. In 2016, the Marr family sold 55% of SCL to an international media conglomerate. Shortly after that, Donna Kerr was appointed as editor with a remit to "liven up the paper, restore revenue, and develop a significant on-line presence". Peter Marr and Charlie George continued to serve on the editorial committee, which met weekly to advise on policy and content. The Marr family retained 30% ownership of the company; the remaining 15% of the shares were owned by a bank. Peter Marr also continued to serve on SCL's board of directors.

When she took over as editor, Donna Kerr was 32 years old. A business graduate from Galway–Mayo Institute of Technology, she had worked for 10 years in news media in the UK. She quickly set about revamping *Firinne,* for example, changing its format from broadsheet to tabloid and introducing a new typeface and layout. The paper continued to focus on high-quality news reporting but it also began to include more photographs, more 'lifestyle' stories and features on 'contemporary culture and technology'. Readership numbers increased, and the profile of the new readers was much younger than the long-established core-customer base. She also revamped the website and set about establishing a strong social-media presence.

In early 2019, there is a lot of public interest in a high-profile court case involving the murder of a celebrity actress, allegedly by her husband. In particular, the tabloids seemed obsessed with a female witness for the prosecution, who has come forward voluntarily and provided the police with some key evidence. In doing so, however, she has revealed that she had an affair with the accused. The witness has been brought into the court to deliver her testimony using an underground entrance, and the media have been unable to obtain her photograph. It was in this context that Donna Kerr calls an emergency meeting of the editorial committee. The following discussion takes place at that meeting:

Donna: Gentlemen! Exciting news: we've got some photographs of the witness. We've also sourced some new background information to enable us to spin stories to go with the photos; the usual stuff about her work, lifestyle, kids and family circumstances. Did you know that she is a long-time friend of a high-profile politician in the area? There is even a hint that she may have had a relationship with him when they were younger. Who knows what else might emerge when we get the story out there. This will be our front-page tomorrow and hopefully for the rest of the week. It's just the kind of story that should really get us on track to becoming a leading national newspaper again.

Charlie: How did we get these photographs and the information?

Donna: Call it good old-fashioned investigative journalism; by talking to people, persistence, following leads and a willingness to take some risks. I've had a couple of guys working on this for the last week and their efforts have paid off big time. I'd prefer not to go into details about what they did, but every fact they supplied is corroborated. We will have to touch-up the photos a bit, but nothing out of the ordinary. One is a fantastic beach shot of her in a bikini.

Charlie: I'm really unhappy and uneasy about this. It goes against everything we stand for. Running this non-story with doctored photographs turns us into just another sleazy supermarket tabloid, a purveyor of half-truths and titillating gossip. What has a beach shot of the witness in a swimsuit got to do with anything? Have we lost all sense of what we are about, all sense of right and wrong?

Donna: Listen, we have to get real. I was hired to boost circulation and save this paper, which was on the verge of closure not so long ago. We're a business trying to make money, and if we don't do that then everyone who works here loses their job. That's the reality of the market. Our task is to serve the public by giving it what it wants. That's why they buy the newspaper. If they want lurid tales of sex and murder then that's what we'll give them. You might not like it but that's what the media game is about today. We're in the entertainment business. If people want to read what you call 'sleaze and gossip', who are we to pass moral judgement on their tastes? The public wants to know, and if something is in the public realm, then they have a right to know. We have to do what we can to get the necessary competitive edge just to survive. Being first with a story like this is really important. After that, it's a question of ensuring our facts are correct and that we stay within the boundaries of the libel laws.

Charlie: I understand the realities of the market very well. But I also under-stand the importance of truth, justice and fairness – of common human decency, empathy and respect for people. The commercial imperative doesn't give us a right to trample all over people's privacy. People have a right not to be harmed and humiliated. We shouldn't manipulate, exploit and mutilate them for the sake of market share and profit. In a few weeks we'll have moved on, but our victims will be left with their shattered reputations. They'll be left to pick up the pieces of their lives after our unwarranted and unforgivable invasion of their privacy. There is no public interest served by publishing lurid photos and faked-up stories about this witness. Are we not concerned about the impact on her and on her family? I understand that she has two young kids. Have we no obligation to them? Remember that she came forward as a witness out of a sense of civic duty. She didn't want her picture in the paper and she has done everything to avoid contact with the press. She hasn't consented to what we propose and she deserves better from us. We may be a business, but *how* we conduct our business is very impor-tant. We should have no part in this media feeding-frenzy.

Donna: I'm glad we are having this discussion and I really respect your views Charlie, but on this occasion, I can't agree with them. It's not our responsibility to define the public interest. We only respond to it. 'Holier-than-thou' morality is a luxury that a modern media organisation simply can't afford. We're not going to break any laws by running the story: if we do, we'll be taken to court and will have to pay the penalty. If the privacy laws don't protect people and are not restrictive enough, then it's up to the government to tighten them up. If we don't report this story, someone else will; it's only a matter of time before our competitors get the photos.

We would lose out in the circulation war and all to no effect. In a media society that values free speech, everyone and everything is fair game. We will give the witness every chance to respond and to tell her side of the story later. For all we know, she has only been avoiding the press in order to negotiate an exclusive and lucrative newspaper deal for herself. What do you think Peter?

Peter: Unfortunately, I have to agree with you, Donna. Personally, I don't like this type of sensational and prurient reporting but we don't seem to have any choice. The changes you already made have worked, so we should trust your judgement. I know that this is the board's view. Going with this story may come at a high cost in terms of the values we have long espoused and cherished, but the world has changed and we must adapt or perish. At the end of the day, it's only business.

Required

Discuss the ethical issues arising in this case. Comment on the decision to publish the photos and the related stories. What would you advise? Make recommendations and explain your reasons.

Case 27
Ailliliu Plc

**Hugh McBride,
Galway–Mayo Institute of Technology**

Ailliliu Plc is a global software solutions business. In addition to a range of standardised products, it devises customised solutions for knowledge monitoring, filtering and retention. Since May 2017, the company has been subjected to widespread criticism in the national and international left-leaning and liberal media for the nature of its business with the government of Simbina. One contract in particular has been singled out for fierce criticism. This involves the design and implementation of specialised software for use by the Simbina government's Internet Surveillance Centre (ISC). The software is, in effect, a mechanism for policing the use of the internet. The ISC's website describes the system as a virtual-policing tool for online oversight aimed at criminal deterrence and law enforcement. A spokesperson for the ISC is quoted, explaining that "the majority of law abiding citizens and organisations have nothing to fear from the system; only criminals and terrorists should have cause for concern." However, human-rights advocates have documented cases in which people were jailed for alleged 'subversive activities' based only on evidence provided by Ailliliu's software. Their alleged crimes included using the internet for "spreading feudal superstition" and for "undermining the honour of national institutions". According to the human-rights advocates the reality is that these so-called 'subversives' were jailed for questioning the authority of the state and for mildly and peacefully challenging the ruling political order.

Ailliliu's critics in the media have argued that the company's involvement with the ISC "goes far beyond the boundaries of what can be considered ethical trading and good corporate citizenship by directly aiding and abetting censorship and human rights abuses by a repressive regime".

They accuse Ailliliu of "commercial opportunism and gross hypocrisy", particularly in view of the company's declared mission and values.

Ailliliu was established in 2004 by two software engineering graduates, Pete Hand and Joe Marr. Both were aged 23, idealistic, visionary, adventurous and fired-up with a driving passion for emerging information technologies. The company's declared mission was encapsulated in the mantra "empowerment through knowledge". Later, it issued a 'Credo Statement' outlining the company's values, which included commitments "to always trade fairly and honestly; to value employee participation and workplace democracy; to enable innate human creativity and innovation; to be an active and responsible corporate citizen of the worldwide communities that we serve."

From the outset, the company eschewed traditional forms of working, organisation and management. It actively fostered an image of being "edgy and alternative" and of seeking to behave "beyond the boundaries of the ordinary". Its recruitment efforts focused on attracting graduates with "critical perspectives, passion, ideals, a strong work ethic and an 'X factor'". One of its recruitment advertisements, for example, stated that "if you consider yourself a bit different to the norm, if you've ever imagined applying your technical genius to benefit millions of people around the world, Ailliliu might just be the place for you". The company's ability to attract and retain high-calibre, talented and committed staff has been a key factor in its success.

The company grew rapidly, establishing a strong international reputation for creativity and innovation in the imaginative design and application of cutting-edge technologies to the solution of clients' needs and problems. It has enjoyed particular success with software designed to monitor and filter internet use. Their products are widely used by parents for child-protection, by organisations to prevent abuse of facilities, and by police for deterring, preventing and detecting terrorism, organised crime and trafficking in child-pornography. The software now being applied in Simbina is a further development of this product range, customised to the requirements of the Simbinese authorities.

By March 2012, when it floated on the Stock Exchange, Ailliliu was already a recognised global brand and an acknowledged market leader. Described at the time in the financial press as "the coolest company with the hottest share price on the planet", the flotation was a great success. The share price continued to enjoy stellar growth until January 2016, when it fell by 12%, at which level it has hovered since. Analysts generally agree that the share-price dip reflected the emerging threat to Ailliliu's future from ever-increasing competition, as well as an over-due correction to technology shares on the wider market. Shares in Ailliliu are primarily held by financial institutions and pension funds. They have also proved popular with ethical investment funds. Hand and Marr remain the largest shareholders, and each continues to own about 14% of the company. Hand is the chief executive officer (CEO) and also the chair of the board; Marr is an executive director and heads up the corporate research & development function.

In August 2017, in a wide-ranging interview with the influential magazine, *International Economist*, Hand defended Ailliliu's involvement with the Simbinese government. Simbina, he explained, is one of the largest and fastest growing markets in the world. For Ailliliu not to get involved would be suicidal for the company's future, to the great detriment of its various stakeholders.

> "All of our competitors are trading there and for us not to seek and avail of the opportunities presented would to be highly irresponsible. Joe and I have been criticised in the past for 'not growing up'. Well, the stock market is a stern master, demanding mature behaviour, and our duty to the shareholders is now paramount. We have always applied our Credo in a real-world context and this requirement is clearly understood and expected. Of course, corporations should act ethically, but they are a force for moral good only in so far as they generate wealth through the provision of goods valued by open, competitive markets. Through our presence there, we are supporting the opening up and development of Simbina. We operate within international and Simbina law. We have insisted on adding a feature to the software, at our own cost, that indicates to internet users that they are under surveillance. What we are doing is no different from any other businesses trading in Simbina. The liberal chatterati criticising Ailliliu are, as usual, very selective in their concerns. Not least, they ignore the reality that nothing can halt the march of technology; as such, it is better to direct it as best one can to ensure it remains a force for long-term good. Are they suggesting, for instance, that there should be no controls on the internet to prevent terrorism or paedophilia? We have always sought to operate with great transparency and a sense of social responsibility and we will continue to do so, going forward."

Despite the publication of the interview, the criticism of the company in parts of the media and among human-rights advocacy organisations has continued. This escalated following the revelations in January 2018 that the company has also been doing business for some time with the governments of Banmara, Samdide and Sauruwa, all alleged to be highly repressive regimes. One human-rights agency has launched an international advocacy campaign, clearly directed at Ailliliu, with the caption: "Empowering *who* with knowledge?" A number of articles by high-profile commentators have appeared recently in the international financial press expressing concern about potential reputation damage to Ailliliu arising from the campaign, and the possible impact on its share price.

In the last week, Hand has received a written request from four of Ailliliu's employees working at its Irish campus. They are Simbinese nationals and members of a small religious sect. They have asked Hand to intervene with the Simbinese government on behalf of some of their relatives who were arrested in Simbina the previous month for some as-yet-unspecified wrong-doing. The employees suspect that it may be connected to their membership of the sect.

Required

Discuss the ethical issues arising in this case.

Case 28

Rachel Forde

Hugh McBride,
Galway–Mayo Institute of Technology

Rachel Forde qualified as a Chartered Accountant just over a year ago, when she joined a prestigious international firm of management consultants. Rachel is ambitious, self-confident, energetic and a technically gifted accountant. Evidence of her ability is that she was actively recruited by the consultancy firm and her current salary is among the highest of her peers. Her professional goal is to become the chief financial officer and executive director of a publicly quoted company within 15 years. In this regard, she considers that the work experience she will get with the consultancy firm should prove invaluable. Furthermore, her CV will be greatly enhanced as a result of working for such a high-profile organisation and brand.

Rachel's current assignment involves a three-month placement with Flog Ltd, a large unquoted company, which though only established seven years, has grown rapidly since its incorporation. At its current rate of development, it expects to be in a position to consider a stock-market flotation within two years. The founder of the business remains the major shareholder and the chief executive. Rachel's assignment involves an evaluation of the financial planning and control systems leading to recommendations for improvement.

In her fifth week on the job, Rachel discovers a series of invoices from a building company for work supposedly carried out on behalf of Flog. The amounts seem excessive and further investigation reveals that much of the work is in fact related to the personal properties of the senior management team and of one significant supplier to the company. It is clear to Rachel that the invoices have been falsified.

She approaches the chief executive about the matter and he is not at all surprised.

"I instructed the building company to invoice us in this way. They had no problem with this. We are worth a lot of business to them so they are willing to play ball."

When Rachel points out to him that the practice is unethical and illegal, he laughs and replies "stuff your ethics. I have a business to run". He advises her not to worry about the matter and to continue with the good work she has carried out to date. "The auditors had no problem with it, so why should you?" he asks rhetorically.

Rachel informs her immediate boss at the consultancy firm about what has transpired. He also advises her to let the matter lie, reminding her that Flog is a valuable client and that the chief executive of Flog is a personal friend of a number of the senior partners in the consultancy firm. He explains to Rachel that her work to date is considered excellent and that the feedback from clients has all been positive. However, Rachel has the distinct feeling that he is hinting strongly that her prospects at the consultancy firm could be greatly damaged if she pursues the matter further. He adds:

"No one likes to stir up trouble in this game. It's damaging to business, to reputations and to careers. Flog has really done nothing unusual. Such minor amendment to invoices is a common enough business practice. It's up to the auditors to police that. Essentially, it's nothing to do with us; it's not what we are paid for. Consultancy is a business like any other. Success is about satisfied customers. This may involve cutting a few corners, turning a blind eye now and again, but everyone in the game accepts this as a matter of course. Everyone does it. My advice to you is to forget the whole thing."

Required

Explain the ethical issues arising in this situation and advise Rachel as to the course of action she should take.

Case 29

Mind your Language

(*In memorium* Philip Roth)

Hugh McBride,
Galway–Mayo Institute of Technology

At the start of the second semester, Pat starts teaching a new group of students with whom he had no previous contact. There are two students on the class list who do not appear for the first two weeks. Pat asks the class whether anyone knows where they are and is told that "they have gone away", to which he remarks good-humouredly: "Ah, intrepid travellers are they? How nice for them to take to the road, anois teacht an Earraigh".

The following week Pat is summoned by the Head of School. An official complaint has been lodged by a student claiming that Pat has spoken derogatorily about her in class. She is from a Traveller background and is finding it hard enough to get through college without the added barrier of racism. The student has been to see the counsellor who is willing, with the student's agreement, to attest to her difficulties. She is also supported by a number of lecturers who are active in a Traveller support group outside the college and who are involved in a self-styled 'concerned lecturers' campaigning group within the college. As one of their projects, they initiated a 'stamp out racism' campaign on campus, which has since been subsumed into a formal staff trade union, student and college partnership forum designed and funded to support and promote diversity.

> "Listen Pat," says the Head, "I know that you are in no way racist in attitude. This was probably an innocent mistake. But in the current PC climate we must all exercise particular care. The student has agreed to withdraw her complaint if you apologise publicly to her in front of the class and also write a letter to her to that effect. That would end the affair quickly and no one loses out."

Before answering the Head, Pat asks about the student's academic track record. "Not that it is of any direct relevance", says the Head, "but she has just about scraped through to date with a certain amount of sympathy and leeway from exam boards. Her attendance has not been great, but it seems that lecturers have been willing to give her the benefit of the doubt given her background." Pat thinks for a moment then responds as follows:

> "I am not going to make any apology because I have done nothing wrong. I knew nothing of this student until today. I intended no comment on her background, nor could I have. It was a mildly humorous remark, a part of ordinary everyday discourse. Is the word 'traveller' in its traditional usage now to be outlawed, annexed by a lobby group in the service of their specific purposes? I refuse to be bullied into compromising my dignity and my academic position because of a bogus threat. I think this student's academic track record may be very relevant here. It seems to me that this is an attempt to compel me into helping her scrape through later in the year."

The Head listens with mounting concern.

> "Standing on your dignity solves nothing, Pat. What difference will it make if you make the apology? If you do, by next week it will all be forgotten about. But if you don't, be aware that there will be powerful forces mobilised against you, not least the concerned lecturers group, who seem to have adopted this girl's case. Are you prepared for all the hassle that will come your way? And for the possibility that the case might go against you and all the consequences that entails? At the very least, this won't look good on your record and could tell against you if, for example, you were to apply for a promotion. This could cause bad feeling in the college and we don't need that right now. Think what the newspapers could do with the story if it leaked out. Why don't you just make the damn apology and have done with it?"

Required

Discuss any ethical issues raised in this case.

Case 30

Brian Mahon

Hugh McBride,
Galway–Mayo Institute of Technology

Brian Mahon, the financial controller of Walker Ltd, has worked at the company for 18 months. He has recently been authorised by the board to purchase, install, test and implement new computer hardware and software to drive the company's information systems. The supplier chosen would also be contractually bound to provide an after-sale service for a four-year period, this to be reviewed at that time. Brian has received two formal bids for the project, both of which appear to meet the specified functionality requirements. One of the bids, however, would involve a much higher initial outlay for Walker. The higher bid was received from a local company, MR Ltd, and the owner, Joe Coy, is one of Brian's oldest friends. Brian phones Joe explaining the situation, suggesting he lower his bid if he wants to win the contract. The following conversation then takes place:

Joe: Listen Brian, it's really important to us that we win the contract, but at the price we have already bid. It may be the key to us obtaining venture capital finance, which is critical for our continued development. At the moment, the negotiations with the potential investors are at a delicate stage. Your contract could tip the balance. And if we don't get the finance, I see difficult times ahead for us.

Brian: Surely it would be worse if you didn't win our contract at all? And I find it hard to believe that one contract, even one as relatively large as ours, could be of such critical importance.

Joe: True, but, as you know, I was hoping to cash in some of my shares and step back from the day-to-day operations of the business very soon. The venture capital investment is vital in that regard. And, by the way, with the venture capital in place, I would finally be able to bring you on that golf trip to Portugal that I promised would happen if ever I struck it rich.

Brian: I suppose the fact that you are a local company may prove to be an advantage. You would certainly be in a better position to fulfil the on-going after-sale service obligations; if anything went wrong, you would at least be easy to get hold of, unlike the other company bidding for the contract, which is based in Budapest. That difference might be a justification for the higher bid.

Joe: Budapest? All the more reason to award us the contract. Surely we should all be trying to support local industry and keep jobs at home?

Brian: That is a point. It can't be wrong to support your own. And I doubt if the Hungarian company will make a fuss if they don't win the bid. Indeed, it is unlikely that anyone will raise any questions at all. And if anyone does, sure I can justify accepting your bid on the basis of the potential better after-sale service. I think you should be planning to book that golf trip for later this year.

Required

Do you agree with Brian's decision to award the contract to MR Ltd? Explain your reasons with specific reference to standards of professional conduct that should be expected from someone in Brian's role.

Scenarios 1 to 8

Personal Morality and Business Decisions

Hugh McBride,
Galway–Mayo Institute of Technology

Scenario 1

A senior bank manager is considering whether to approve a loan application for €5 million from a company involved in publishing 'adult' magazines. The magazines are on sale in news agents throughout the country including at all airports and train stations.

The finance will be used by the company for new product development and an expansion of its distribution network. The company has enjoyed steady growth for 10 years, has had relatively high profitability and the management team are considered to be excellent. It plans to float on the stock market within one year; preparations are well advanced and provisional approval has been indicated by the relevant stock exchange. The company's ability to repay the loan is unquestionable.

The bank manager has some personal concerns, based on her religious and moral views, about sanctioning the loan. She also has some concerns about potential reputational damage to the bank.

Required

Should the bank manager approve the loan? What are the ethical issues (if any) involved? Consider the following in the context of the above scenario:

- Do you agree that pornography is 'just a business like any other'?
- Would it matter if the bank manager's personal concerns were instead from a secular liberal perspective?
- Are managers obliged not to let personal morality influence their decision-making?

Scenario 2

A senior bank executive proposes that the bank request an evangelical group, Christian Call, to close its account because of its anti-homosexual views. Christian Call have had an account with the bank for the past 11 years. In a written submission, the executive explains that the Christian Call website is "full of blatant homophobia" and that its "discriminatory pronouncements based on the grounds of sexual orientation are incompatible with the stated values of this bank, which publicly supports diversity and dignity in all its forms for our staff, customers and other stakeholders. We believe in respect for all sectors of society. My proposal regarding the Christian Call account is based purely on the issue of respect for diversity; I have no issues with religion."

Pointing out that the bank has sponsored a number of gay pride festivals in recent years, the executive continues to argue in his submission that "anyone who regards homosexuality as sinful has no place banking with us. This bank is not a natural port of call for those who take a biblical view of sexual orientation. When the account was originally opened, the bank was unaware of the views of Christian Call on these matters."

However, there is also a note of caution in the bank executive's written submission regarding the possibility of some adverse publicity surrounding his proposal. It could be portrayed, he says, by certain sections of the media as "politically correct religion-bashing". Furthermore, it may mean having to ask other Christian, Jewish and Muslim religious groups holding broadly similar opinions to also close their accounts.

Required

Should Christian Call be asked to close their account? What are the ethical issues (if any) involved? Consider the following in the context of the above scenario:

- Do you agree that a business should be prepared to compromise on its stated values if its profitability is threatened?
- Do you think that a services business should care about the views and behaviour of its customers?
- Should a business concern itself with how its customers use its products or services?

Scenario 3

A gay couple are kissing in a pub when they are approached by a staff member who politely asks them to leave, saying their behaviour is "bothering" him and some of the older and regular customers. The couple think the request objectionable and demand loudly to speak to the owner. The landlady, who has witnessed the encounter from the far side of the room, then gets involved, saying she also finds the couple's behaviour "indecent and obscene", that she agrees with the staff member and the other customers, and asks them again to leave. She also states that she has in the past asked heterosexual couples to leave the pub for similar "over-the-top and unacceptable" behaviour in a public place.

Required

Comment on the ethical issues (if any) arising. Consider the following in the context of the above scenario:

- In an event that many people are "bothered" by the opinions or behaviour of another person that they consider be "indecent and obscene", are there valid grounds for imposing restrictions on the freedom of the person to express the opinions or to engage in the behaviour?

Scenario 4

The manager of a publicly funded arts & culture centre has been asked by a delegation of employees to withdraw the centre's advertising from a magazine that carries personal adverts and occasional feature articles that the employees consider "objectionable" on the grounds of being "demeaning to women". The magazine is a long-established publication with an eclectic readership across all demographics. It contains a broad selection of articles and photos about everyday life and opinion, aimed at informing and entertaining its readership. It is particularly popular among young professional people and students from the country living in rented accommodation in urban areas. Surveys indicate that it serves as a valuable source of public information about events at the arts centre. The publishers of the magazine have recently invested heavily in developing a strong online presence which has proven successful to date.

Required

What would you advise the manager of the arts & culture centre to do? Comment on the ethical issues (if any) arising. Consider the following in the context of the above scenario:

- Does the nature and general content of the magazine matter?
- Should the opinion of the employees outweigh the manager's obligation to the arts centre and to the public it serves?

Scenario 5

The CEO of a fast-growing, high-potential SME is considering promoting Inge to the post of senior marketing executive. Inge has worked at the company for just over two years and has been an outstanding employee. At a recent meeting, the HR manager described Inge as the "brightest of the many bright young things working for us". However, following receipt of an anonymous letter, the CEO asks the HR manager to recheck Inge's CV that is held on file. It transpires that it contains two false claims that were missed when she was originally hired. One claim relates to a qualification she does not have, the other to job experience she claimed to have but did not. When the CEO asks Inge about this, she agrees that the claims were misleading, adding:

> "It was the only way I could get a chance to prove my worth. Everyone inflates their CV nowadays; it's what people do and everyone in the game knows and understands this. I've worked hard for the company and proven I'm great at the job: that should be the only basis for deciding on the promotion."

Following this conversation, the CEO advises the HR manager that Inge's employment contract should be terminated.

Required

Do you agree with the CEO's decision? Comment on the ethical issues arising. Consider the following in the context of the above scenario:

- Do you consider that it is ever permissible to tell a lie?
- Should it matter that 'everyone does it'?

Scenario 6

John is the owner of a small business that is struggling to survive. He has been trying to replace a key employee who resigned to take up a new position abroad. The employee who left was highly skilled and experienced in a specialised area. John has had difficulties in recruiting someone suitable. Most applicants have generic skills rather than specialist ones required, and lack experience.

He decides to offer the job to Uli Beck, the best candidate from among the applicants. She seems highly capable, but will need training in the specialist area and close supervision for the first year as she gains experience and improves on her standard of spoken English. Thereafter, John considers that she should be able to work autonomously in the role and will prove to be a valuable asset. He phones her to tell her that he will be offering her the job, and that she should receive a formal letter of offer within a week.

Shortly after this John gets a call from Dermot, a close friend. Dermot's nephew has just returned from Australia, having lived there for four years, and is now looking for a job. Dermot asks whether John has any suitable vacancies. His nephew has some experience working in the same area as the employee who left; however, he is not as strong a candidate as Uli Beck. John tells Dermot that as a "special favour to him" he will offer his nephew a job. The following week, John writes to Uli Beck explaining that the job is no longer available.

Required

Do you agree with John's decision? Comment on the ethical issues arising. Consider the following in the context of the above scenario:

- Would it matter if John were the CEO of the business, but not the owner?
- Do you consider that it is ever permissible to break a promise?

Scenario 7

A friend has offered to show you how to access a 'pirate' movie-streaming website. You often go to the cinema and already subscribe to a legitimate online streaming service. However, the pirate site offers free access to a range of films and box sets that are not available on the legitimate site. According to your friend, the law about streaming movies is ambiguous and its illegality has not been conclusively established.

"Most people we know do it. A lot of the time, people stream movies they have already paid to see in the cinema. And the prices of subscribing to the official sites are a big rip off; their charges are way too high in Ireland, especially when compared to other countries. People using the pirates will force them to rethink their pricing and that can only be a good thing. Besides which, you'll mainly be streaming content that they don't offer anyway. So the official sites aren't losing out. You'd be foolish not to do it. No one gets hurt, and the service is not easily traceable to you so you won't get caught."

Required

Do you agree with your friend's viewpoint? Comment on the ethical issues (if any) arising. Consider the following in the context of the above scenario:

- Would your views be the same if you were a young actor trying to break into film?

Scenario 8

You buy and sell second-hand cars. A group of youths have offered you €1,200 for a 14-year-old car that you have had on your books for over five months. It has one month left on its current NCT approval. It is unlikely to pass the next NCT as it was involved in a serious accident before you bought it. Your initial interest in buying the car was as a possible source of spare parts. You have informed the youths fully about the state of the car. One of the youths has an identity card indicating that she is over 18; the others are all aged around 16 (you suspect). You have asked them what they want the car for but they are, to put it politely, uncommunicative on this score.

Required

Should you sell them the car? Are there any ethical issues arising? Consider the following in the context of the above scenario:

- If you are selling a second-hand car, should you always disclose the full truth about the state of the car to the potential buyer?
- In general, what do you consider constitutes a 'fair price' for a product or service?

Scenarios 9 to 12

Ethical Issues from 'Over There'

Hugh McBride,
Galway–Mayo Institute of Technology

Scenario 9

A development aid agency has admitted making undocumented cash payments to armed militia groups in a North African country. This, they claim, was done in order to ensure the security and safety of their employees working in "a conflict zone". Their employees are involved in the organisation and delivery of medical, food and other essential supplies to refugees fleeing from conflict in a neighbouring country. The admission followed an exposure of such practices by an investigative documentary on television. The aid agency claims that such "aid divergence" has been normal practice for all agencies operating in the region for many years. They describe it as "a necessary and accepted part of operating in the region". The documentary alleged that some of the militia groups to whom payments were made are involved in supporting terrorist atrocities in Europe.

Required

Do you consider the aid agency's practice of making payments to militia groups acceptable? Comment on the ethical issues (if any) arising. Consider the following in the context of the above scenario:

- What should the responsibility of a development aid agency be for the security and safety of its employees on overseas assignments?
- Is payment of 'protection money' to armed groups in conflict zones acceptable for this purpose?

Scenario 10

A development aid agency has been asked by a well-known human rights advocacy group to refuse a substantial donation from a large corporation that the advocacy group alleges is involved in supporting a repressive government in a Central Asian country. The issues the advocacy group refer to have been reported in the international media. Critics have argued that the products and services supplied by the corporation have sustained the regime and contributed to the repression of its people. Others have argued that trade should be separated from politics. The aid agency intends to use the money donated by the corporation to support their poverty relief work, including with victims of a recent typhoon in Haiti, which requires an immediate on-the-ground response.

Required

What would you recommend that the aid agency should do? Comment on the ethical issues (if any) arising in the above scenario.

Consider the following in the context of the above scenario:

- Would it be acceptable for a development aid charity to accept a financial donation from a corporation involved in: (i) the design and manufacture of armaments; (ii) using animals for testing its products; (iii) cigarette manufacturing; (iv) coal mining?
- Should the source of sponsorship or money raised by a development aid agency matter, provided the funds are used wisely and efficiently to alleviate suffering?

Scenario 11

Bean Ltd is a high-potential Irish engineering company that is trying to break into the lucrative Middle-Eastern market with the active support of the state enterprise development agency. Mary is Bean's most experienced and knowledgeable sales executive and has been with the company since it started. She has played a key role in winning most of the company's major international contracts to date and is well regarded by clients and her colleagues.

However, she was recently asked by the new CEO to withdraw from the employee team that is scheduled to travel as part of a trade delegation to a Middle-Eastern country. "I have spent a long time working in the Arab world", he says to Mary "and it is my informed view they really don't like doing business with women. You will just be made feel uncomfortable the whole time you are there and we are less likely to win the contracts we have targeted." The CEO indicates that he wants a male subordinate of Mary's to go instead. Mary protests that she is the most qualified person for the job, but the CEO is adamant. "Don't take this personally or treat it as a gender issue", he says. "It's strictly a matter of good business practice; 'when in Rome' and all that. We have to respect their culture if we are going to do good business over there."

Required

Do you agree with the CEO's decision? What are the ethical issues (if any) involved?

Consider the following in the context of the above scenario:

- Would there be any ethical concerns arising if an Irish university advertised for a lecturing position that was only open to male candidates? (The job is in an overseas campus under a partnership agreement for programme delivery between the university and the foreign government. The agreement specifies that only male teaching staff will be employed.)

Scenario 12

A caller to a national radio programme expresses serious concern about major retail outlets selling clothes made in Banmara. Her concerns arise from the dreadful persecution of the Tirc people in that country, which in her opinion amounts to "ethnic cleansing and maybe even genocide".

She is strongly of the view that people should not buy these products for two reasons: to avoid complicity in the persecution and to help to end it.

> "A person must do what they can, particularly as it costs us so relatively little to do the right thing. I know that the clothes are of good quality and are very cheap, and probably better value than anything else on the market at the moment. And I know that it's expensive to kit children out for school and that lots of families are still having difficulties making ends. But the least we should be expected to do is not to support a country like Banmara by buying their exports."

She also states that if the retailers acted responsibly, they would not stock the clothes for sale as "they are in effect profiting from human misery when they are in a strong position to exert pressure to end the persecution". She states that she will not shop in any stores that carry the clothes, and while she suggests that others should consider doing likewise, she stops short of calling for a consumer boycott of the retailers.

Required

Do you agree with the caller's position? Comment on the ethical issues (if any) involved. Consider the following in the context of the above scenario:

- Do you agree that end consumers have an obligation to actively seek to change corporate behaviour for the better?